Love to
Grandma
Christmas 2001.
x x

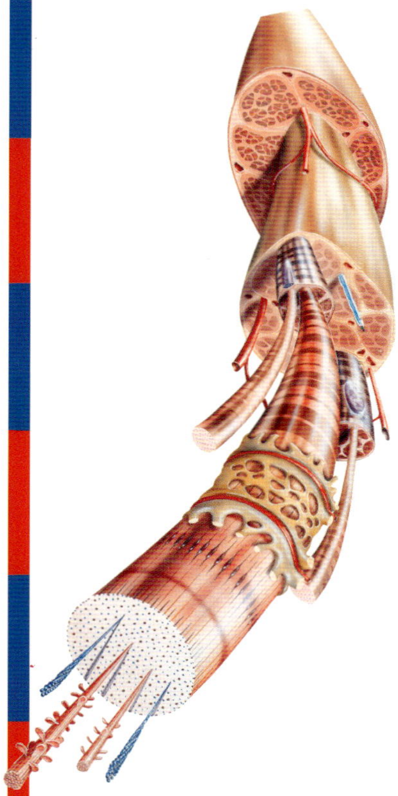

DID YOU KNOW?

p

This is a Parragon Book
First published in 2000

Parragon
Queen Street House
4 Queen Street
Bath BA1 1HE, UK

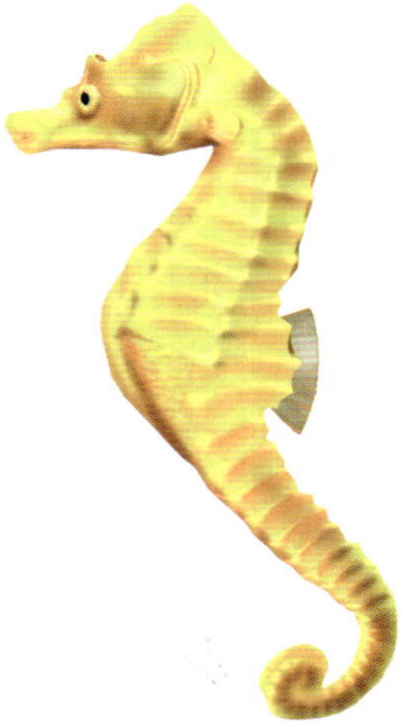

Produced by
Monkey Puzzle Media Ltd
Gissing's Farm
Fressingfield
Suffolk IP21 5SH
UK

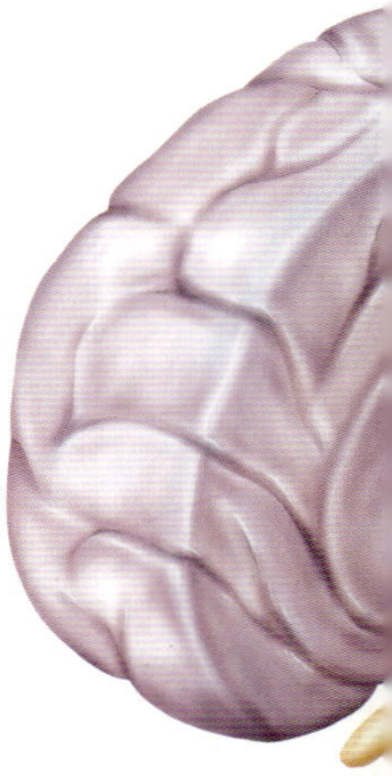

ISBN 0-75254-486-1

Printed in Hong Kong

Authors
Peter Eldin, Jason Hook and Jillian Powell

Illustrators
Michael Posen, David McAllister, Mike Atkinson, Julian Baker, Andrew Farmer, Rob Jakeway, John James and Roger Kent

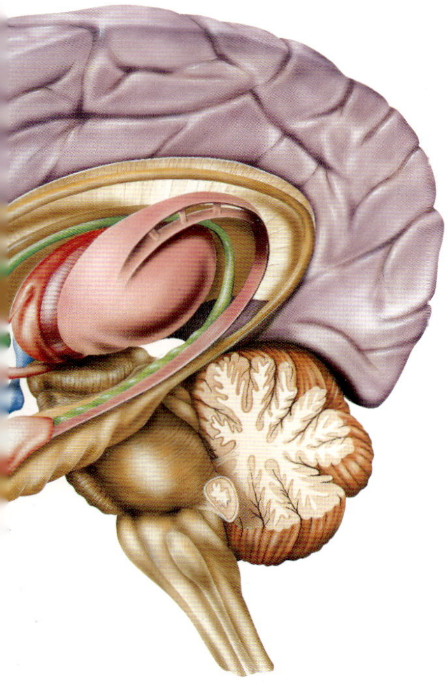

Designers
Cobalt Information Design

Editor
Louisa Somerville

Additional Editorial Assistance
Jenny Siklós, Lynda Lines and Caroline Hamilton

Contents

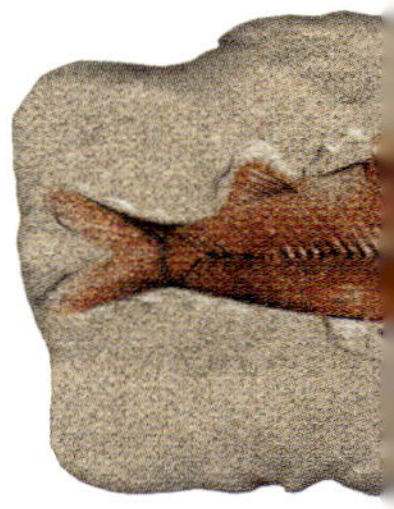

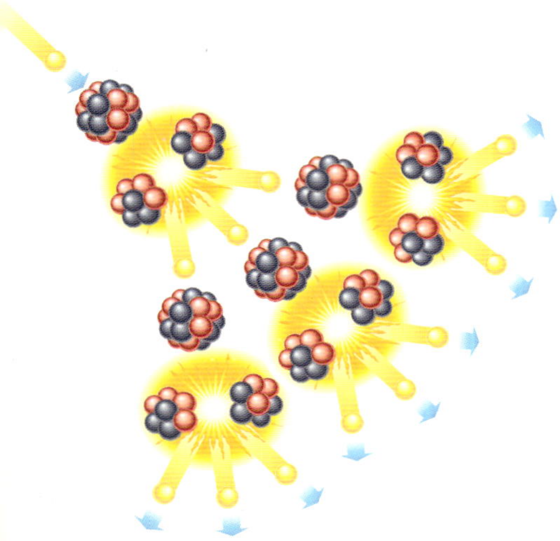

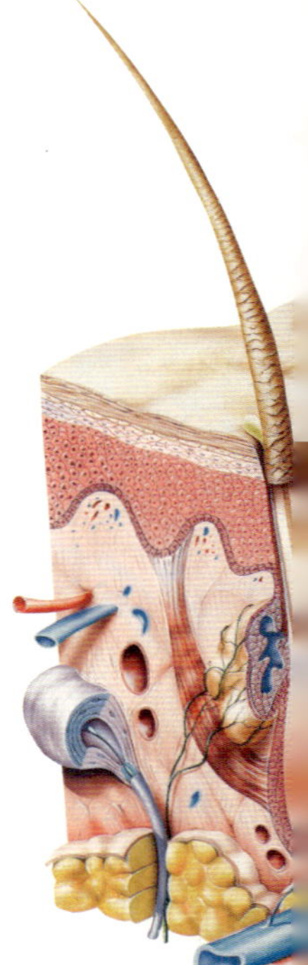

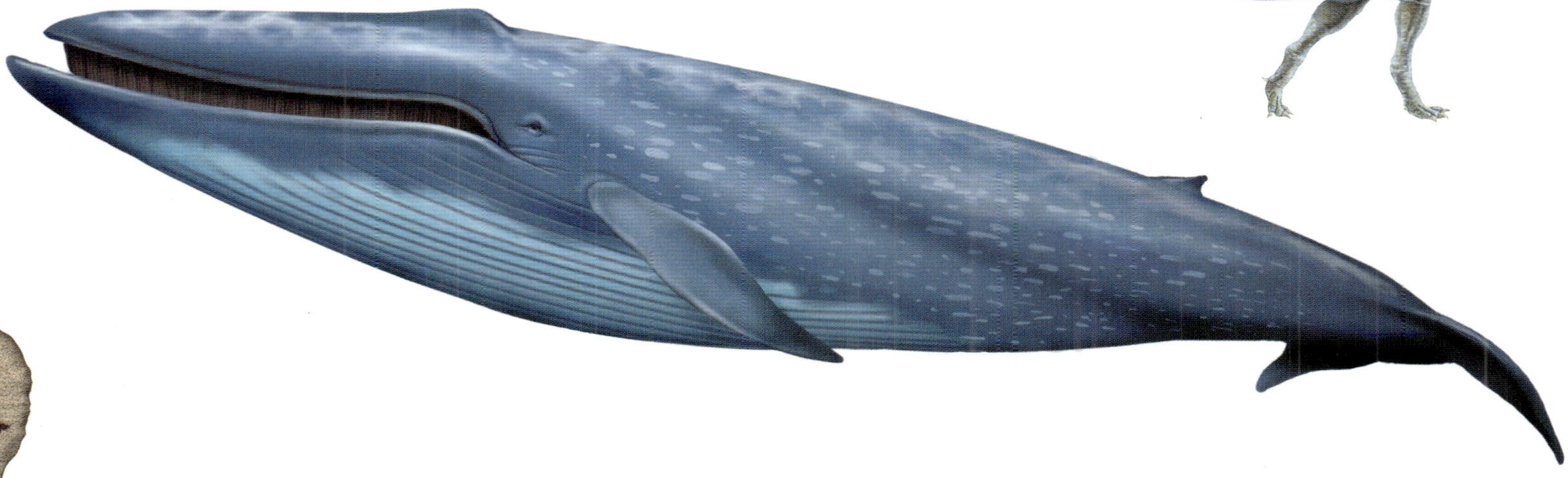
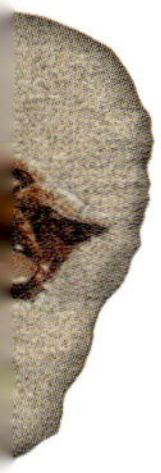

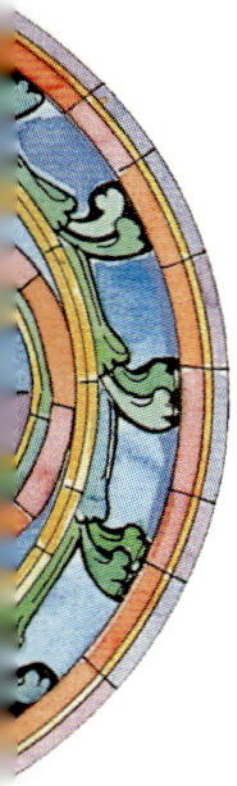
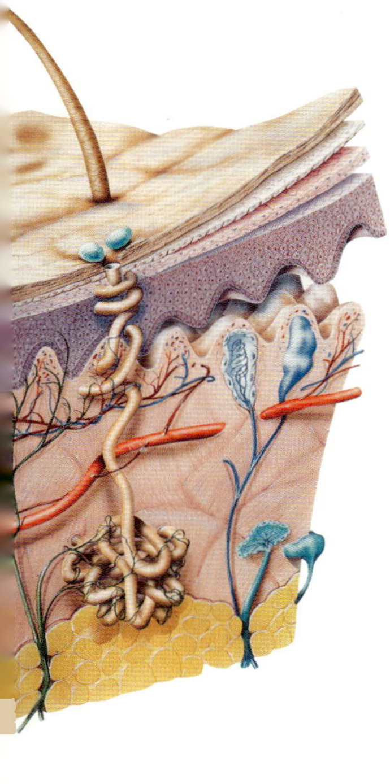

The Universe

The Big Bang

The universe is made up of millions of stars and planets, huge clouds of dust and gas, and vast empty spaces. Everything that exists in space is part of the universe. No-one knows how big the universe is. It is so vast that scientists measure it in light years. One light year is the distance light travels in a year — about 9,460,000 million km (5,910,000 million mi). However, we may still only have discovered about ten percent of the universe.

The Universe Began With A Big Bang

Scientists believe that the universe began with a vast explosion called Big Bang about 15 billion years ago. Powerful radio telescopes have detected weak signals that could be echoes of the Big Bang. Scientists believe that time, space and all the matter in the universe began with Big Bang. Within minutes of the explosion, atomic particles joined together to make the gases helium and hydrogen. Over millions of years, these gases formed the universe and all the stars and galaxies within it. The universe started to expand after Big Bang and has gone on getting bigger. Even today, parts of the universe are still forming. Scientists used to think that the universe was curved in shape, but now they believe it is probably flat. Some scientists think that in billions of years, the universe will come together in a Big Crunch, or will just stop expanding.

Artist's impression of the Big Bang

The Milky Way

Stars Began As Huge Clouds Of Gas After Big Bang

As the universe expanded and cooled after Big Bang, the force of gravity pulled matter together to form billions of stars. Stars are grouped together in galaxies which form different shapes. About a third of all galaxies are spiral shaped.

There Are Millions Of Galaxies In The Universe

The Sun — the Earth's star — s part of a galaxy called the Milky Way. Scientists used to think that the Milky Way was the only galaxy in the universe. They now know there are at least 100,000 million other galaxies. Like all galaxies, the Milky Way is moving, and the stars inside it move around its centre. It takes a ray of starlight about 100,000 years tc cross the Milky Way. The Milky Way gets its name because it looks like a splash of milk in the night sky. Ir ancient Greek mythology, the goddess Juno was feeding her baby Hercules when he spilt some milk.

Did You Know?

★

The Milky Way is a vast spiral containing over 100 billion stars.

A light year is the distance light travels in a year – over 9 trillion kilometres. The Milky Way is 10C,000 light years across. That's quite big!

The universe might be infinite! Can you imagine what that means?

Modern telescopes can collect light that has been travelling for 25,000 years.

After the first millisecond of the Big Bang, the expanding universe was 50 billion times denser than lead, and 30 million times hotter than the Sun.

Scientists have discovered twenty planets with a Sun like ours, which might contain alien life!

The Stars

There are billions of stars in every galaxy. Each star is a spinning ball of hot gases. Nuclear reactions in the hot core produce heat and light, which we see as starlight. Stars begin as clouds of gas and dust that slowly come together from atoms scattered in space. They vary in size and brightness.

The Sun Is The Earth's Star

The closest star to Planet Earth is the Sun. It is about 150 million km (94 million mi) away from Earth and its rays take 8.3 minutes to reach us. The next nearest star to Earth is called Proxima Centauri, and is about 40 million million km (25 million million mi) away.

Birth of a star

New Stars Are Born All The Time

New stars form from huge clouds of spinning gas and dust. The clouds swirl around until the force of gravity pulls them together into clumps of matter which get tighter and hotter until nuclear reactions are sparked off, turning hydrogen into helium which burns and shines. Most new stars are very hot and bright. As starlight passes through the Earth's atmosphere, the rays are bent at different angles, depending on the temperature of the air. As light passes through both hot and cold air, it shines in many different directions at once. This is what makes stars appear to twinkle.

Stars Turn Red Before They Die

Stars eventually die when the gases inside them burn out. The bigger a star is, the faster it burns up its hydrogen gas. Big stars blow up into vast red supergiants then explode into supernovas. The supernova throws shells of gas into space at up to 40 km (25 mi) a second. It leaves behind expanding layers of gas and dust with a small spinning star at the certre. Smaller stars blow up and turn red, then blow away their outer layers of gas to leave a dead star, called a white dwarf, which cools and fades.

Stars Race Through Space At High Speed

Stars look as though they are fixed in the night sky but really they are moving through space at high speed. They are just too far away for us to detect their movement, except using powerful equipment. Although they are moving, stars form patterns called constellations. There are 88 different constellations. Many of them have names from Greek mythology.

Did You Know?

The earliest recorded observations of the stars were made in China in about 3000 BC.

The signs of the zodiac are dot-to-dot pictures made in the night sky by the stars of different groups or 'constellations'.

Many constellations were given their names by the ancient Greeks.

Rock paintings in Arizona and New Mexico were made by Native Americans to record a supernova in the Taurus constellation in 1054.

The Sun is only a medium-sized star. It is 100 times bigger than the Earth, but some stars are 1,000 times bigger again!

The brightest star that can be seen from Earth is the 'Dog Star', Sirius, which gives off thirty times more light than the Sun.

The Solar System

The Sun, and everything in its orbit, make up the Solar System. Scientists believe that the Solar System began to form at the edge of the Milky Way Galaxy about 10 billion years ago, after Big Bang. As well as the Sun, planets and moons, the Solar System contains lumps of ice and rock and vast clouds of dust. All of these are held together by the force of the Sun's gravity.

Jupiter

Jupiter Could Hold Over 1,000 Planet Earths

Jupiter is the biggest planet in the Solar System. It is over 1,000 times larger than Earth. It is made mainly of gas, but its mass is so large its gravity acts like a giant vacuum cleaner, sucking lumps of rock, such as asteroids, into its atmosphere.

Comets Are Like Dirty Snowballs In Space

Comets are lumps of ice mixed with dust and grit that orbit the Sun. They are 'space litter' left over from when the Solar System formed. The solid part of a comet is surrounded by a cloud of glowing gas. When a comet's orbit takes it near the Sun so that it begins to melt, gas and dust stream out to form the comet's tail. This is why comets were once known as "hairy stars." Comets have vast orbits and some can only be seen from Planet Earth every few thousand years. Most are named after the astronomers who discovered them, such as the Hale-Bopp Comet, which came into view from Earth between 1995 and 1997.

The Earth Is One Of Nine Planets That Orbit The Sun

All the planets in the Solar System travel in the same direction but at different speeds. The four closest planets to the Sun are small and rocky. They are Earth, Mars, Mercury and Venus. The planets further away are made of ice, gas and liquids. They are Jupiter, Saturn, Neptune, Uranus and Pluto.

There May Be A Mystery Planet X

Some scientists believe there is a tenth planet still to be discovered in our Solar System. They believe Planet X is bigger than Pluto and that its gravity affects Uranus and Neptune, but it may be too far away for us to detect, even with the most powerful equipment.

Did You Know?

In 1987, the space probe Pioneer 10 became the first man-made object to leave the solar system.

When the Italian astronomer Galileo looked at Jupiter in 1610, it was the first time a planet had been studied through a telescope.

Io, one of Jupiter's sixteen moons, is the most volcanic body in the solar system, throwing up lava spouts 140 km high.

On Mars, there is a volcano over twice the height of Everest.

There is a picture of Halley's Comet on the Bayeux Tapestry, because it appeared in 1066.

Mercury is the fastest-moving planet in the solar system, and was named after the ancient Roman messenger of the gods.

The Moon

The Moon is the nearest object in space to Planet Earth. It is a ball of rock about a quarter of the Earth's size. Earth's gravity makes the Moon spin round on its axis as it orbits the planet. Astronomers don't know for certain how the Moon formed. Billions of years ago, it may have been a planet itself.

The Moon Causes The Ocean Tides

The gravity of the Moon pulls at the water in the Earth's oceans to make it swell into a high tide. As the Earth spins every 24 hours, each part has a high tide twice a day. The highest tides are called spring tides. They happen when the Moon is in line with the Sun and the Earth, and the sun's gravity pulls at the oceans too.

There Are Many Moons In The Universe

Many other planets in the solar system have moons that orbit them. Mars has two moons, and Saturn has at least 18 moons. Some moons are globes like the Earth's Moon, others look like lumps of rock. Some have craters, mountains and valleys. Moons may once have been planets that have been pulled into the orbit of another planet by gravity.

Moonlight Is Really Reflected Sunlight

The Moon has no light of its own, but it is the brightest thing we see in the night sky because it reflects the light of the Sun. As the Moon orbits Earth, we see different amounts of its sunlit face, from a tiny crescent to a full moon. When the side of the Moon that faces Earth has no sunlight on it, it is a new moon that we can't see. The time it takes from a new moon to a full moon is 29 1/2 days, or one lunar month. The different stages are known as the phases of the Moon.

Phases of the Moon

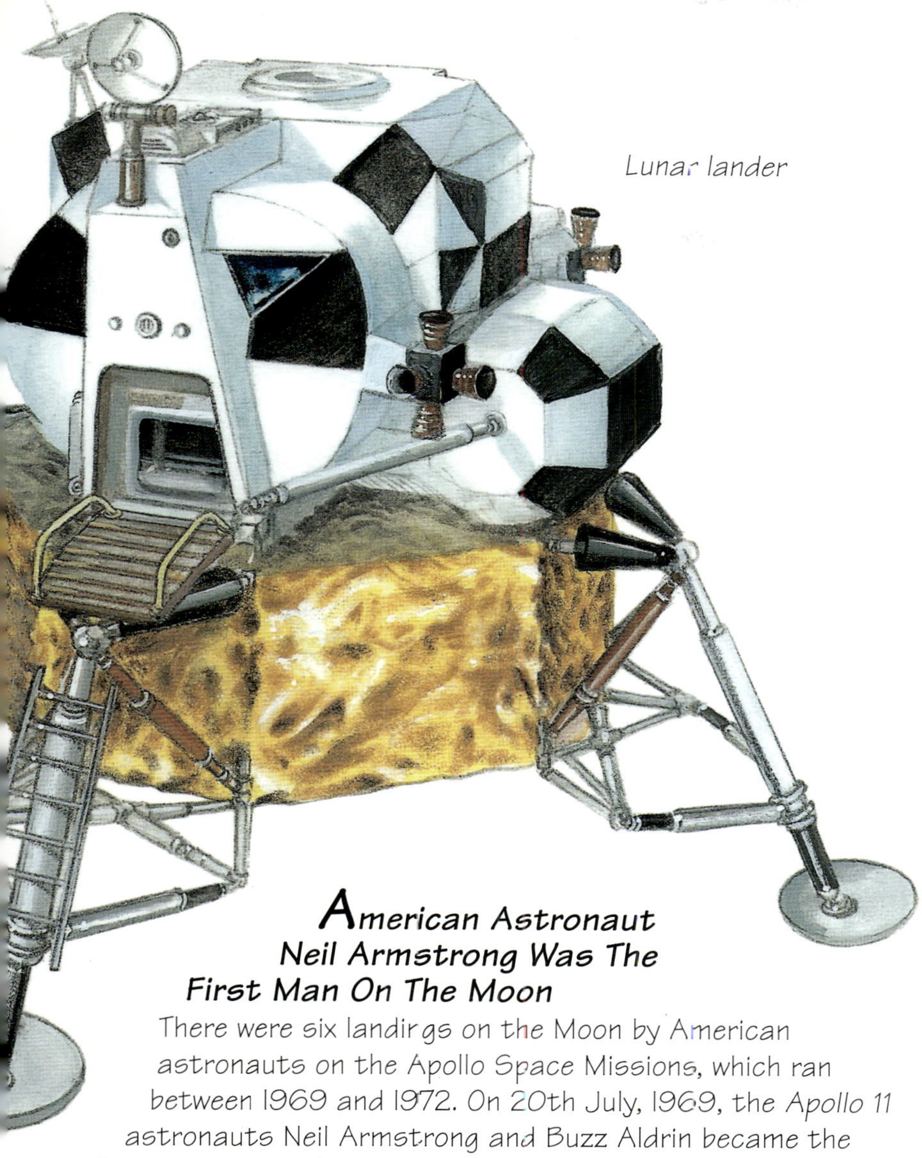

Lunar lander

American Astronaut Neil Armstrong Was The First Man On The Moon

There were six landings on the Moon by American astronauts on the Apollo Space Missions, which ran between 1969 and 1972. On 20th July, 1969, the *Apollo 11* astronauts Neil Armstrong and Buzz Aldrin became the first men to set foot on the Moon. They brought back rock samples and left scientific instruments on the Moon to send information back to Earth. TV footage shows them jumping on the Moon's surface. Gravity on the Moon is one sixth of the Earth's gravity, so people can jump six times higher on the Moon than on the Earth.

Did You Know?

Priests in ancient Mesapotamia recorded lunar eclipses in 2000 BC.

About one-fifth of Earth's population heard Neil Armstrong, the first man on the Moon, say: 'That's one small step for man, one giant leap for mankind.'

Sir Isaac Newton invented the reflecting telescope in 1668, then explained why the Moon's motion affected Earth's tides.

Because of gravity, a child who weighs 28 kg (62 lb) on Earth would weigh less than 5 kg (11 lb) on the Moon

Many of the craters on the Moon were created when it was struck by meteors and asteroids.

The gravitational pull of the Moon can cause the North American continent to rise 15 cm (6 in) when the Moon is above it.

The Sun

The Sun, like all stars, is a ball of hot, spinning gases. It is the brightest star in our sky because it is the nearest to Earth. The warmth and heat that the Sun provides gives energy to plants and animals on Earth. Without the Sun, there would be no life on Earth.

The Sun Is A Middle-Aged Star

The Sun formed about 5 billion years ago and is about half way through its life. After Big Bang, tiny particles of hydrogen gas joined together to make helium gas, giving off heat and light which we call sunshine. At is core, the Sun's temperature is about 14,000,000 °C (25,000,000 °F).The Sun will burn up all its hydrogen in about 6 billion years. Scientists believe it will then explode into a supernova, destroying everything in the solar system, including Earth.

Solar Eclipses Happen When The Moon Blocks Out The Sun

A solar eclipse only happens when the Moon is directly between the Sun and the Earth. The Sun is 400 times bigger than the Moon, but it is also 400 times further away, so the Moon is big enough to block out its light. Total eclipses only happen once every few years and last just a few minutes. Because they happen in a different part of the world each time, astronomers travel all over the world to view them using special equipment.

The Sun Could Hold Over A Million Planet Earths

The Sun is bigger than everything else in the solar system put together. It measures about 1.4 million km (875,000 mi) across. Its mass is so large it acts like a magnet and pulls everything else in the solar system into its orbit, including the Earth.

The Temperature On The Sun's Surface Is Around 6,000° C (10,800° F).

Astronomers can sometimes detect dark patches on the surface of the Sun, which they call sunspots. These are patches of gas that look darker because they are cooler than the surface temperature. Occasionally, they group together to form a dark cluster. The largest one ever seen measured about 18,130 million square km (7,000 square mi).

Cutaway view of the Sun

Planet Earth

The Living Planet

Earth is the only planet in the Solar System that can support life. Its atmosphere contains the gases oxygen and nitrogen, which plants and animals need to breathe and grow new cells. Earth's distance from the Sun means that water can exist as a liquid rather than just as ice or water vapour, and the Sun's warmth and light provide energy for all living things.

Some Parts Of The Earth Spin Faster Than Others

The Sun's gravity makes the Earth spin round on its axis once every 24 hours. It turns towards the Sun, then away again, giving us day and night. The Earth always spins towards the east so we see the Sun rise in the east and set in the west. Everywhere on Earth takes 24 hours to spin round, but different parts spin at different speeds. Near the North and South Poles, the Earth hardly moves. But at its widest part, round the Equator, Earth moves at over 1,600 km (1,000 mi) every hour or 40,000 km (25,000 mi) every day. As well as spinning on its axis, the Earth is journeying round the Sun every year, travelling at a speed of about 10,458 kph (6,500 mph).

Did You Know?

You may feel like you are standing still, but the Earth is orbiting the Sun at over 107,000 kph (66,500 mph)!

According to an ancient Hindu belief, the Earth was held up by elephants standing on the back of a giant turtle.

In 250 BC, an ancient Greek astronomer called Eratosthenes accurately calculated the Earth's circumference by measuring shadows cast by the Sun.

When a comet struck Siberia in 1908, a 60 km (37 mi) area of forest was flattened and the shockwaves were felt in London!

In 1650, the Christian Church accepted Archbishop James Ussher's findings that Earth had been created at 9 am on Sunday 23 October, 4004 BC.

The fact that the Earth is magnetic was established by Queen Elizabeth I's physician William Gilbert.

Planet Earth as it appears from space

Seasons Happen Because The Earth Is Tilted

As it spins on its axis, the Earth is tilted at an angle of 23.5°. As Earth circles the Sun, for half the year the northern half is tilted towards the Sun, while the southern half tilts away. For the other half of the year, it is the northern half that tilts away from the Sun. This gives us our seasons. At the Equator, the Earth's tilt makes little difference to the amount of Sun so there are no seasons. At the Poles, there are only winter and summer.

Earth Is About 5 Billion Years Old

Planet Earth formed after the Big Bang, from a spinning cloud of gas and dust in space. Like all the planets in the Solar System, Earth is made up of layers. The crust, or outer layer, is a thin layer of hard rock. Beneath that is the mantle, which is part solid and part iquid, and beneath that is a solid metal core which is surrounded by hot liquid metal. You would have to dig down 6,378 km (4,000 mi) to reach the centre of the Earth.

The Continents

The Earth's surface is divided into about 20 pieces, or plates, like the panels of a football. Scientists call them tectonic plates. These plates are constantly moving and rearranging themselves, and as they move they carry the continents of land and ocean floors with them. Movements in the Earth's plates shape the continents, build up or destroy mountains, and cause earthquakes and volcanoes.

Africa And South America Were Once Joined

In the 1960s, scientists realised that the continents are moving around the surface of the planet. This is known as 'continental drift'. For over 300 years, scientists had noticed that the shapes of some continents, such as the west coast of Africa and the east coast of South America, would fit together like pieces of a jigsaw. This suggested they had once been joined together as part of a larger continent.

Did You Know?

★

If the ice at the polar caps was to melt, the oceans would rise by nearly 100 metres (330 ft).

The levels of the oceans were so much lower 15,000 years ago that the first Native Americans were able to walk from Siberia into North America.

The seas contain 60,000,000,000,000,000,000,000,000,000,000,000,000,000,000,000,000 water molecules!

In the 1700s, scientists called Neptunists claimed that the entire earth had once been covered by a thick, soupy ocean.

Scandinavia is believed to have risen 300 m (almost 1,000 ft) since the glaciers that pressed down on it melted over 9,000 years ago.

The longest mountain range in the world is actually underwater. It is called the Mid-Ocean Ridge.

The Land Beneath Your Feet Is Moving

The movement of the Earth's plates means that the continents are still drifting slowly apart. North America is about 10 m (30 ft) further away from Europe than it was when it was first discovered around 500 years ago, and the Atlantic Ocean gets wider by a few centimetres (inches) every year. Millions of years from now, North America may break away from South America, and Australia may drift further northwards. A map of the world in the future might look as strange to us as a map of the world from millions of years ago.

There Was Once Only One Supercontinent

Scientists now believe that there were once very different continents scattered around the globe. Slowly, they moved together until, around 300 million years ago, they joined together to form a vast supercontinent which scientists call Pangaea, or 'all land'. Then, around 100 million years later, this continent began to break up into the continents we have today. This explains why scientists have found parts of the same ancient mountain ranges, and fossils of the same animals, scattered on different continents, and why Europe once had a very different climate — because it was once in the Tropics.

280 million years ago

180 million years ago

65 million years ago

The world today

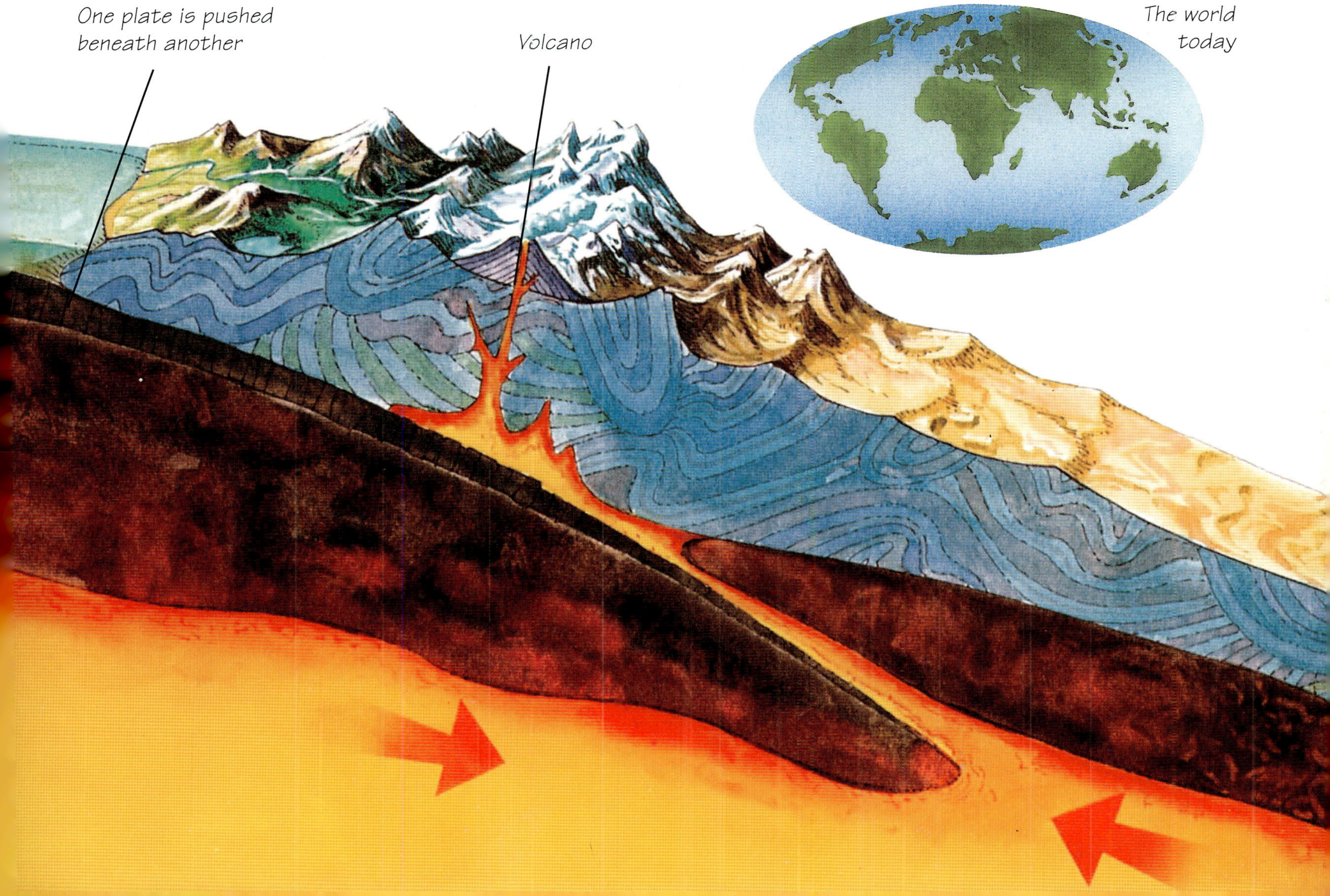

Earthquakes

When the Earth's plates collide together or pull apart, we feel the movement as earthquakes. Most earthquakes happen along the edges of tectonic plates. In a small quake, the plates move just a fraction, but a major earthquake can shake the ground so violently that buildings collapse and many people may be injured or killed. There can be after-shocks for days, or months, after a major earthquake.

Did You Know?

Over one million people are believed to have died in an earthquake that struck Syria in 1201.

The most powerful earthquake ever recorded measured 9.5 on the Richter Scale, and struck Chile on 22 May 1960.

Earthquakes beneath the oceans release powerful 'tsunamis', or tidal waves, which lift up ships and dump them in the middle of towns. They can travel at over 900 kph (560 mph) and reach 300 m (1,000 feet) high.

Nearly 3 million earthquakes occur each year, though most of them are too small to be felt.

After an earthquake, the earth vibrates like a giant gong – creating a note twenty octaves lower than middle C!

Three earthquakes that struck New Madrid, Missouri in 1811 and 1812 were so powerful that they changed the course of the Mississippi River.

Tidal Waves Are Caused By Earthquakes Under The Sea

When an earthquake shakes land under the sea, the vibrations it causes can set off tidal waves called tsunamis. Tsunamis can cross oceans and flood land far away from the earthquake's epicentre. They can travel at speeds of several hundred kilometres (miles) an hour and when they reach shallow water near a coastline, they can build up waves 30 m (90 ft) high, which flood the land causing havoc and destruction. A tsunami that hit the coast of Bengal in 1873 killed 200,000 people.

Movements In The Earth's Crust Cause Earthquakes

Earthquakes are also caused by movements in the Earth's crust, making rocks crack into blocks and slide past each other. These cracks are called faults. One famous fault is the San Andreas Fault in California, USA.

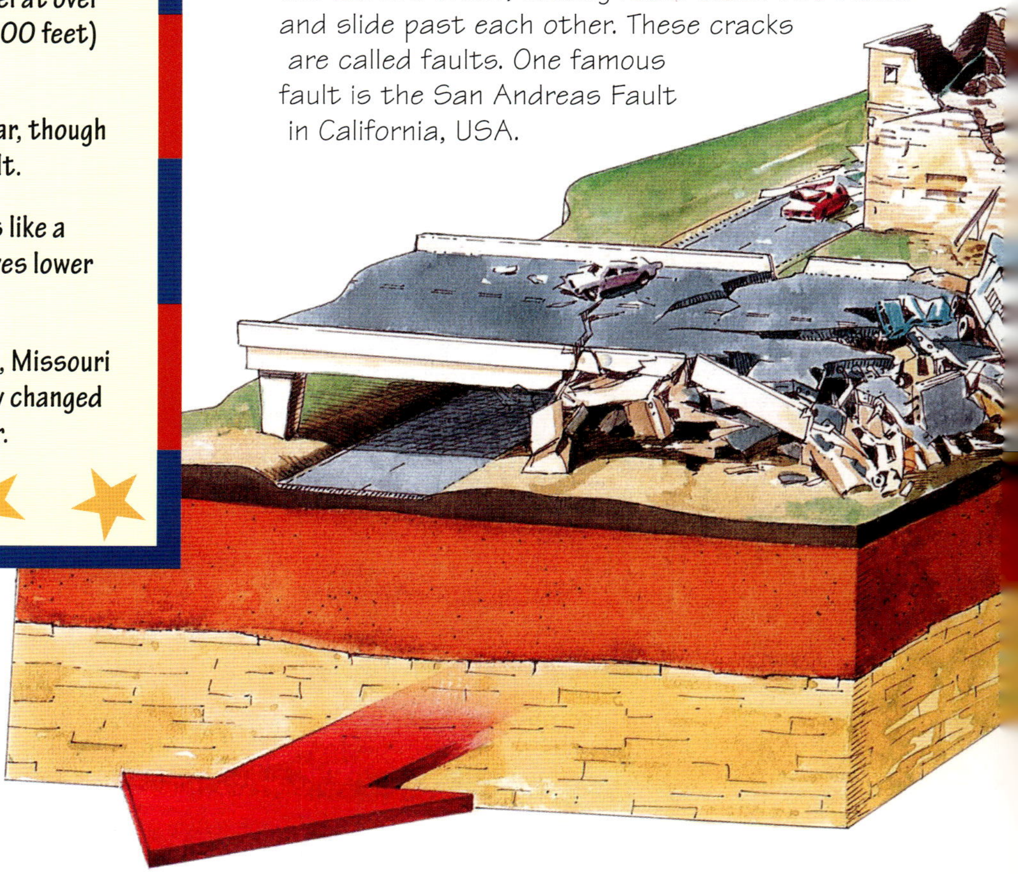

The Pacific Ocean Is Surrounded By A Ring Of Fire

The zone around the Pacific Ocean is known as the 'Ring of Fire' because most of the world's earthquakes and volcanoes happen here, where several of the Earth's tectonic plates meet.

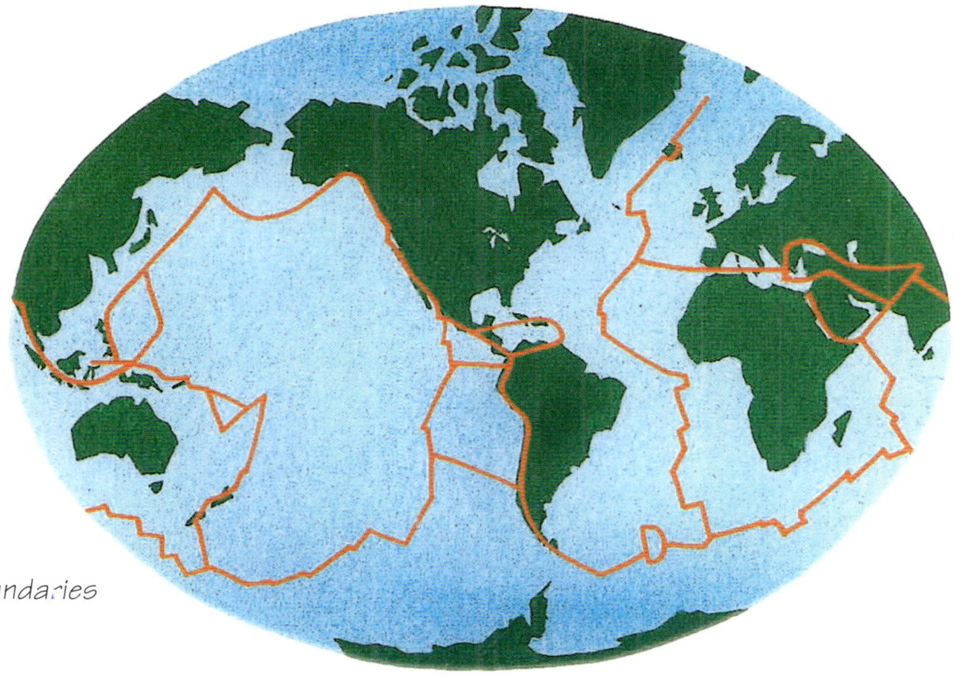

Plate boundaries

Scientists Predict When Earthquakes Will Happen

For thousands of years, people have tried to predict when earthquakes will happen. They looked for signs in nature, such as animals behaving strangely. The ancient Chinese were the first to invent instruments to detect earthquakes. Today scientists use satellites to detect hotspots on the Earth's surface where earthquakes or volcanoes may happen. They use seismographs and seismometers to detect and measure vibrations made by earthquakes. In 1935, the scientist Charles F. Richter (1900 – 1985) worked out a scale for measuring the energy released during earthquakes. On the Richter scale, earthquakes are measured in magnitudes, with each one 30 times greater than the last. Another scale of measurement, the Mercalli scale, is based on the effects of earthquakes. A Mercalli III earthquake rattles windows, while the top of the scale, Mercalli XII, destroys whole areas.

Volcanoes

The Earth's core contains great heat and pressure, like a giant powerhouse. Volcanoes erupt when hot, liquid rock and gas burst out of cracks in the Earth's surface. Most volcanoes erupt along the edges of the Earth's tectonic plates, but some punch through hotspots in the Earth's crust.

There Are Hundreds Of Active Volcanoes On Earth

There are around 1,300 active volcanoes on Earth. The most violent eruptions happen where two of the Earth's plates collide. Pressure builds up until liquid rock, called magma, bursts out of a mountain as lava, or explodes into clouds of dust and lava bombs. Some volcanoes blast holes in mountain sides. Others, like those on the Hawaiian islands, burst out as 'mantle plumes' through cracks in the ground. Some volcanoes remain dormant (inactive) for hundreds of years before they erupt. When a volcano stops erupting altogether, it becomes extinct.

Did You Know?

When Krakatoa, in Indonesia, erupted on 26 August 1883, the explosions were heard in Australia, over 3,000 km (1,850 mi) away.

So much dust was blown into the atmosphere by Krakatoa that the sunlight was blocked out and temperatures dropped worldwide.

The word 'volcano' comes from Vulcan, the Roman god of fire. The Romans believed Vulcan lived beneath the volcanic island of Vulcano, off the Italian coast.

Since its boiling lava destroyed and preserved the city of Pompeii in AD 79, Vesuvius has erupted a further eighty times.

The famous ancient Roman writer Pliny the Elder was killed by the poisonous fumes from Vesuvius – when he landed his ship in an attempt to get a better view of the eruption!

Volcanoes Have Different Shapes

The shape of a volcano depends on how it erupts and the kind of lava it throws out. Some produce runny lava that spreads into a low shield shape. Others shoot out a sticky lava that builds up into a steep cone. When magma cools to form a plug in a dormant volcano, the rocky plug can last long after the rest of the volcano has worn away. The Devil's Tower in Wyoming, USA, and the Sugar Loaf mountain in Rio de Janeiro, Brazil, are both the remains of volcanoes.

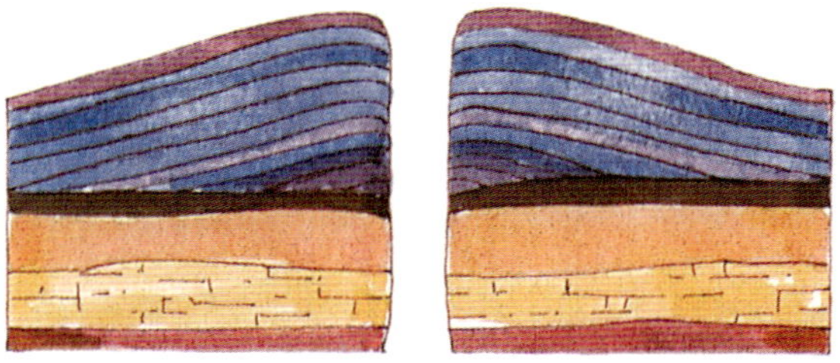

Shield-shaped volcano

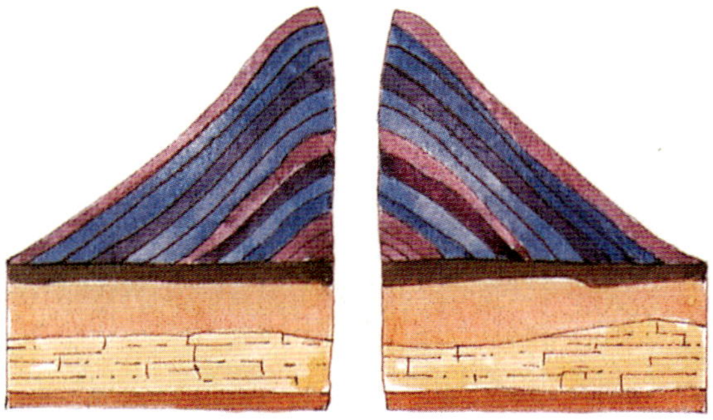

Cone-shaped volcano

Volcanoes Erupt In Space

The biggest known volcano is on Mars. Olympus Mons is 24 km (15mi) high, three times the height of Mount Everest, the highest mountain on Earth. Some of the most active volcanoes in space are found on Io, one of Jupiter's 16 moons. Io has little gravity, so gases reach great heights as they shoot out of the volcano at 1,000 kph (650 mph).

The Roman City of Pompeii Was Buried When Vesuvius Erupted

In 79 AD, the volcano Vesuvius erupted, covering the Roman city of Pompeii under 6 m (18 ft) of hot ash. Many people were just having lunch when the volcano erupted. When the city was uncovered in 1711, fossilized remains of food including bread, olives and figs were found, with the bodies of people and animals just as they were when they tried to escape.

People Once Thought Volcanic Eruptions Were Caused By Angry Gods

Before scientists understood what caused volcanoes to erupt, people believed they were the work of angry gods or goddesses, or of giants or evil spirits. Sometimes people or animals were thrown into volcanic craters as sacrifices, to try to calm the gods' anger.

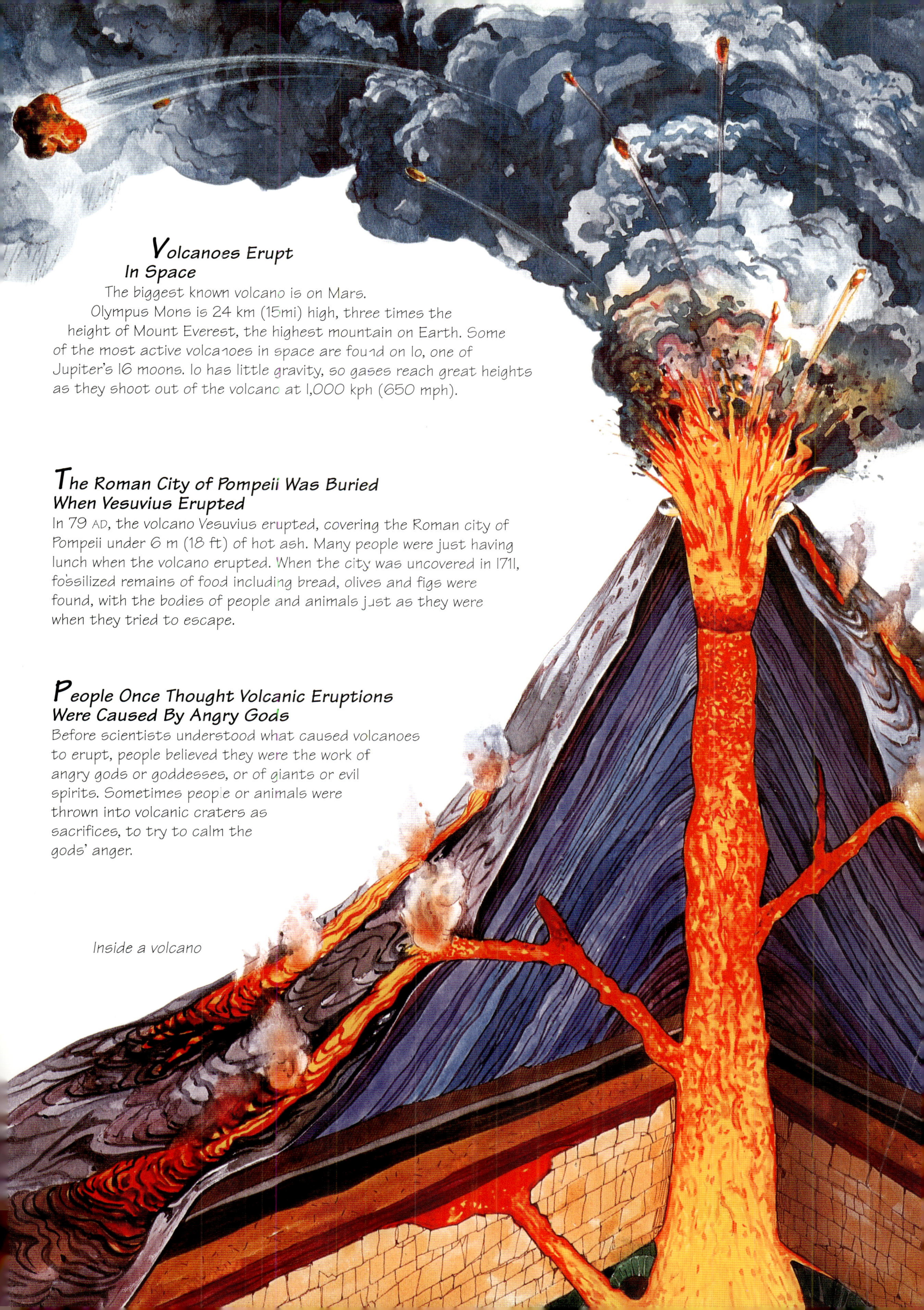

Inside a volcano

Shaping the Landscape

Rivers, seas and ice, and the weather, are constantly shaping and changing our landscape. Without water, Planet Earth would be jagged and cratered like the Moon. Rivers and streams, and glaciers of ice, slowly carve out valleys and plains. Wind and water shape rocks, cliffs and dunes.

Wind-blown sand can shape rocks

The wind blows sand along the ground to form sand dunes

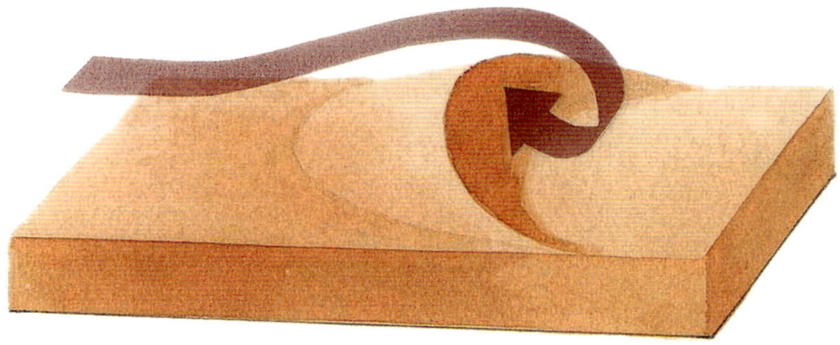

Wind And Rain Shape Rocks

The rocks on the Earth's surface are constantly being worn away and shaped by water, ice and wind. Wind piles sand into dunes, or blasts it at rocks, slowly wearing them away into shapes like sculptures. The sun heats up rocks so that the minerals inside them expand, then at night they cool down and contract. Different minerals expand and contract at different rates, causing the rocks to crack and crumble. Minerals can also be worn from rock by rain. As rain falls, it absorbs gases from the air which make it into a weak acid which eats away at a rock surface. Water can also seep into cracks in a rock then freeze and expand, forcing the rock to split open.

The Norwegian Fjords Were Made By Glaciers In The Last Ice Age

Glaciers are rivers of ice that form when snow builds up and slowly presses down into solid ice. Some form as ice sheets and others as valley glaciers. When glaciers form in mountain valleys, the weight of the ice can make them slide slowly downhill. Some can flow up to 100 m (300 ft) a year. As the ice carries bits of stone and rock with it, it wears away deep valleys and bowls in mountain sides, and builds up mounds of rock called moraines. In the last ice age, ice carried huge boulders from Norway 800 km (500 mi) to the east coast of England.

Did You Know?

Niagara Falls was originally at Lewiston, N.Y., but has gradually moved 11 km (7 mi) further upstream, by eroding the gorge it flows into.

The Mississippi River washes over 600 million tonnes of rock and mud into the Gulf of Mexico each year.

One of the fastest glaciers on record was the Bruarjokull Glacier in Iceland, which slid its enormous bulk along at 125 m (410 ft) a day for two months.

Over 45,000 billion tonnes of salt are dissolved in our oceans.

Greenland's glaciers can be over 3,000 m (1,000 ft) thick, move over 40 m (130 ft) a year, and produce 40,000 icebergs annually.

The Grand Canyon is growing one metre deeper every 6,000 years, as the Colorado River erodes it.

Rivers Shape Valleys And Plains

As rivers and streams slowly wind through the landscape, they wear away solid rock to form deep valleys, and carry mud and silt which they build up into plains and deltas. A delta forms when a river slows down as it flows into the sea. It deposits mud and silt as swampy land, where grasses take root. In Bangladesh, millions of people live on the islands in the delta of the river Ganges.

River running from mountains to the sea

Waves Shape The Coastline

Coastal landscapes change quickly as waves and sea water wear away rock to create cliffs, and build up or wash away sand and stones. Waves can cut into rock to carve out sea caves, or create arches of rock. As these are worn away and crumble, they can leave pillars of rock called stacks.

Natural Wonders of the World

Around the world are natural wonders that have become landmarks and tourist attractions. Many are record breaking natural features, such as the tallest mountain or the highest waterfall. Others are unusual or spectacular landforms that have been created by the weather, or by movements in the Earth's crust.

Movements In The Earth's Crust Formed Ayers Rock

Wind-blown sands have shaped Ayers Rock, in the Australian outback. Movements in the Earth's crust formed a red sandstone hill about 500 million years ago. Aboriginal people call the rock Uluru and for them every cliff, boulder and cave has sacred meaning.

Uluru

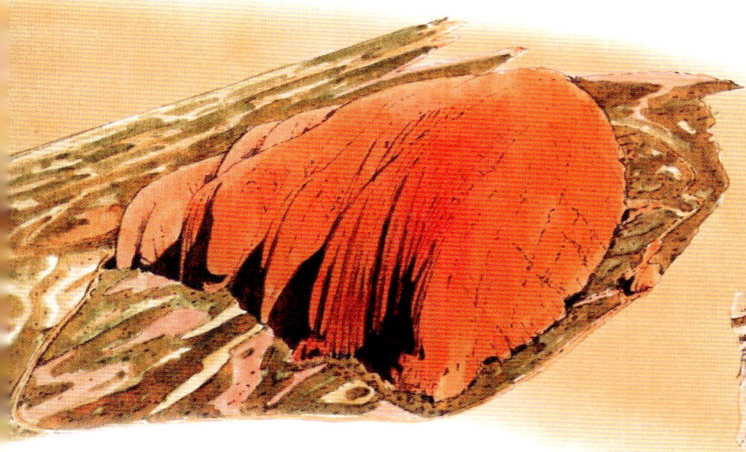

Grand Canyon

Victoria Falls

It Took Six Million Years For The Colorado River To Form The Grand Canyon

Over millions of years, rivers can carve canyons thousands of metres (feet) deep through solid rock. The Grand Canyon in Arizona, USA is the world's longest land gorge. It stretches for 450 km (280 mi) and is 1.6 km (1 mi) deep. Its walls have been described as a cross-section through time, as each layer of rock is older than the one above it. The oldest rocks, at the foot of the Canyon, are at least 2 billion years old.

Niagara Falls First Formed 12,000 Years Ago

A waterfall is a vertical drop of rock over which a river falls. Waterfalls form when rivers pass over hard rock, then over a layer of softer rock. As the softer rock wears away, a vertical face of hard rock is left behind. Spray from Victoria Falls on the river Zambezi, in Africa, reaches heights of 500m (1,650 ft). In the rainy season, the water flows at the rate of 550 million litres (120 million gal) a minute, over the rock face. At Niagara Falls on the US-Canadian border, water falls at 80 km (50 mi) an hour, wearing away about a metre (3 ft) of rock every year. The Falls are now 11 km (7 mi) further upriver than they were when they first formed about 12,000 years ago. The world's highest waterfall is Angel Falls in Venezuela, which have a total drop of 979 m (3,212 ft).

Rocks and Minerals

The Earth's Rocks

The Earth is covered in a thin crust of rocks. There are many types of rock, from hard granite to soft chalk. The rocks themselves are made up of substances called minerals. Most rocks contain several minerals, such as quartz or gypsum. There are thousands of minerals on Earth but only about 30 of them form rocks.

Did You Know?

A type of sandstone found in India, called itacolumite, can be bent by hand.

Pumice is filled with so many air-holes that it will float in water.

Carbon-dating was used to prove that the Dead Sea Scrolls – the oldest surviving version of the Bible – were written around the time of Christ.

Granite found near Dodoma in Tanzania has been dated at 3.6 billion years old.

Scientists have used carbon-dating on fragments of meteorites, and found them to be 4.5 billion years old.

A Greek philosopher called Theophrastus wrote a study of rocks, minerals and fossils in about 300 BC, called 'Concerning Stones'.

Rocks Are Formed From Minerals

Mineral deposits form underground when heat and pressure change rock into hot, runny magma. As the magma cools, crystals appear, which harden to form rocks. Minerals can also be worn from rocks by wind, water or ice, and washed into rivers and streams.

Greenland Has The Oldest Rocks

Geologists (people who study rocks) can tell how old rocks are by studying the radioactive minerals in them. When a rock forms, it contains some radioactive elements, which decay over time. Geologists have worked out the rate at which elements decay, so they can tell the age of a rock by the amount of radioactive elements that remain. The oldest rocks so far dated are in Greenland. They are about 3,800 million years old.

Sand, silt and mud are washed into lakes and seas, where they pile up in layers. Over millions of years, the layers harden to form sedimentary rocks.

Rocks Can Take Millions Of Years To Form

There are three main kinds of rock. Igneous rocks form when hot, runny rock called magma cools underground, or pours out of volcanoes or cracks in the Earth to harden on the surface as lava. Sedimentary rocks form from layers of sediment (small bits of rock). Wind, water and ice wear away older rocks, then fragments get washed away and slowly build up in layers. Over time, the layers harden into new rocks. Metamorphic rocks form when older rocks change by being heated or squashed. Most rocks take millions of years to form.

The Grand Canyon's Oldest Rocks Are At The Bottom

The Grand Canyon in Arizona, USA was carved out by the Colorado River. It took around 2,000 million years to form. The further down the canyon you climb, the older the rocks are.

The Rocks In The Earth Are Recycled

Rocks slowly change from one kind into another. This is called the rock cycle. Igneous rocks are worn away by water, wind and ice and build up into new layers of sedimentary rocks. Heat and pressure change these rocks into metamorphic rocks. They in turn can heat up to form new magma, which forms igneous rocks, to start the cycle again.

A Mineral Is Named After Three Astronauts

When astronauts went to the Moon in the 1960s and 70s, they brought back rock samples. Most of the minerals in the rocks were similar to those on Earth, but one new mineral was found. It was named armacolite after Armstrong, Aldrin and Collins, the first astronauts to set foot on the Moon in 1969.

Rock Forms and Features

All over the Earth rocks have formed different types of landscape from mountains and canyons to sand dunes and flat plains. These natural features form when rocks are made, or are worn away by water, wind or ice. For thousands of years, rocks have also been shaped by people as stone for buildings, tombs, statues and more.

Columns Of Basalt Look Like Giant Stepping Stones

The Giant's Causeway, on the coast of County Antrim, Northern Ireland, was formed about 60 million years ago. The continents of North America and Europe, which had been joined together, began to split apart. Lava poured up from the ocean floor, making a dark, igneous rock called basalt. As it cooled, the basalt shrank into thousands of six-sided columns, which wind and water have worn away to look like giant steps. Legend says that the columns were put there as stepping stones by a giant called Finn MacCool.

The Giant's Causeway

Did You Know?

Finn MacCool, who legends say built the Giant's Causeway to get from Ireland to Scotland, used to get his ideas by sucking his thumb.

The earth is made up of dense rocks, making it the heaviest planet in the solar system. The lightest planet is Saturn, which would float in water – if you could find a tank big enough.

The world's tallest stalagmite is found in Krasnohorska Cave, in the Czech Republic, and is a mighty 32 m tall.

The Great Stalactite in a cave at Pol an Ionain, Republic of Ireland, hangs down a tight-fitting 6.2 metres.

Until the 1750s, Christian people believed that fossils were the remains of plants and animals drowned during the Great Flood.

The Egyptian Pyramids Are Lined With Granite

Granite is one of the hardest building stones. The ancient Egyptians used it to line the pyramids that they built as tombs for the pharaohs. The city of Aberdeen, Scotland, is known as the granite city because it is also mainly built from granite. Granite is an igneous rock that forms deep under ground. It contains minerals, including grey quartz and pink and white feldspars, and polishes to a high shine. Granite is quarried by drilling into the rock and driving in steel wedges to break off blocks of stone, or by using dynamite. The granite rock of Mount Rushmore in South Dakota, USA, was carved by dynamite and drilling to form the heads of four US Presidents. Each head is 18 m (60 ft) high and can be seen from 96 km (60 miles) away.

Stalagmites and stalactites

The World's Biggest Cave System Is In Kentucky, USA.

In China's south-western Yunnan Province is the Lunan Stone forest. This 'forest' of stone pillars, up to 30 m (90 feet) high, formed millions of years ago, when movements in the Earth's crust pushed up and folded a bed of limestone. Limestone is a sedimentary rock, made from calcium carbonate. Rainwater can dissolve it away, forming steps and pillars above ground or creating passages, potholes and caves underground. The largest cave system in the world is Mammoth Cave in Kentucky, USA, which has around 530 km (330 mi) of caves and passageways.

Some Stalagmites Are 10,000 Years Old

Inside limestone caves, rainwater dissolves the mineral calcite, dripping from the ceiling and onto the ground to form stalactites (growing downwards) and stalagmites (growing upwards). Stalagmites can take 200 years to grow as thick as a finger. Some are 10,000 years old and measure several metres high.

Fossilized fish

Fossils Are Millions Of Years Old

Fossils are the remains of animals or plants preserved in rocks for millions of years. They can be a whole skeleton, a single bone or a set of footprints. Many fossils can be found in limestone rock.

The Taj Mahal Is Built From Marble

Marble is a metamorphic rock that forms when other rocks, mainly limestone, are changed by heat and pressure. It is easily carved and ranges in colour from white to pink, red, grey or green, but it is also easily damaged by pollution and acid rain. Some of the world's most beautiful buildings, such as the Parthenon in Greece, and the Taj Mahal in India, are built from marble.

Precious Stones

Precious stones, or gemstones, are minerals that are prized because they are rare, beautiful and hard-wearing. They include diamonds, emeralds, rubies and sapphires. There are over 3,000 different minerals, but only about 50 are valued as gemstones. Most are crystals that form when magma cools slowly deep in the Earth's crust. They are found by mining and quarrying, or by sifting the mud from the beds of rivers and streams.

A Diamond Is Cut To Give It Its 'Fire'

When a diamond is first mined, it is called a rough diamond. Rough diamonds vary in shape, and sometimes have to be split before they are cut and polished. Most diamonds are cut using a method, called brilliant cutting, invented by an Italian jeweller in the 17th century. The diamond is cut by a revolving metal plate covered in diamond dust. The faces, or facets, are angled to reflect as much light as possible, giving the diamond its 'fire'. When Queen Victoria was presented with the Koh-i-Nor diamond in 1850, she was disappointed with its sparkle, and had it brilliant cut, which reduced its weight by nearly 80 carats.

Gemstones Are Thought To Have Magic Powers

Gemstones have been collected and worn for thousands of years. In the Middle Ages, many were believed to have healing powers, and were worn as lucky charms. During times of plague in Europe, people believed that if someone wore an opal, it would shine if they became sick, and turn dull if they died. Nowadays, some people believe in the healing power of crystals. According to the ancient Chinese art of Feng Shui, the light they reflect carries positive energy, bringing good health and fortune.

Diamond Is The Hardest Mineral

Diamonds are the most prized gems of all. They form when carbon crystallizes under great heat and pressure about 100 km (62 mi) below the Earth's surface. They are the hardest of all known minerals, and are used not just for jewellery, but have industrial uses, such as drilling and polishing. People once worked out the value of gemstones by weighing them against the seeds of the carob tree. This is the origin of the word 'carat', the measure used to weigh gems nowadays. One carat weighs 0.20 g (3/4 oz).

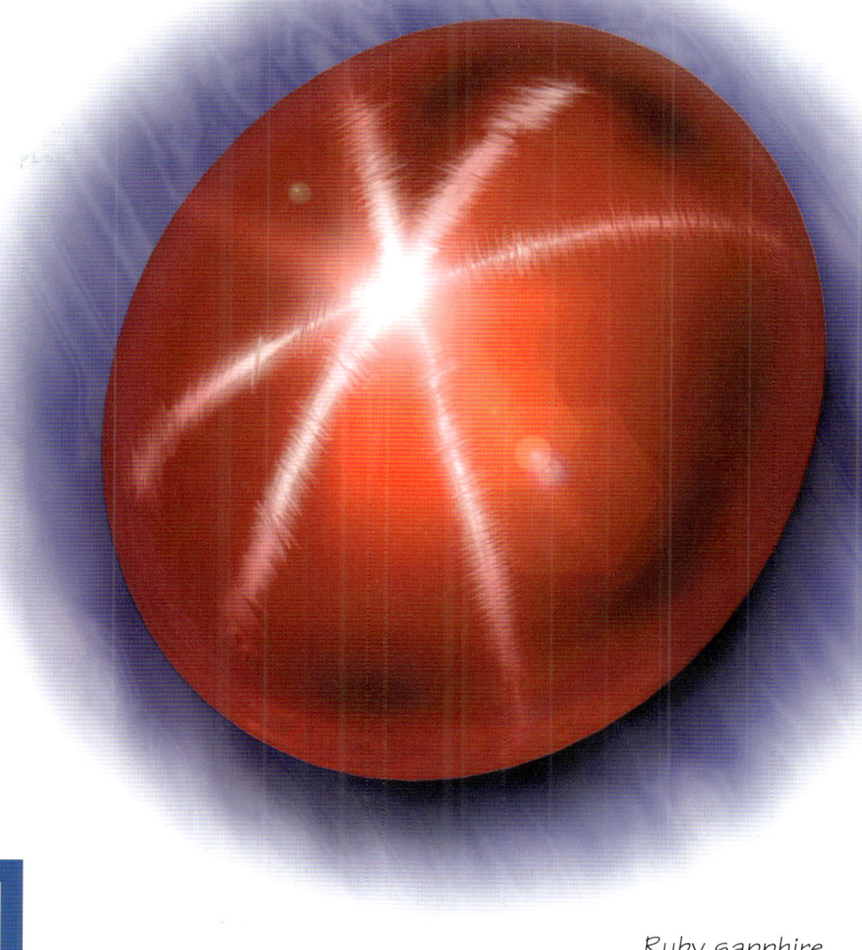

Ruby sapphire

Did You Know?

★

The world's biggest natural diamond was the Cullinan Diamond, mined in Pretoria, South Africa, on 26 January 1905. It weighed in at 3,106 carats or 621 g.

The world's largest cut diamond, the 530-carat Great Star of Africa, was cut from the Cullinan Diamond. It is set in Queen Elizabeth's sceptre, kept in the Tower of London.

Diamonds were mined in India as early as 800 BC, and used as blades in tools and knives.

The Kimberley Diamond Mines in South Africa were discovered when a farmer's boy discovered a 'pretty pebble' in 1867. They produced £78 million of diamonds in the next 26 years.

Owners of the famous Hope Diamond have been cursed with bankruptcy, scandal, suicide and murder.

'Pigeon's Blood' Rubies Are The Most Prized

Rubies are a red form of the mineral corundum. Many are mined in Thailand, but the most prized 'pigeon's blood' colour is found only in rubies from the Mogok mines in Myanmar (Burma). Known as 'the Valley of Rubies', they have been mined for about 1,500 years. Tradition says that the miners used to be paid in small stones by the King who owned the mines, and that this encouraged them to cut larger stones into small pieces. The star rubies from Sri Lanka were once believed to ward off illness and bad luck. They get their name because when they are cut into a dome shape, they reflect a shining star of light.

The World's Biggest Diamond Is The Cullinan Diamond

The main diamond mines are in South Africa and Australia. Diamonds are valued by their weight, their colour, their cut and their clarity. The biggest white diamond ever dug was the Cullinan diamond, which was found in a mine near Pretoria in South Africa in 1905. It weighed 3,106 carats, or 621.2 g (1lb 5oz), and was so big it was cut into nine large stones and 96 smaller ones. Another famous diamond is the Koh-i-Nor, which means 'Mountain of Light', from India. Legend says it belonged to the child of a sun god, before it passed down through generations of Indian emperors. It was shipped to England in the 19th century as a gift for Queen Victoria.

Metals

Many of the things we use everyday, from cars to cutlery, are made from metals. Most metals are found scattered in rocks called ores. Only a few metals, such as gold and silver, are found in pure form. The ore usually has to be crushed and heated to extract the metal.

Chryscolla – a copper ore

Copper And Tin Mixed Together Makes Bronze

Early peoples mined rocks using simple tools, such as sharpened deer antlers and flint axes. They found that by heating ores in a fire with charcoal, made from burnt wood, they could melt and extract copper and tin, which they used to make tools and weapons. Some time before 4,000 BC, they learned that by mixing copper and tin, they could make a stronger metal alloy, called bronze. This was the start of the Bronze Age.

Malachite is an ore of copper

Aluminium Is One Of The Most Common Metals In The Earth's Crust

Aluminium is a very light metal. It is found in bauxite ore. It makes up about eight percent of the Earth's crust, but it has only been used for about 100 years, because it needs very high temperatures to melt the ore. The bauxite is heated and melts into aluminium oxide, then an electric current is passed through which removes oxygen, leaving the metal. Today, aluminium has many uses. Many cars are made from aluminium because it is strong and light and does not rust.

Did You Know?

Lithium is the lightest metal, and was discovered in 1817 by a Swedish chemist.

Bronze was the first alloy made by humans, when they mixed copper with tin to produce a substance that could be used for tools and weapons.

In ancient Greece, around 400 BC, the 'laughing philosopher' Democritus suggested that all matter was made up of an infinite number of unsplittable atoms.

Atoms can in fact be split – and splitting the atoms in uranium generates three million times more energy than the same weight of coal could produce.

To stay healthy, the human body needs tiny amounts of metals including iron, magnesium, chromium, copper and zinc.

Iron Age sword

Iron First Came From Outer Space

It was not until around 1500 BC that people were able to make iron by heating, or 'smelting', iron ore. However, iron jewellery has been found in tombs in the Middle East dating from as early as 3,000 BC. This iron came from lumps of metal in meteorites that fell to Earth from outer space. People called the meteorites 'metal from the sky'. Today, iron is made by smelting iron ore with coke and limestone in huge ovens called blast furnaces.

Peacock ore

Steel Was First Made In 1856

Most iron is used to make steel, which is strong and easy to shape. Steel is made by removing carbon from iron ore. The first steelmaking converter was made by a British inventor called Henry Bessemer in 1856. He found that by blowing air through the furnace, carbon combined with oxygen and escaped as a gas, leaving steel behind.

Oxygen In The Air Makes Steel Go Rusty

Stainless steel was discovered by accident in 1913, during experiments to find a steel alloy that could be used to make gun barrels. Steel rusts because it reacts with oxygen in the air to make iron oxides, which are red in colour. Adding chromium to steel makes a tough, rust-free alloy. Stainless steel is used to make everything from space rockets and milk tankers, to cutlery and razor blades.

Precious Metals

Precious metals are those that are valued because they are rare and attractive, and are not easily scratched or worn away. Precious metals include gold, silver and platinum. They are found in pure form, either by mining or by sifting the mud from river beds and streams.

Gold Is Used To Make Spacesuits

Platinum, gold and silver are all prized for making into jewellery, but they also have many other uses. Platinum is used to make electronic circuits because it does not rust or wear out. Thin films of gold are used to reflect heat rays from visors on spacesuits and from the windows of skyscrapers. Silver is used in chemistry, medicine and photography. Photographic films and paper have a thin coating of silver which is sensitive to light.

Gold prospectors

Hallmarks Were Invented To Stop Silversmiths Cheating

In the 14th century, a system of testing and stamping silver was introduced. This was to stop silversmiths from dishonestly mixing silver with cheaper metals. The system, called hallmarking, has been used for precious metals ever since. Every silver article over 15.5 g ($1/2$ oz) must be tested and marked — although sometimes hallmarks can be forged!

Gold Can Cause A Stampede

In 1848, a saw mill owner in the Sierra Nevada Mountains in California, USA, was digging out a stream to power his mill, when he found grains of gold. The news leaked out, starting the biggest gold rush in history. People rushed from all over the USA, hoping to strike rich. Gold prospectors panned for gold by swilling pans in streams or rivers, so that sand and gravel floated away, leaving heavier grains of gold behind. Gold remains so rare that some people estimate that all the gold ever mined would fit into a cube 18 m (60 ft) square.

Plants

About Plants

Plants were the first living things to appear on Earth, millions of years before any form of animal life. The first plants consisted of single-celled algae, microscopic plants that live on the surface of water or cling to wet rocks. Plants need three things to make them grow — sunlight, air and water. The biggest difference between plants and animals is that plants make their own food, whereas animals do not.

Plants Feed On Sugar

Green plants make their own food. The leaves take in sunlight and carbon dioxide from the air. The roots draw up water from the soil. Cells inside the leaves use the energy from the sunlight to change the water, carbon dioxide and a chemical inside the leaf, called chlorophyll, into the plant's food, a type of sugar called glucose. At the same time, the plant gives out oxygen through its leaves. This process is called photosynthesis, which means 'making by light'.

Cells inside a leaf

All Flowers Produce Seeds

The purpose of a flower is to produce seeds that will grow into new plants. As the flower develops the bud opens to reveal the petals. In the centre of the flower are the seeds. In some flowers, such as the poppy, the seeds ripen inside a hard case, which protects the seeds until they are ready to be dispersed. The seed case 'explodes' or splits open, scattering seeds in all directions. Each seed will grow into a new plant.

Seed case of a poppy

Stages of a poppy bud opening out into a flower

Did You Know?

There are over a quarter of a million species of plant.

Mangrove trees have their roots in mid-air, because they can't take in oxygen through the mud they grow in.

The Venus flytrap eats insects, which it catches by snapping its jaws shut.

Ancient people first began to grow crops, rather than live on wild varieties, about 10,000 years ago in the Middle East.

In 1839, China and England fought a war over the smuggling of opium – a drug made from poppies.

In 1987, scientists genetically modified a tomato plant to make it resistant to caterpillars.

Roots Keep A Plant Fixed In The Soil

Roots anchor a plant in the ground and absorb water and mineral salts from it. These are transported up through the plant's stem (or tree trunk). Some plants have a main root, called the tap root, with smaller branch roots (known as fibrous roots) spreading out from it. Others plants have fibrous roots that are all more or less the same size as the tap root.

Plants Grow Towards The Light

Plants grow upwards towards sunlight, which they need to make food. Normally a plant will grow vertically but if it is in a shaded position with the light coming from just one direction, the plant will turn towards the light. Without sunlight the leaves cannot develop chlorophyll — the substance that makes plants green — or convert sunlight into food that the plant needs to grow.

Pollination and Seeds

All plants must reproduce themselves in order for the species to survive. There are several ways in which plants do this. Simple plants reproduce by splitting themselves in two. Other plants, such as fungi, send out spores which float away on the air, to eventually settle and grow. Some plants have roots or stems that divide to reproduce. Most flowering plants produce seeds that will grow into new plants.

Inside a flower

Most Flowers Have The Same Structure

Although flowers vary hugely in colour, shape and size, most have the same basic structure. Outside the petals there are small green leaves, called sepals, which protected the flower when it was in bud. The petals of the flower can vary in number according to the species. In the centre of the petals are a number of small stalks, called stamens, which produce pollen. Right in the centre of the flower are the carpels, the reproductive part of the plant. The lower part of the carpel is the ovule, which develops into seeds when the flower has been pollinated.

Some Plants Use Insects For Pollination

Flowers attract insects with their bright colours and scent. Insects pollinate plants as they feed on a sugary liquid, called nectar, produced inside the flower. Nectar is an important source of energy for many insects. The insect visits one flower and picks up the pollen on its body and the pollen is transferred to the carpel of another plant when the insect visits it.

Pollen Can Be Spread By Wind Or Water

Many plants, such as grasses, rely upon the wind as a means of pollination. Some water plants rely on the water to carry the pollen to other plants. Because this is a more random procedure than insect pollination, these plants usually produce a large amount of pollen.

Strawberries Reproduce Without Seeds

Some plants, such as the strawberry, put out stems called runners, at the end of which are small plantlets. These plantlets take root and eventually become a separate plant.

Did You Know?

Some flowers smell like rotting flesh, to attract the flies they need to carry their pollen.

An Australian mammal called the honey possum lives on the pollen and nectar of flowers.

The flowers of some orchids look and smell like female bees – they have no trouble attracting bees to pollinate them!

An ancient Oriental lotus seed preserved in a peat bog near Tokyo successfully sprouted into a flower 2,000 years later.

In Greek myths, there is a land of 'lotus eaters' who live on the fruit of the lotus tree. Any strangers who eat this fruit forget about their home.

The seeds of coconut trees can spread from one island to another – by floating across the sea in coconuts!

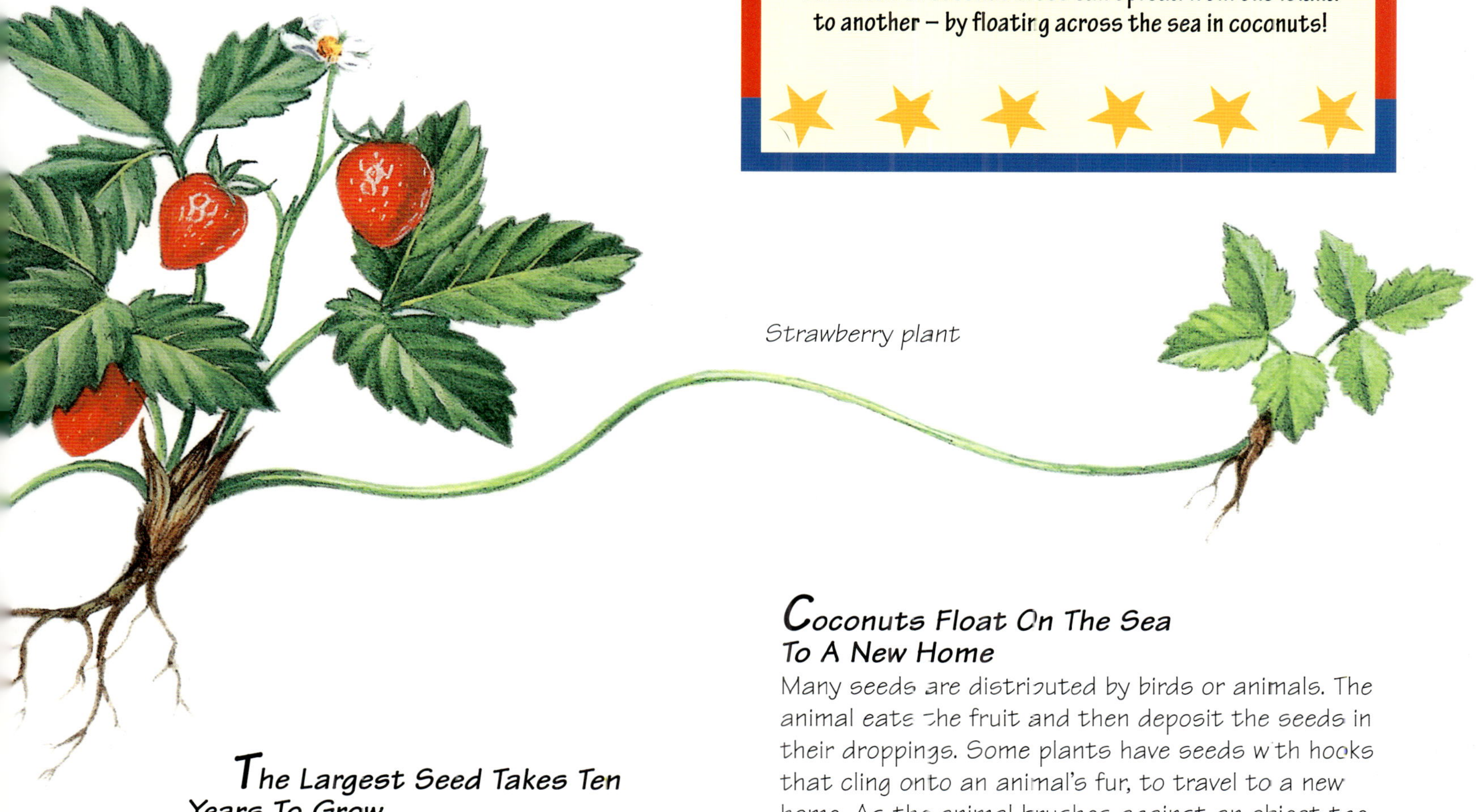

Strawberry plant

The Largest Seed Takes Ten Years To Grow

The largest seed is that of the coco de mer palm that grows in the Seychelle Islands. It takes ten years to mature and may weigh up to 18 kg (40 lb). It is sometimes called the double coconut because it looks like two coconuts joined together.

Coconuts Float On The Sea To A New Home

Many seeds are distributed by birds or animals. The animal eats the fruit and then deposit the seeds in their droppings. Some plants have seeds with hooks that cling onto an animal's fur, to travel to a new home. As the animal brushes against an object the seed drops off. Some seeds can be carried to new areas by water. Coconuts, for example, often grow near the sea. The coconut falls from the tree into the water and then floats to another place where it grows into a new tree.

Desert Plants

The hot and dry conditions found in deserts are far from ideal for plants, which need water to grow. Yet several types of plants have adapted themselves to these hostile environments.

Cactus in flower

Cacti Are Adapted To Hold Water

Cacti have long roots that lie close to the surface, which enables them to take in any available water quickly. The stem of a cactus is designed to hold water and the spines — which are actually the leaves — are designed to lose as little water as possible through evaporation. The spines also help to protect the plant from animals that may try to eat it. If a piece of a cactus plant gets knocked off, it can take root in the sand and grow into a new plant.

The Saguaro Cactus Lives For Over 200 Years

The saguaro cactus of the Arizona and Mexican deserts takes 10 years to grow to a height of 2.5 cm (1 in). Often it will not flower until it is 50, or even 75, years old. By the end of its life, which is about 200 years, it will have reached 15 m (50 ft) which makes it the largest member of the cactus family.

Many Desert Plants Only Bloom After It Has Rained

Many desert plants remain dormant (inactive) until the rains come, when they burst into life creating a lush and beautiful landscape. The plants grow quickly, flower, create new seeds and die in a very short time. Resurrection plants are brown and shrivelled when it is dry, to conserve water, but when it rains the leaves expand and turn green again. Living stones, desert plants of southern Africa, look just like stones until they flower after it has rained.

Did You Know?

★

The world's largest cactus is the Saguaro of Mexico and California. It can grow to 16 m (52 ft), weigh 10,000 kg (10 tons), and store 3,000 litres (660 gal) of water.

Some Native Americans of Mexico follow a religion based on the visions caused by taking a drug made from the mescal cactus.

The American pygmy cedar lives entirely on water vapour absorbed from the air.

Certain cacti can store enough water to live for a year without rain.

The guayule plant that grows in the deserts of Mexico leaks acid from its roots to prevent other plants growing near it!

Because desert plants all wait for rain to germinate, deserts can become a blaze of colour for a few days after rainfall.

Desert Plants Have Ways To Conserve Water

Because there is very little rain in desert regions, many desert plants store water in some way, in their stems, their leaves, or their roots to last them through periods of drought. Some of these plants also have a thick, waxy skin that lessens the amount of water lost through evaporation. All these desert plants, that include cacti, are known as succulents.

Some Desert Plants Get Water From Air

The caper plant which lives in the Sahara Desert can survive without taking up any water from its roots. It gets its water from vapour in the air. Another desert plant that gets most of its water from the atmosphere is the welwitschia, which grows in the coastal deserts of south-west Africa.

North American desert

Trees

A tree is a large plant with a thick, woody stem — the trunk. Trees are the largest and longest living plants on Earth. They are found all over the world, except in deserts, the Polar regions and on the tops of high mountains. There are two basic types of tree: those that have broad leaves, and those that have needle-like leaves.

Did You Know?

★

Legends of the Bolivian rain forest say the trees walk towards the sun – because their large roots grow towards the sunlight.

Trees are the oldest living things. The bristle cone pine of the Rocky Mountains can live for 5,000 years. Maidenhair trees have been in existence since the age of the dinosaurs.

The ombu tree of Argentina has such a spongy bark that it is virtually impossible to cut it down!

The banyan tree grows in the branches of other trees, sending roots down to the ground and gradually strangling its supporting tree.

A banyan has many trunks, and can develop into a one-tree forest! The largest example, in Sri Lanka, has over 350 main trunks.

Deciduous Trees Lose Their Leaves In Winter

Many trees are deciduous — they lose their leaves in winter. In autumn, the leaves wither and fall. The fallen leaves are replaced by new leaves that grow each spring. This does not happen with evergreens which, as their name suggests, keep their leaves throughout the winter months.

Woodland Trees Are Home To Many Creatures

In a wood there are thousands of creatures. Some live underground, some live on the woodland floor and some live in the trees. Birds nest in tree branches, and in holes in trunks. Squirrels also nest in holes in trees. The leaves and bark are home to numerous caterpillars and insects. Even dead trees are full of life, for they are home to beetles and other minibeasts, slugs, worms, small mammals and birds.

The Tallest Trees Are Redwoods

The Coastal Redwoods of California, USA, are the tallest trees in the world. They can be as high as 83 m (272 ft) or more and one in the Humboldt Redwoods State Park in California is over 111 m (364 ft) high!

Rings Tell A Tree's Age

A cross-section of a tree shows alternate light and dark rings of wood. The light rings are the tree's summer growth each year and the dark rings are winter growth. By counting these pairs of rings, scientists can calculate the age of the tree. The width of the rings are also an indication of the weather — narrow rings indicate poor conditions and wider rings denote good weather. Nowadays, scientists use a more accurate method of dating trees, called carbon dating, which measures radioactivity.

Trees Provide Us With Lots Of Useful Things

Apart from various types of timber used in all manner of building and construction, trees also yield many other products useful to humans. Trees provide us with a wide variety of edible fruits. Rubber and cork also come from trees, as do a range of products used in medicines.

Trees Help Prevent Soil Erosion

The roots of trees help to hold the soil together. Where large areas of trees have been cut down, the soil is eroded — it is washed away by water or blown away by the wind. Trees also provide homes and shelter for animals and birds, and help to make the world an attractive place in which to live.

Rainforest tree

Fantastic Flowers

The world's largest flower has mottled orange-brown and white petals and often reaches a diameter of about 90 cm (3 ft) and can be 2 cm (3/4 in) thick. Found in the jungles of south-east Asia, the flower is popularly called the stinking corpse lily because it smells like rotting flesh! Its scientific name is *Rafflesia arnoldi*, after Sir John Raffles and Dr. Arnold, the British botanists who discovered the plant in 1818.

Duckweeds Are The Smallest Flowering Plants

Duckweeds, tiny plants that live on the surface of ponds and lakes, are the smallest flowering plants in the world. The flowers are less than 1 mm (1/30 in) across.

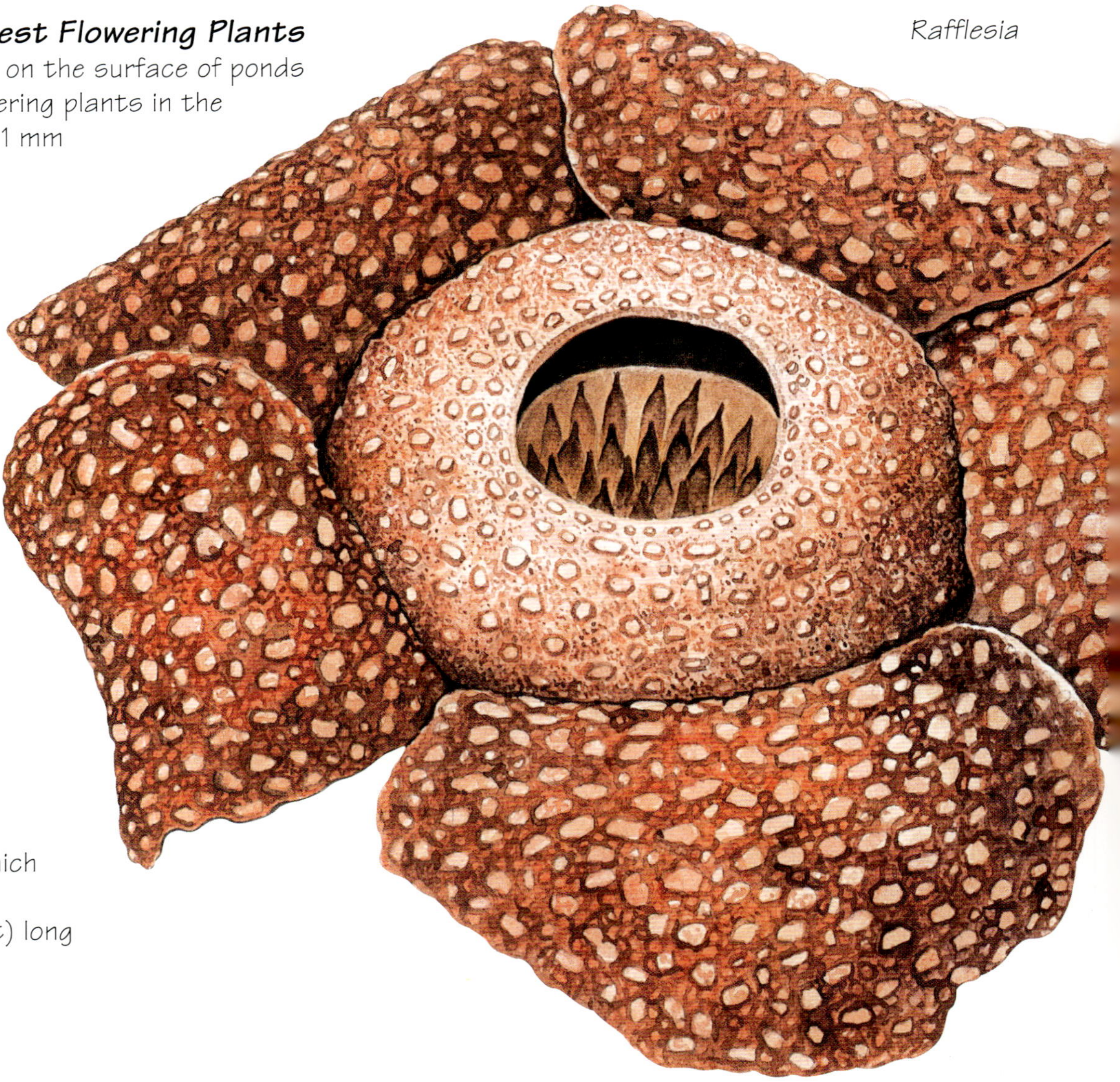

Rafflesia

The Slowest Growing Plant Lives In Mexico

The record for being the slowest growing flowering plant, is the fern-like dioon, which grows in Mexico. A single specimen, known to be almost 1,000 years old, attained a height of only 2 m (6 ft).

Raffia Palms Have The Biggest Leaves

The leaves of the raffia palm, which is found on islands in the Indian Ocean, can be up to 20 m (65ft) long

Some Plants Eat Meat

The best known of the carnivorous, or meat-eating, plants is the Venus fly trap from the swamplands of Carolina, USA. Inside its leaves are a series of spikes. When these are brushed by a fly, the leaves close shut around the insect, which is then digested. Once the fly has been digested, the flower opens again to catch another one.

Pitcher Plants Drown Their Prey

Pitcher plants are so called because they form the shape of a water pitcher. Insects are attracted to the plant, but because the inside of the pitcher is slippery, they slide to the bottom of the pitcher which contains water. The insects drown and are then digested by the plant.

The Ginko Is The World's Oldest Plant

The ginkgo tree, sometimes called the maidenhair tree, first appeared some 180 million years ago during the Jurassic period. It is the earliest known plant that is still in existence.

Animals

The Animal Kingdom

The animal kingdom contains over a million species – ranging in size from microscopic organisms right up to the massive blue whale. Animals can be classified into vertebrates (those with a spine) and invertebrates (those without). There are five main classes of vertebrates – there are the fishes, then come the amphibians, reptiles, birds and the more advanced mammals, which include humans. Animals are found all over the world. They have had to adapt to local conditions and food supplies, so creatures in the same family often have special characteristics suited to their environment and way of life.

The Tallest Animal

Giraffes can be from 5 m (16.5 ft) tall, making them the tallest animals in the world. Giraffes live in the dry savannah of Africa. Their long necks enable them to feed from tall bushes and trees. Unlike other animals, giraffes sleep standing up.

Fastest And Slowest Animals

The fastest land animal is the cheetah which can run at 101 kph (63 mph) for short level distances of up to 500 m (1640 ft). Over a longer distance the pronghorn antelope, on the plains of Mexico and North America, can really travel – it can keep up a speed of 56 kph (35 mph) over a distance of 6 km (4 mi). At the other end of the speed scale is the three-toed sloth, which takes a whole minute to cover 2 m (6.5 ft). That is actually slower than an ordinary snail! There are five species of sloth, all of which live in the rainforests of South and Central America. They live in trees and spend much of their time hanging upside-down doing absolutley nothing. They can even sleep upside-down.

Cheetah

Did You Know?

A cheetah has an acceleration of 0–80 kph (0–50 mph) in 2 seconds!

The peculiar-looking aardvark is the only member of the order of mammals called tubulidentata.

The duck-billed platypus and the echidna are the only two mammals that lay eggs.

In the Swiss Alps, stone chests from 100,000 years ago have been found containing the carefully arranged bones of cave-bears.

The Roman emperor Octavius Augustus kept 420 tigers, 260 lions and one rhinoceros. The rhinoceros must have been rather lonely.

Zoos of exotic animals were kept in the 13th century by English kings and queens in the Tower of London, and by the Kubla Khan (the emperor) in China.

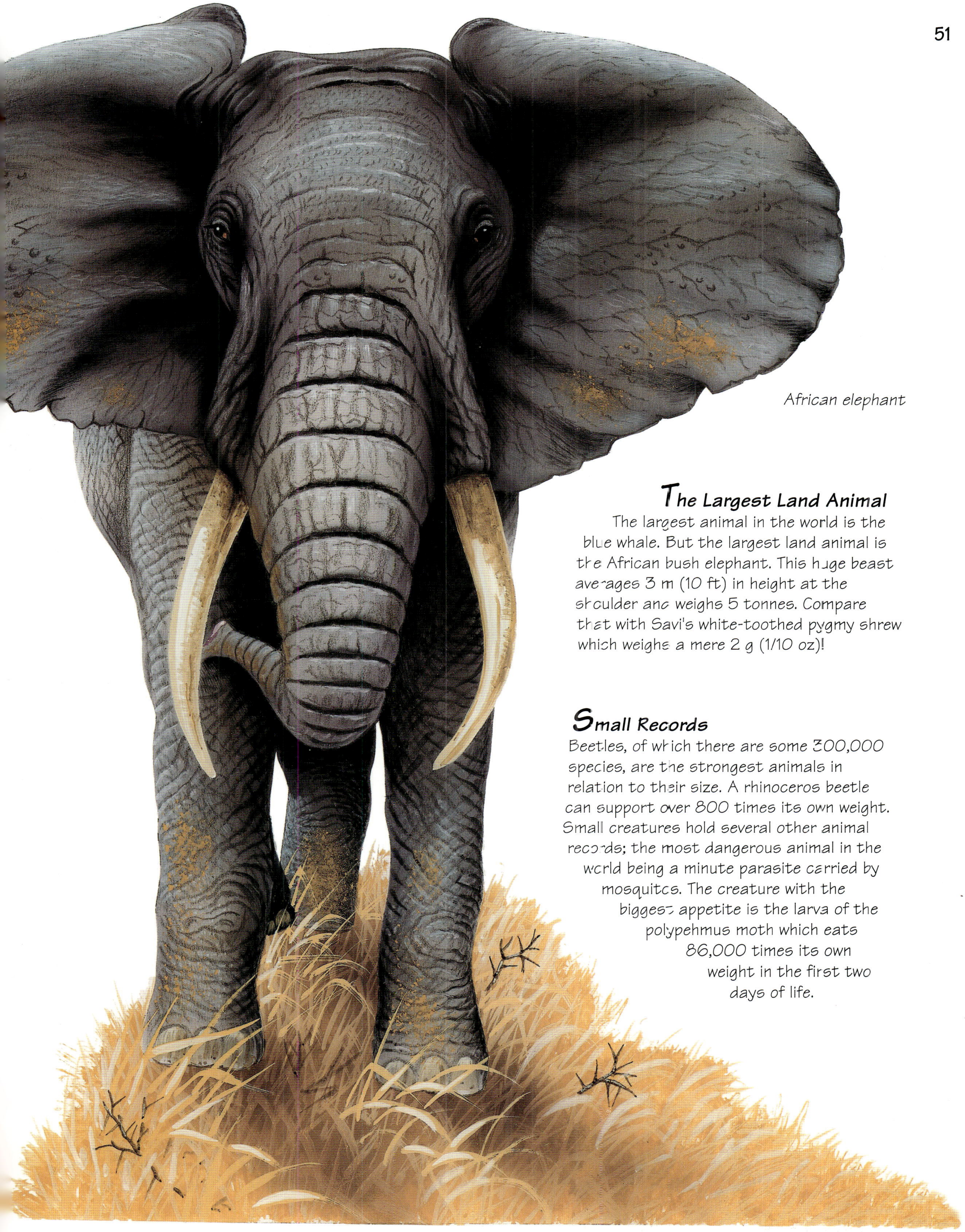

African elephant

The Largest Land Animal

The largest animal in the world is the blue whale. But the largest land animal is the African bush elephant. This huge beast averages 3 m (10 ft) in height at the shoulder and weighs 5 tonnes. Compare that with Savi's white-toothed pygmy shrew which weighs a mere 2 g (1/10 oz)!

Small Records

Beetles, of which there are some 300,000 species, are the strongest animals in relation to their size. A rhinoceros beetle can support over 800 times its own weight. Small creatures hold several other animal records; the most dangerous animal in the world being a minute parasite carried by mosquitos. The creature with the biggest appetite is the larva of the polypehmus moth which eats 86,000 times its own weight in the first two days of life.

The Big Cats

Wild species of the cat family are found all over the world, except for in Antarctica and Australia. They are all carnivores (meat eaters) and all hunt by stalking their prey and then pouncing. There are 37 species of wild cat. Larger members of the family, such as the lion, tiger and leopard, are known as the big cats. Smaller members of the family include the ocelot, the lynx and the serval.

The Biggest Cat

Biggest and most powerful member of the cat family is the tiger, which lives mainly in the rich forest areas of India, south-east China and Indonesia. In the heat of the midday sun, the tiger will take to the shade or rest in water to keep cool. Most members of the cat family dislike water, but tigers love it and are good swimmers.

Tiger

Iriomote cat

Big, Wild And Domestic Cats

Big cats are related to and similar in appearance to wild cats and domestic cats. The European wild cat looks very much like the domestic tabby cat, as does the rare iriomote cat, and the caffer cat.

King Of The Jungle

The best known of the big cats is undoubtedly the lion, often called 'the king of the jungle'. At one time lions roamed all over Europe, Africa and Asia, but now they are found only in parts of Africa and a small area of India. Lions usually hunt in a group and although it is usually the female that kills the prey, it is the male, the head of the pride (group), that gets to eat first.

The Beautiful Leopard

Leopards are very agile big cats that live in Africa and Asia. They climb trees well and sometimes store their dead prey in trees. The spots on a leopard are more like rosettes than spots, especially along the back, and those of the African species are smaller than those on the Asian variety. Some leopards are completely black and are known as panthers.
A relative of the leopard is the jaguar of Central America which always lives close to water and is an excellent swimmer. The rosettes on its body are quite distinctive because they have a black spot in the centre.

The snow leopard, or ounce, of Asia is a beautiful creature. It has white spots on a whitish background. It hunts wild sheep and boar in the mountains of central Asia and the Himalayas.

Snow leopard

Did You Know?

In prehistoric times, sabre-toothed tigers attacked prey with their enormous, curved canine teeth.

Leopards often drag the carcass of their prey up a tree – to be eaten later!

While a cheetah is the fastest sprinter, the pronghorn antelope of North America would outrun it over a longer distance.

Lions sometimes climb into trees to stop flies biting them.

Ancient kings in Asia used cheetahs to hunt other animals.

The ancient Egyptian pharaoh Amenhotep III was said to have shot and killed 102 lions with a bow and arrow.

Two Species of Elephant

There are two species of elephant: the Indian elephant and the African elephant. In both continents they live in herds in the forests and grassy plains. The elephant uses its long trunk to breathe, to smell and to gather food. Its trunk is very good for holding things, and it is so sensitive that it can even pick up very small objects. The trunk is also used for drawing up water, which is then transferred to the elephant's mouth for drinking. Its tusks are actually enlarged incisor teeth. They are used for digging up roots, boring for water and for fighting. The elephant does not have very good eyesight. It does, however have a keen sense of smell and excellent hearing. An African elephant seldom lives for more than 50 years and 70 is about average for an Indian elephant.

African elephant

Differences Between The Species

The main difference between the two species is that the Indian is the smaller of the two. Only the males of the Indian elephant have tusks, whereas both male and female African elephants have them. The tusks of an Indian elephant are smaller.

The elephant flaps its large ears to cool its body. African elephants have bigger ears than Indian elephants. There is also a difference in the 'lips' at the end of the trunk. Indian elephants have just one, African elephants have two. The feet are also slightly different between the two species. The Indian elephant has five digits on its front feet, the African has only four.

Indian elephant

Did You Know?

When an elephant calf dies, its mourning mother will carry its body around for several days.

An elephant pregnancy lasts for 22 months.

An adult elephant can hold 4.5 litres (1 gallon) of water in its trunk. It needs to drink about 20 trunkfuls a day!

An elephant's trunk contains over 40,000 muscles.

The famous African general, Hannibal, used elephants to carry heavy loads in his army when he crossed the Alps in 218 BC to invade the Roman Empire.

A popular Hindu god, called Ganesh, has the head of an elephant.

The Elephant's Closest Relation

Strangely, the closest living relative of the elephant is a small rodent-like creature, the hyrax, which looks more like a guinea pig than an elephant!

Why Elephants Bathe In Mud

Elephants love to bathe, rolling around in the water. They use their trunks to draw up water which they then shower all over their body. They also enjoy dust baths, again using the trunk to gather up the dust and blow it over themselves. This gets rid of flies and ticks. Although the elephants' skin is thick, it is very sensitive and flies and ticks bother it.

The Bear Facts

There are seven species of bear, the largest of which is the Alaskan brown bear which is also known as the Kodiak bear. Other brown bears are found in North America, the best known being the grizzly, which gets it name from the grizzled appearance of its fur. The smallest member of the bear family is the honey bear, or sun bear, of Malaysia. It spends most of the day in its nest in a tree and searches for food at night. The only bear to live in the Arctic is the polar bear. Apart from the polar bear, which feeds almost solely on fish, seals and walruses, bears eat a wide variety of plants and animals. Two animals often thought to be bears are the panda and the koala. In fact neither are bears, the panda is a relative of the racoon and the koala is a marsupial.

A Bear That Wears Spectacles

The spectacled bear of the Andes is the only bear to live in South America. It has white or tawny rings around its eyes which have given rise to its name. In spite of the spectacles, this bear, in common with other bears, does not have very good eyesight but makes up for this by a good sense of smell.

Spectacled bear

Kodiak bear

The World's Biggest Bear

The Kodiak bear, found on Kodiak Island and other nearby islands off Alaska, is the largest member of the bear family. An average adult male can be up to 2 m (6.5 ft) long and weighs around 500 kg (1,100 lb). In spite of the fact that it (in common with other bears) is classed as a carnivore (meat eater), its main diet is vegetable matter, although it does catch and eat salmon as they swim up river in the summer.

Brown bear

Did You Know?

★

When it is hibernating, a bear's body temperature can drop by up to 5 °C (41 °F).

In India, sloth bears get drunk by chewing fermenting madhuca flowers, then they hang upside down from trees!

For centuries, bear-baiting was a popular sport across the world. Now it is illegal in many countries.

The smallest bear, the sun bear, likes to spend its days sunbathing.

Some Native American warriors tied their hair into knots like a bear's ears to ask for the bear's sacred protection.

Bears Love Fish And Honey

There are brown bears in Europe and Asia, although the number of brown bears in Europe is now quite low. The brown bear loves honey and will open a wild hive to get at it, while ignoring the stinging bees. After eating the bear rolls on the ground or rubs itself against a tree to get rid of the bees. Brown bears will also go into a river to catch fish as do other bears.

How Animals Use Camouflage

To hide from their enemies or potential prey, animals have many ways of camouflaging themselves. The spotted and blotched pattern on the body of a giraffe breaks up its outline so it becomes almost invisible in dappled sunlight beneath the trees. The spots on a leopard fulfil the same function. Many creatures are so well camouflaged that you do not know they are there until they move.

Some Animals Can Change Their Colour

The chameleon can change its colour to blend in with the background. The praying mantis of Malaysia changes its colour too, to look like a flower and attract insects. The European tree-frog can also change its colour to match its surroundings.

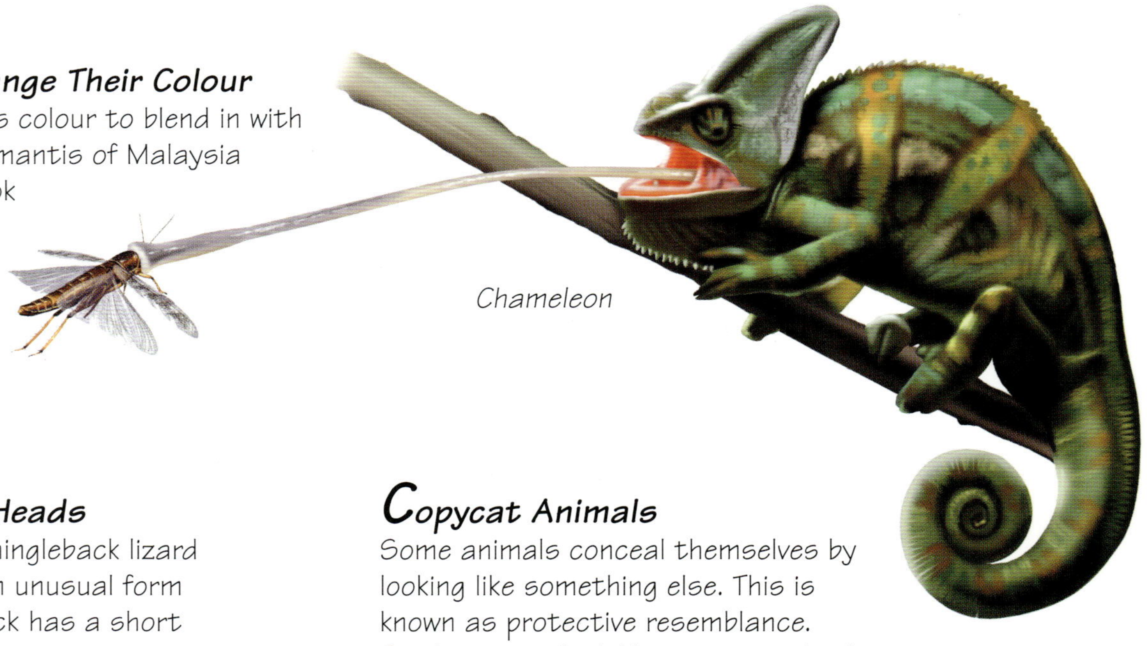

Chameleon

The Creature With Two Heads

Predators that attack the shingleback lizard of Australia are faced with an unusual form of protection – the shingleback has a short plump tail that is similar in appearance to its head. As the creature seems to have two heads, the predator does not know which end to attack!

Copycat Animals

Some animals conceal themselves by looking like something else. This is known as protective resemblance. Stick insects look like twigs, as do the caterpillars of the light emerald moth which even have little twig-like bumps along their surface. There are many species of insect which look like the leaves of a tree.

A Sloth Goes Green

An unusual form of camouflage helps the sloth of the South American jungles. Its coarse hair is grooved, and in these grooves grows a simple green algae, the colour of which helps to conceal the sloth.

Shingleback lizard

Some Creatures Mimic Others

For protection, some creatures try to look like others. For example, a harmless creature will look like a poisonous or distasteful one that bears warning colours. Many hover flies look like bees and wasps which helps to keep predators at bay because they believe the harmless hover fly may sting them.

Dinosaurs

The Coming of the Dinosaurs

Dinosaurs lived on Earth for 160 million years. The word dinosaur means 'terrible lizard' and was first used by the British palaeontologist Richard Owen in 1842. We tend to think of dinosaurs as enormous creatures but they came in all sizes. The first dinosaurs appeared over 220 million years ago and were quite small. The smallest of the dinosaurs was *Compsognathus* which was only 90 cm (3 ft) long and weighed just 3 kg (6.6 lb). *Diplodocus* was the longest, in fact the longest animal that has ever lived, with a length of 25 m (82 ft). The heaviest creature that ever lived was *Brachiosaurus* which weighed over 50 tonnes.

Brachiosaurus

Two Types Of Dinosaur

Scientists have divided dinosaurs into two main groups: *Saurischia*, meaning 'reptile-hipped' because their hips are similar to those of crocodiles and other reptiles; and *Ornithischia* (bird-hipped) because their hip bones are arranged like those of birds. In fact it is quite possible that the first birds evolved from the *Ornithischia* dinosaurs.

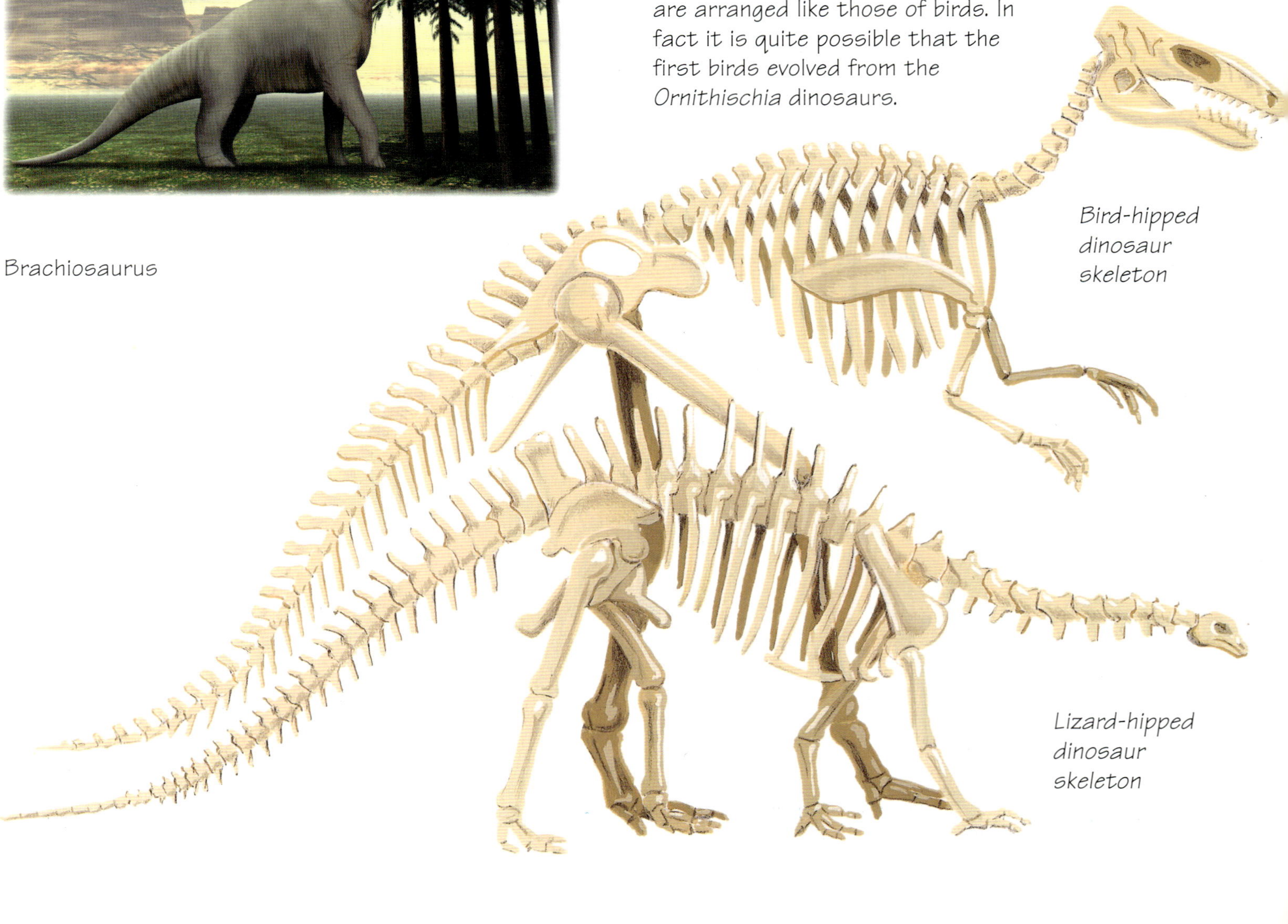

Bird-hipped dinosaur skeleton

Lizard-hipped dinosaur skeleton

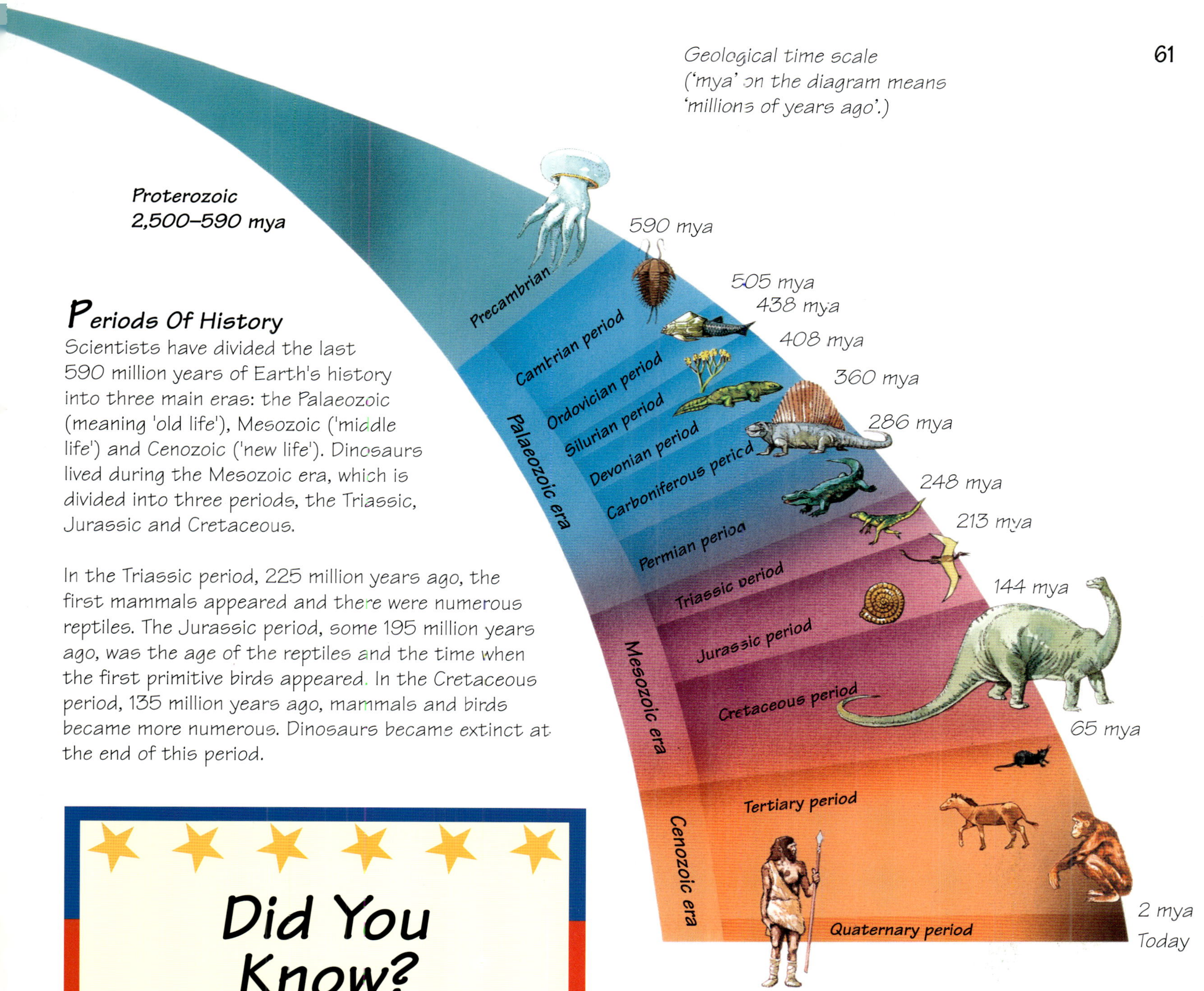

Geological time scale ('mya' on the diagram means 'millions of years ago'.)

Periods Of History

Scientists have divided the last 590 million years of Earth's history into three main eras: the Palaeozoic (meaning 'old life'), Mesozoic ('middle life') and Cenozoic ('new life'). Dinosaurs lived during the Mesozoic era, which is divided into three periods, the Triassic, Jurassic and Cretaceous.

In the Triassic period, 225 million years ago, the first mammals appeared and there were numerous reptiles. The Jurassic period, some 195 million years ago, was the age of the reptiles and the time when the first primitive birds appeared. In the Cretaceous period, 135 million years ago, mammals and birds became more numerous. Dinosaurs became extinct at the end of this period.

Did You Know?

★

The oldest animal fossils are about 700 million years old. Human beings did not exist for about another 698 million years!

Soft-bodied animals such as worms, jellyfish, corals and molluscs evolved 500 million years ago.

The first fish had no jaws, and had to suck food into their bodies!

Many kinds of fish first appeared 420 million years ago, including the ancestors of today's sharks.

Prehistoric insects were much larger than today's versions. Dragonflies had a wingspan of over 60 cm (24 in)!

First Living Things

Life began in the seas some 2,000 million years ago. The earliest form of life consisted of particles of protoplasm, the basis of all living matter. From this evolved simple single-celled organisms, similar to the amoeba, which gradually developed, over many millions of years, into many-celled organisms – simple creatures such as microscopic bacteria.

More complex creatures, such as sponges and jellyfish, began appearing perhaps 600 million years ago. The jellyfish was one of the first animals to have a mouth and a stomach. All life at this time was in the sea and it was not until around 400 million years ago that simple plants and insects probably began inhabiting the shore line. By 345 million years ago some primitive amphibians were beginning to venture onto land and the first reptiles began developing.

How Dinosaurs Evolved

No-one on this Earth has ever seen a living dinosaur, so how do we know what they looked like? The first clues come from fossils which have been found in rocks. Fossils are usually formed by the animal's skeleton, but they can also be formed from footprints. Scientists have gained many clues about dinosaurs from fossilised footprints and eggs that have been found. The fossilised teeth can give an indication as to what dinosaurs ate because feeding habits affect the way that teeth are worn down. Plant eaters had blunt teeth but meat eaters had sharp teeth to tear into flesh.

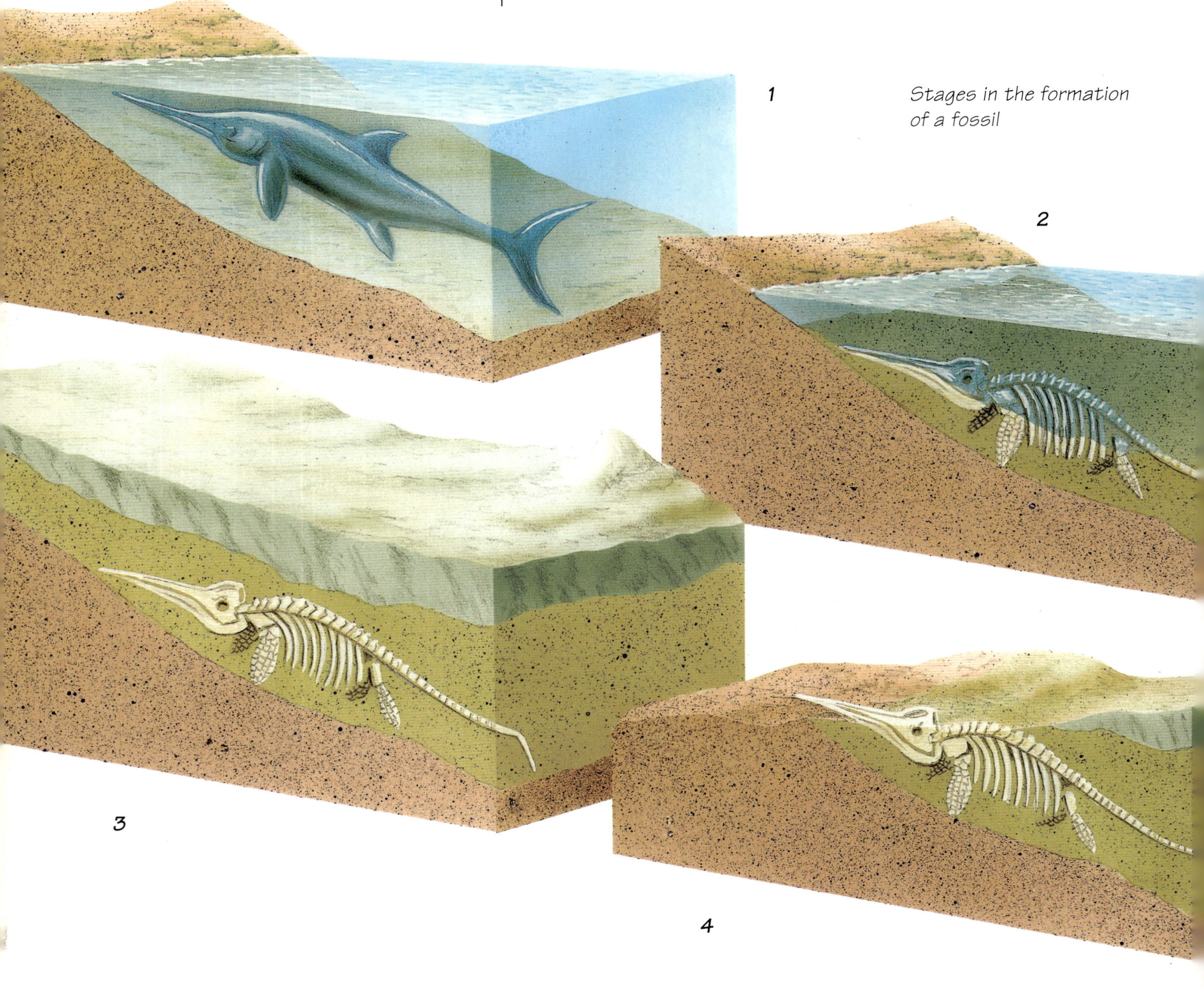

Stages in the formation of a fossil

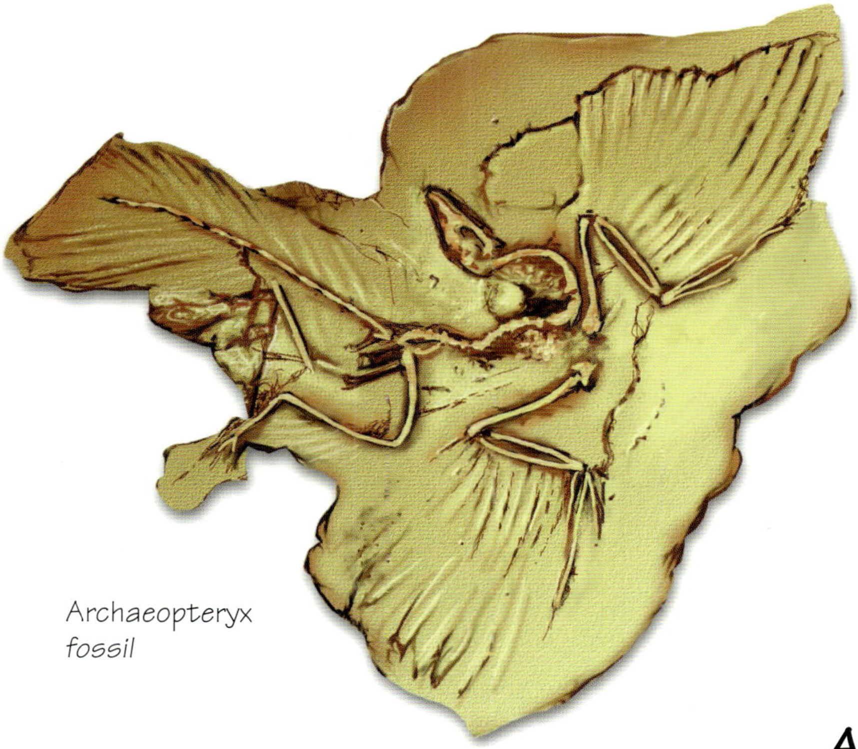

Archaeopteryx fossil

First Dinosaur Discovery

Nothing was known about dinosaurs until the 19th century. No doubt bones and fossils had been seen before, but no-one knew what they were. The first to be discovered and recognised as a large reptile was *Megalosaurus* or 'large lizard' in 1818. It was not, however, the first to be named. That honour belongs to the *Iguanodon*, the teeth of which were discovered by Mary Mantell, wife of Dr Gideon Mantell, in England in 1823. The teeth puzzled scientists until a large number of skeletons, over half of which were complete, were discovered at Bernissart, Belgium in 1878 and the full picture of the dinosaur was assembled.

How A Fossil Is Formed

A fossil is formed when a buried skeleton is replaced by stone. This happens when minerals from water in the ground penetrate the pores in the bones and gradually harden into stone. Sometimes the creature, especially smaller ones, may be completely eaten away by the water, leaving a hole in the same form as the creature. This hole forms a mould which then fills up with minerals and solidifies. Fossilised footprints are formed when the mud in which the prints were made hardens into rock.

A Discovery Yet To Be Made

One thing that is not known for certain is what colour dinosaurs were. Like present-day animals, dinosaurs probably evolved colours according to how and where they lived.

How Dinosaurs Evolved

Dinosaurs evolved from reptiles, the first creatures to live on land all of the time. This happened during the Triassic period. These reptiles, the thecodonts, named after the type of teeth they had (socket toothed), looked rather like modern crocodiles. Some actually developed into crocodiles. Others developed frog-like movements of their hind legs, and over a period of perhaps a million years they gradually changed their form until they were able to walk upright some of the time. Other Thecodonts developed into pterosaurs – lizards that could glide from tree to tree.

Did You Know?

Scientists celebrated the first life-size reconstruction of a dinosaur by having a banquet inside it!

The first dinosaur to be identified was Megalosaurus ('Big Reptile'), which the clergyman William Buckland described in 1824 from its fossilized jawbone.

The dinosaur Iguanodon was identified in 1825, and 30 complete skeletons were found in a Belgian coalmine 53 years later.

When Sir Richard Owen invented the term Dinosauria in 1841, only a few types of dinosaur were known.

Fossils of dinosaur droppings can tell us what dinosaurs ate!

There are fossils of dinosaur bones, teeth, droppings, eggs and footprints.

The Triassic Period

The Triassic period was the period between 248 and 213 million years ago. Scientists called it Triassic (from the Latin word *trias*, meaning 'in threes') because remains of the first dinosaurs were found in a three-layered system of rocks.

Two early dinosaurs

The Earliest Dinosaurs

Towards the end of the Triassic period, some 200 million years ago, creatures developed that were quite different from their thecodont ancestors. These were the first dinosaurs. Among them were two small meat eaters, *Herrerasuarus* and *Staurikosaurus*. Both were about 2 or 3 m (6.5—9 ft) long and walked upright, but little is known about them because very few fossils exist from this period.

Dinosaurs Versus Mammals

Many other animals, as well as dinosaurs, lived in the Triassic period. There were creatures both on land and in the water. The first mammals, warm-blooded animals that feed their young with milk, appeared about the same time as the dinosaurs. But it seems that the dinosaurs were better adapted to the conditions at the time and thrived, whereas the earliest mammals soon died out. This situation remained unchanged until the dinosaurs became extinct at the end of the Cretaceous period, and the mammals then took over the land.

Did You Know?

★

Dinosaurs ruled the earth for 160 million years before becoming extinct.

Dinosaurs can be divided into two groups, depending on whether their hip-bone looks like a bird's or a reptile's.

The discovery of dinosaur bones in the 1700s was ignored because the Christian Church said God would not allow any creature to become extinct.

The biggest dinosaur discovered is Seismosaurus. It reached 36 m (118 ft) tall, and weighed 80 tonnes. It wasn't at all ferocious, it just munched quietly on plants!

Some scientists believe the biggest Brachiosaurus may have weighed 190 tonnes.

Some dinosaurs swallowed stones to break up food in their stomachs.

Life In The Seas

During the Triassic period, life in the seas continued to flourish. The first ichthyosaurs, placodonts and nothosaurs thrived at this time. Ichthyosaurs were fish-shaped reptiles ranging from 1—9 m (3—30 ft) long with limbs shaped like paddles. They also had a dorsal fin and a fish-like tail. Placodonts were armour-plated and jawed, most of them were quite small. Nothosaurs, ancestors of the Plesiosaurs, had feet which were used for swimming, but possibly for scrambling on shore as well.

Not All Dinosaurs Walked Upright

Staurikosaurus, *Herrarasaurus* and many other early dinosaurs could walk upright. This was important for these plant eaters because they could reach high branches and they could also see around them. Other plant eaters walked on four legs but usually had long necks so they were still tall enough to eat from high branches and look around for danger.

The meat-eater Tyrannosaurus makes a meal out of a plant-eater.

The Jurassic Period

During the Jurassic period, some 195 to 135 million years ago, many large dinosaurs flourished. Jungles were lush and the seas were plentiful. Dinosaurs were the dominant creatures of land, sea and even the sky throughout this period. The name Jurassic comes from the type of rock in which dinosaur records have been found, which is the same as the limestone rock of the Jura mountains on the French-Swiss border.

The First Bird

Archaeopteryx, the earliest known bird, was actually a link between reptiles and birds, for it had features belonging to both. Its body and jaw were like those of a reptile, but it bore feathers on its wings and tail. It could not fly off the ground like proper birds but probably had the ability to fly from tree to tree if it launched itself from a high perch. The name *Archaeopteryx* comes from Greek words meaning 'ancient wing'. A feather belonging to *Archaeopteryx* was discovered in Germany in 1860 and skeletons were found in the following year.

Archaeopteryx

Did You Know?

★

The first dinosaurs lived in a world with just one giant continent.

At the beginning of the age of dinosaurs, there were trees and ferns, but no flowers!

Huge dinosaurs had giant holes in their skulls, to make them lighter to carry!

The wings of the earliest 'bird', the Archaeopteryx, have been beautifully preserved as fossils.

The 'Ostrich-mimic' dinosaur, Struthiomimus, looked like a scaly ostrich, and could run twice as fast as an Olympic sprinter.

Not all dinosaurs were huge – the Compsognathus ('Elegant Jaw') dinosaur was the size of a turkey!

Shonisaurus

Life In The Seas

The seas abounded with swimming reptiles. Some land levels had fallen by this time and the seas had invaded large areas. As a result many land-living reptiles such as the plesiosaurs returned to life in the water. Although they now lived in the sea, they came onto land to lay their eggs in holes in the sand, in the same way that some turtles do today.

Ichthyosaurs continued to flourish, the largest being the dolphin-like Shonisaurus which was 15 m (49 ft) long.

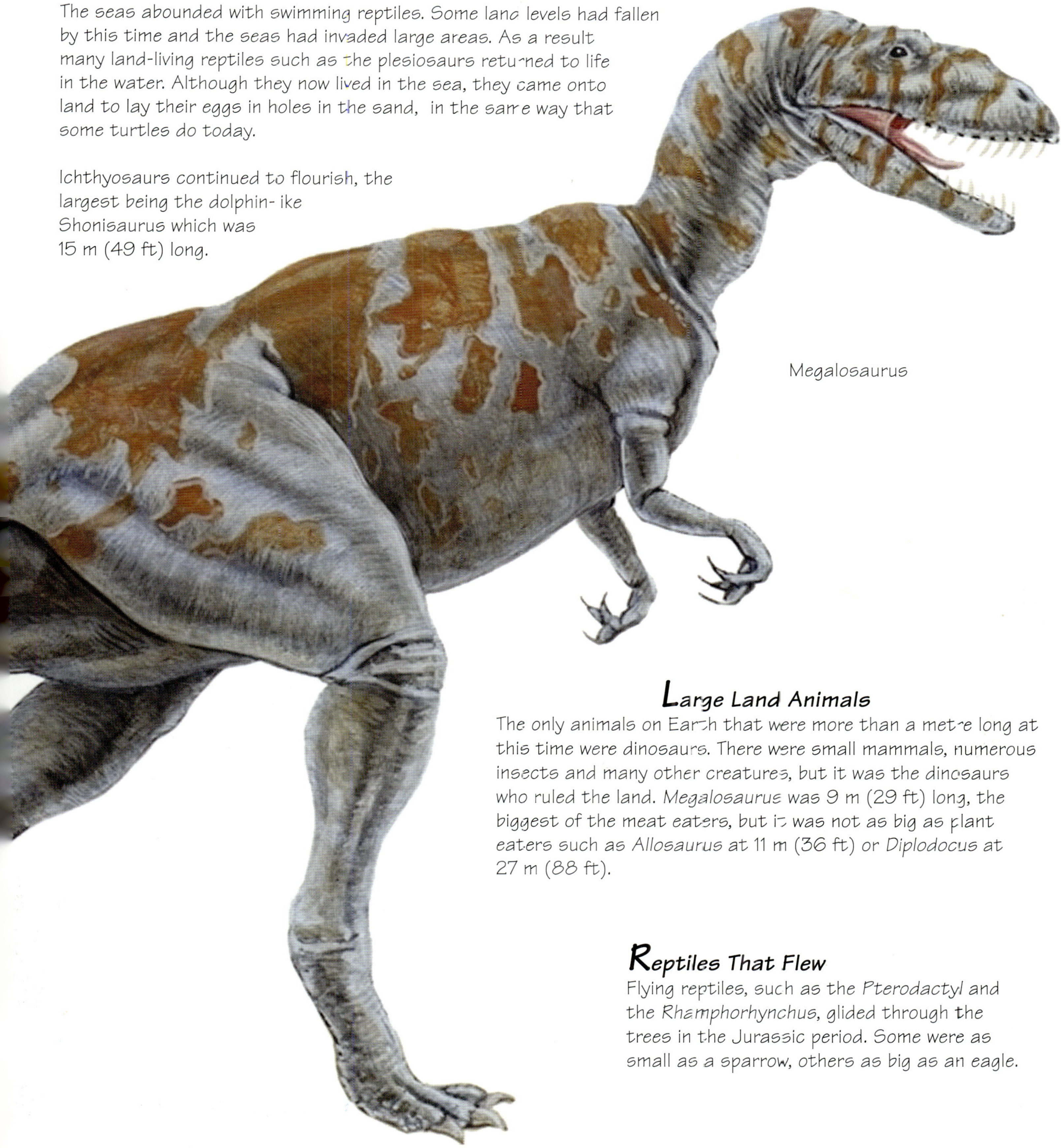

Megalosaurus

Large Land Animals

The only animals on Earth that were more than a metre long at this time were dinosaurs. There were small mammals, numerous insects and many other creatures, but it was the dinosaurs who ruled the land. *Megalosaurus* was 9 m (29 ft) long, the biggest of the meat eaters, but it was not as big as plant eaters such as *Allosaurus* at 11 m (36 ft) or *Diplodocus* at 27 m (88 ft).

Reptiles That Flew

Flying reptiles, such as the *Pterodactyl* and the *Rhamphorhynchus*, glided through the trees in the Jurassic period. Some were as small as a sparrow, others as big as an eagle.

Life in the Cretaceous Period

Cretaceous means 'chalky' and dinosaurs from this period (144 to 65 million years ago) are found in the chalk beds that were forming on Earth at this time. Great changes were taking place in the world. What had been one great land mass was breaking up into the continents we know today. Climatic changes were also taking place and the Earth began to have seasons. More and more flowering plants appeared. Dinosaurs continued to flourish until the end of this period when they became extinct.

Tyrannosaurus rex

The Birth Of Tyrannosaurus

Tyrannosaurus rex ('king tyrant lizard'), perhaps the best known of all the dinosaurs, was the biggest of the meat-eating dinosaurs of the Jurassic and Cretaceous periods. It was 10 to 12 m (35 to 40 ft) long and could rear up to a height of 5 m (16 ft). It probably weighed as much as two elephants. The skull of *Tyrannosaurus* was over a metre long and its mouth contained 60 large teeth, some of which were 15 cm (6 in) long. In spite of its enormous size, it is thought that *Tyrannosaurus* could have moved at 30 kph (18 mph) or more.

Iguanodon

The famous *Iguanodon* lived at this time in Europe. It was a plant eater about 10 m (33 ft) long. It could crouch on all fours to eat low lying vegetation but could rear up to some 4 m (14 ft) to reach higher branches. One feature that has intrigued scientists is the bony spike on its thumb, which was possibly used to defend itself.

Cretaceous Sea Creatures

In the seas around what is now called Australia lived *Kronosaurus*, a descendant of the plesiosaurs. In actual fact *Kronosaurus* was a pliosaur — a short-necked plesiosaur. Pliosaurs were the largest of all the sea reptiles and *Kronosaurus* was about 12 m (40 ft) long.

Also in the seas at this time was *Archelon*, the biggest member of the turtle family. Its shell was 3 m (10 ft) long — much larger than the turtles of today, although very similar in appearance.

Kronosaurus

Other Animals Of The Period

Ostrich dinosaurs appeared during the Cretaceous period. One such creature was *Struthiomimus* ('ostrich mimic') which was very similar to the modern ostrich, but it had no feathers and it had a long tail. It could run very fast — just like the ostriches of today.

Snakes also made their appearance in the Cretaceous period and mammals were developing too, but they were still very small.

Iguanodon

Did You Know?

During the age of dinosaurs, the land divided into different continents and the first flowers evolved.

Barosaurus ('Heavy Lizard') had such a long neck that some scientists have suggested it needed 8 hearts to pump blood to its brain!

The terrifying Tyrannosaurus ('Terrible Lizard') was the largest flesh-eating animal ever to walk the earth.

The Tyrannosaurus tore up other dinosaurs with 15 cm (6 in) long fangs.

Dinosaurs were not as stupid as people say — their brains were big and complex by reptile standards.

Some underwater reptiles had even bigger skulls than the Tyrannosaurus.

Death of the Dinosaurs

At the end of the Cretaceous period several reptile groups suddenly died out, some 65 million years ago — 60 million years before the appearance of the first human. It is not known what caused this. One theory is that a large meteor may have hit the earth. The impact caused an enormous dust cloud that blocked out the sun causing such a dramatic drop in temperature that most animals could not survive.

Dinosaurs Still To Be Discovered

Over 1,000 different types of dinosaur are now known to have existed, but this number is increasing every year as more discoveries are made by palaeontologists (scientists who make a study of fossils).

Piecing together all the evidence is a slow and painstaking job. In the early days of palaeontology bones were simply collected, but now everything is reccrded, detailed notes are made of finds and their locations and photographic and other evidence is also used. Perhaps we will never know everything about the life of dinosaurs, but each day brings exciting new discoveries that are increasing our knowledge of these fascinating creatures.

Palaeontologists studying dinosaur fossils

Other Animals That Disappeared

Many other creatures disappeared at the same time as the dinosaurs. These included the pterosaurs and the plesiosaurs. They all had one thing in common — they all needed a warm environment to survive, which caused scientists to think there may have been a sudden change in climate for them to have disappeared.

All living things have to adapt to changing conditions to survive. Throughout the Mesozoic era, dinosaurs had proved they could adapt, but this took place over a very long period. A sudden change in conditions would not allow the animal enough time to adapt.

The Time Of Mammals

With the disappearance of the dinosaurs mammals began to flourish, giving rise to the many different mammals that we know today.

The death of the dinosaurs

Sea Creatures

Fish Facts

Most fish have a torpedo-shaped, cylindrical and streamlined body that tapers towards the tail. Many fish are dark on their upper side so that they blend in with the surrounding sea when seen from above, and have light undersides to match the sky when seen from below. Many fish sport a wide variety of colours — sometimes for camouflage, to attract a mate, or maybe even to warn off predators.

Lion fish

How A Fish Swims

A fish swims by bending its muscular body from side to side while moving its tail, which helps it to swim in a straight line. The dorsal fins on the top of the body and the anal fin on the underside near the tail keep the fish stable. The pectoral fins near the head and the pelvic fins on the underside are normally used for steering or propulsion. Most fish have a gas-filled swim bladder inside their bodies, which helps them to keep buoyant. By altering the amount of gas in the swim bladder, the fish can rest at any depth in the water.

Fish Take Oxygen Through Their Gills

Fish get oxygen into their bodies by passing water through feathery structures behind the head, called gills. The gills absorb oxygen into the bloodstream and remove carbon dioxide.

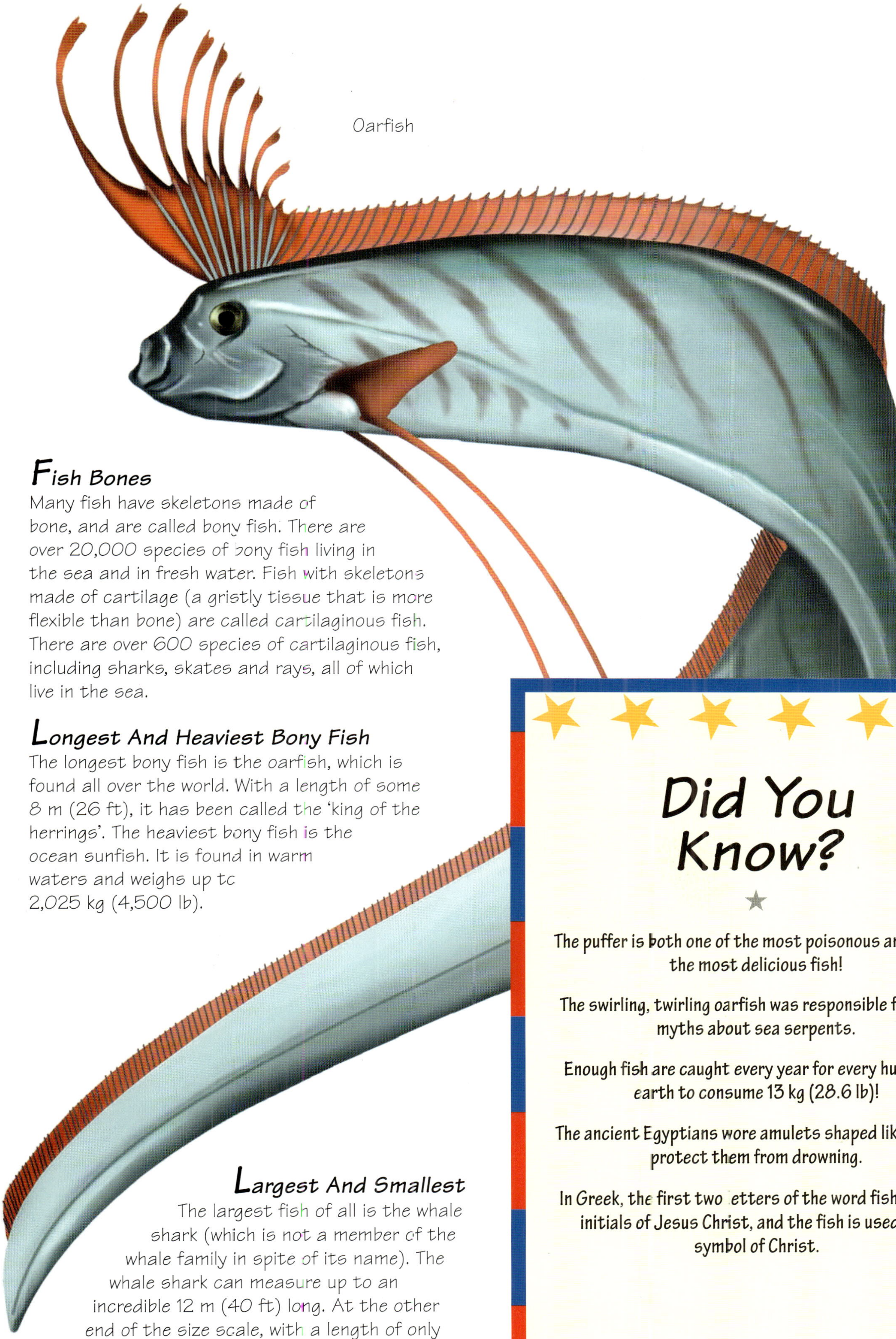
Oarfish

Fish Bones

Many fish have skeletons made of bone, and are called bony fish. There are over 20,000 species of bony fish living in the sea and in fresh water. Fish with skeletons made of cartilage (a gristly tissue that is more flexible than bone) are called cartilaginous fish. There are over 600 species of cartilaginous fish, including sharks, skates and rays, all of which live in the sea.

Longest And Heaviest Bony Fish

The longest bony fish is the oarfish, which is found all over the world. With a length of some 8 m (26 ft), it has been called the 'king of the herrings'. The heaviest bony fish is the ocean sunfish. It is found in warm waters and weighs up to 2,025 kg (4,500 lb).

Largest And Smallest

The largest fish of all is the whale shark (which is not a member of the whale family in spite of its name). The whale shark can measure up to an incredible 12 m (40 ft) long. At the other end of the size scale, with a length of only 8 mm ($1/3$ in), is the dwarf goby found in the Indian Ocean.

Did You Know?

The puffer is both one of the most poisonous and one of the most delicious fish!

The swirling, twirling oarfish was responsible for early myths about sea serpents.

Enough fish are caught every year for every human on earth to consume 13 kg (28.6 lb)!

The ancient Egyptians wore amulets shaped like fish to protect them from drowning.

In Greek, the first two letters of the word fish are the initials of Jesus Christ, and the fish is used as a symbol of Christ.

The Most Feared Sharks

Sharks are the most feared creatures in the sea, with a reputation for being ferocious killers. They are certainly well equipped for killing, with their strong jaws and tough teeth. They have an excellent sense of smell. A line of sensory cells running along the body and over the head can detect vibrations in the water. A shark also has a streamlined body, strong muscles and a large tail that enables it to swim very fast.

Hammerhead shark

Head Like A Hammer

The hammerhead shark is so called because the front of its head is in the shape of a hammer. About 6 m (20 ft) long, it is a very dangerous and aggressive, greyish coloured shark that lives in most warm waters. Its eyes are at the ends of the 'hammer', which gives it a wide range of vision.

Arctic Hunters

Greenland sharks have very small teeth but they are turned inwards to improve the bite — something that comes in useful when they attack whales. Greenland sharks grow up to 6 m (20 ft) long and normally live in warm seas. However, they visit Arctic waters to hunt for seals and small whales.

Most Sharks Are Harmless

There are about 250 different species of shark. About ten species are known to attack humans, but the majority are quite harmless. Some are just scavengers, feeding on what they can find, while others live on plankton. The majority are flesh eaters that feed mainly on fish, but if they are hungry or excited. they are liable to bite anything that comes near.

Sharks Have A Bad Reputation

That sharks have a bad reputation is largely due to the great white shark which is regarded as the deadliest shark of all. It is about 11 m (36 ft) long. Although encounters with humans are rare, they often prove fatal for the person concerned. The shark that attacks more people than any other kind is the whale shark which lives along the Australian coast.

A Shark With A Grin

Another shark that is regarded as a maneater is the tiger shark, which lives in tropical waters. It has a fold of skin at the corners of its mouth, which makes it look as though it is grinning, adding a sinister touch to its gruesome reputation. This 6 m (20 ft) long shark also eats other sharks, sea turtles and carrion.

Did You Know?

The largest fish, the whale shark, lives on some of the smallest creatures – plankton!

The chances of being attacked by a shark are 300 million to one. Even less if you stay out of the water!

If you are attacked by a great white, watch out – it can smell one drop of human blood in 100 million drops of water.

The cookie-cutter shark bites then revolves like a tin-opener – and has left perfect circular bites on the domes of submarines!

The shark has the most powerful bite ever measured.

Modern swimmers have started to break records by wearing special swim-suits based on a shark's rough skin.

Great white shark

Fantastic Fish

When searching for food, the mudskipper — found around the coasts of Africa, Asia and Australia — will come out of the water, using its specially adapted fins as legs. It seems to like being out of the water — it will bask in the sun and will often climb trees to find a sunny spot. Another fish that 'walks' is the tripod fish. Its two chest fins and its tail fin have evolved into long, stiff spines on which the fish walks along the sea-bed.

Mudskipper

Did You Know?

The European eel travels over land when it makes its 6,000 km (3,700 mi) journey to the Sargasso Sea to spawn.

Lung fish can survive out of water for up to four years – by not doing very much!

The male angler fish weighs one thousand times less than the female, and lives off the female like a parasite!

Deep-sea life was first observed in 1934, when scientist William Beebe descended to 923 m (3,028 ft) in a machine called a 'bathysphere'.

An archer fish can judge the distance of its 'shots' because it is the only fish with eyes that point forwards!

Archer fish will line up to shoot at the same target – like contestants at a rifle range.

A Fish Can Give An Electric Shock

One member of the catfish family is capable of giving out an electric shock to ward off danger. This is the electric catfish which is found in the seas of Africa. Although it can give a powerful shock, it is a delicacy in the Middle East, where it is known as the raad, or thunder fish.

A Fish Can Kill A Person

Several species of fish can make electricity, using specially adpated muscles which create electric impulses instead of movement. Fish are the only creatures that can do this. Electric rays, of which there are about 30 species, can create enough power to disable a person temporarily. However, it is a freshwater creature that produces the most electricity of all. The electric eel found in the rivers of South America, can produce enough power to kill a person outright.

Fish Go Fishing

Attached to the head of the angler fish is a small piece of flesh which looks like a worm. The angler fish waves this lure until some unsuspecting fish takes a bite at it, at which point the angler fish promptly gobbles up its prey. Two relatives of the angler fish use similar tricks. The sargassum fish hides in seaweed — some actually look like seaweed — and wait for another fish to take the worm-like bait. The bat fish hides its lure in a tube above its mouth until it goes fishing. Then the lure pops out.

A Mouthful Of Fish

After laying some 50 to 100 eggs, the female Egyptian mouth brooder carries them around in her mouth for safety. Even after they have hatched, the young fish continue to use their mother's mouth to escape from danger. This goes on for only a few days, for once the young fish grow bigger, the mother is likely to eat them! Another fish that uses its mouth in this way is the sea catfish, but in this case it is the male that looks after the eggs.

Sea catfish

Crabs and Lobsters

Crabs, prawns, shrimps and lobsters are members of the group of animals known as crustaceans. The largest crustacean is the giant spider crab of Japan which can, measure up to 3 m (9 ft) between the tips of its outstretched legs. Pea crabs, of which there are over 200 species, are the smallest known crabs. They hide inside the shells of mussels and oysters for protection.

Hermit crab

Shells For Protection

Although protected by their shells, crabs have several enemies, including humans, and have to find other ways to protect themselves. For example, most spider crabs camouflage themselves with seaweed and pieces of sponge so they cannot be seen easily. Some crabs look like their surroundings, or hide under rocks or seaweeds. A lot of crabs burrow into the sand so that only their antennae are visible. The hermit crab often lets a sea anemone ride on its back. The anemone has stinging tentacles. so the crab is protected, too. The greenadier crab goes one step further by carrying a sea anemone in each claw!

Hermit Crabs Live In Other Crabs' Shells

The hermit crab does not have a hard shell so it makes its home in the empty shell of some other sea creature. As the crab grows, it has to find larger and larger shells in which to live. It changes from shell to shell very quickly because it is afraid of being attacked.

Lobsters

Lobsters are generally bigger than crabs and their tails are stretched out behind them, whereas a crab's tail is tucked under its body. To swim, the lobster curls its tail under its body quickly and with such force that the lobster shoots backwards in the water. To help it, the lobster can fan out the end of its tail for greater thrust.

Lobsters Walk In Single File

One American lobster migrates in an unusual way. Every autumn, the spiny lobsters of Florida and the Caribbean march in single file to deeper waters further south to avoid stormy weather.

Crab Legs

Crabs have five pairs of legs, the first pair of which are equipped with large claws. It uses eight of its legs for walking. A crab walks sideways because otherwise its legs would get tangled up. If a crab traps one of its limbs, the limb snaps off and the crab grows a new one.

Crab Claws

The male fiddler crab has one gigantic claw that is much larger than the others — it is the largest crab claw of all. It is often coloured differently to the rest of the body and has two purposes — for fighting other males to defend its territory, and to attract a mate.

Did You Know?

A boxer crab defends itself by holding anemones in its pincers, like two fluffy pink boxing gloves!

Long-legged guano crabs live on bat droppings or 'guano'. Yuk!

Rock crabs on the Galapagos Islands clean ticks from the bodies of iguanas.

The decorator crab wears 'fancy dress', hooking plants on to its body to camouflage it.

Spider crabs have changed little since the age of dinosaurs.

In mythology, a crab nipped the hero Hercules on the foot. It was rewarded by his enemies with a place in the heavens, and formed the Cancer constellation.

Male fiddler crab

Magnificent Whales

There are about 80 species of whale, among which are the largest creatures to have inhabited Earth. They appear to be very intelligent, social creatures who communicate with each other with a complicated system of sounds. Although whales live in the sea they are mammals, not fish. This means that they are warm blooded and give birth to live young who feed on their mother's milk. The young are born tail first so that they do not drown.

Killer whale

Different Kinds Of Whales

Right whales were named by whalers because they were the 'right' whales to catch for their oil. There are three types of right whale: the Greenland right whale, the black right whales and the pygmy right whales. All right whales are rare because they have been over hunted.

The largest of the toothed whales are the sperm whales. They can grow up to 17 m (56 ft) in length. There are also two sperm whales, the pygmy sperm whale and the dwarf sperm whale, that are among the smallest of the toothed whales.

One very unusual looking whale is the narwhal. The male narwhal has an enlarged tooth that grows straight out to form a spiral tusk about 3 m (10 ft) long.

The black and white killer whale is the most dangerous of all the whales. As well as fish, they will eat seals, penguins and even dolphins and porpoises to which they are closely related. The killer whale is the largest member of the dolphin family.

Grey whale

Two Groups Of Whales

There are two groups of whales — the whalebone, or baleen, whales and the toothed whales. There are more toothed whales, which are usually smaller than baleen whales. Baleen whales live on plankton, which is made up of tiny sea creatures and plants. The whale strains plankton out of the water by sieving it through the comb-like plates of stiff material called baleen, that hang from the whale's top jaw. Toothed whales use their teeth to catch and kill all types of fish. Baleen whales include blue, right, humpback, grey, sei and fin whales. Killer whales, sperm whales, porpoises and dolphins are all toothed whales.

Blue whale

Biggest Creature In The World

The blue whale is the largest creature in the world, in fact it is the largest ever to have lived. It is larger even than the biggest of the dinosaurs. Although it feeds only on tiny, shrimp-like krill, the stomach of a blue whale can hold about two tonnes of food. Sometimes it is called the sulphur-bottom whale because of the yellowish algae that may appear on its belly.

Did You Know?

The Bahamonde's beaked whale, whose bones were washed ashore in 1986, has never actually been seen alive!

Whales evolved from the same ancestors as deer, camels, pigs, cows and hippos.

The blue whale is the biggest creature in the world. It is as long as a Boeing 737, and weighs more than twenty elephants.

Whales can communicate at 188 decibels, the loudest noise made by any animal.

Swindlers used to sell narwhal horns as the horn of the mythical unicorn.

In the Bible, the prophet Jonah is swallowed by a whale and lives in its belly for three days and nights.

Fish of Many Colours

Deep sea fish tend to be very dark with few obvious markings. As there is little light in the ocean depths, this lack of colour helps hide the fish from predators, and from prey. Fish that live nearer the surface usually have a light belly, silvery sides and a green-blue top whereas those that live among weeds or on the bottom are often well marked on the top and plain underneath.

Some Fish Can Change Colour

Flatfish, such as sole, plaice or flounders, can merge so exactly with their background that they are impossible to see. Some fish can actually change colour to suit their surroundings. Several tropical fish are able to change colour in an instance. In these fish, the cells containing the colours, or pigments, can contract to hide the pigment, or expand to make it stand out. The cells can also combine some colours, rather like an artist combining different paints.

Pipefish

Carpet shark

Masters Of Disguise

The slender, dark green pipefish, a relative of the sea horse, is almost invisible among the seaweed in which it lives. It feeds by standing on its nose so it, too, looks like seaweed. The sea dragon, a type of sea horse that lives in warm Australian waters, has leaf-like flaps of skin, so that it blends in with the seaweed. The leaf fish of South America is a master of disguise — it is very thin and brown, and looks just like a leaf. To add to this deception it drifts in the water, exactly like a dead leaf.

Fish Use Colours To Attract A Mate

Many of the fish that live among colourful coral reefs are themselves brightly coloured. Colourful patterns are probably used by fish to recognize their own species, or sometimes to attract a mate. The pattern of different colours on the fish's body also helps break up its outline so that it is more difficult to see. This technique, which is used by many land creatures as well, is known as disruptive colouration.

Reptiles

What is a Reptile?

Reptiles have been on earth for over 300 million years. They are vertebrates (animals with backbones) and are usually covered with scales, or plates, which are rather like plates of armour. Some have short legs, while others have no legs at all. Reptiles are cold-blooded. This does not mean that their blood is cold — it means that their body temperature depends on their surroundings, so in cold weather, for example, a reptile feels cold. Most reptiles lay eggs, but there are some lizards and snakes, such as rattlesnakes, that give birth to live young.

One Reptile Is The Size Of A Paperclip

The smallest reptile is a gecko from the West Indies. At 19 mm (3/4 in) long, it is a bit shorter than a paperclip. At the other end of the reptilian scale is the reticulated python, which can grow to a gigantic 6 m (18 ft) — long enough to stretch all the way from the ground to the roof of a three-storey house. The world's heaviest reptile is the saltwater crocodile, which can weigh as much as 1,000 kg (2,200 lb).

Gecko

Many Lizards Have A Third Eye

The brains of reptiles are quite small and not very well developed. This means that most lizards move quite slowly, with simple movements. Many lizards have a light-sensitive area in the top of their heads just beneath the skin. This area is called the pineal eye, and is sometimes also known as the 'third eye'. It is thought to register solar power and is probably used to control some behaviour that is dependent upon light. Vipers, pit vipers and rattlesnakes have special cells in their heads that can detect heat. The snakes use these cells to hunt their prey in the dark.

Nile crocodile

Did You Know?

The South American snake, the anaconda, is the longest reptile, reaching over 9 m (30 ft)!

A tortoise presented by the English explorer James Cook to the Tongan royal family in the 1770s lived until the 1960s. If tortoises could only speak!

The reptile most eaten by humans is the green turtle.

The giant Galapagos turtle nearly became extinct in the nineteenth century because passing sailors kept dining on it.

Different Types Of Reptile

There are about 6,500 species of reptiles in the world. They belong to four main groups, or orders: crocodiles and alligators; turtles, tortoises and terrapins; lizards and snakes; and the tuatara. There are three main types of reptile body: lizards, alligators and crocodiles have a long body and a long tail; snakes have a very long body with a very short tail; turtles and tortoises have a rounded, shell-covered body and a short tail.

The tuatara is a fossil

The tuatara, which lives on small islands off New Zealand, is nicknamed the 'living fossil' because it is the only living member of a group of reptiles that is related to the dinosaurs. It is olive green or grey in colour and about 60 cm (2 ft) long. It looks like a lizard but its skull is a different shape.

Where Reptiles Live

Reptiles live in many parts of the world but, because they are cold blooded, many cannot survive in very cold places, such as in the polar regions. Because reptiles are cold blooded they must constantly move from warm places to cooler ones and then back again to maintain their body temperature. Land-based reptiles can raise their body heat by basking in the sun. Reptiles that live in very hot areas hide beneath rocks or in burrows during the extreme heat. Then they have to bask in the early morning and late afternoon sun to boost their body temperature, to help them to survive the cold nights.

Loggerhead turtle

Turtles Are Good Swimmers

A turtle has two things that help it to be an excellent swimmer. Its shell has been streamlined to help it cut through the water, while its legs have evolved into large flippers. Turtles usually breed in the same place every year. Although they find it difficult to walk on land, they make their way up a beach to lay their eggs in a hole in the sand. When the young turtles hatch out they make a dash for the sea. Many of them get eaten by predators before they reach the water.

Reptiles Don't Have Homes

The holes in the sand made by egg-laying turtles and the scraped-out hollow in which crocodiles and alligators lay their eggs are the nearest that any reptile comes to a sort of home. None of the reptiles, with the exception of crocodiles, are very good parents. The young are just left to fend for themselves.

Some Reptiles Hibernate
In some areas of the world, the weather is warm enough for reptiles during the summer but too cold in the winter. They survive by hibernating, hiding away in burrows or nests where they sleep through the winter until warm weather returns.

There Are No Snakes In Ireland
Ireland has no snakes of its own. According to Christian legend, Saint Patrick (AD389–461), patron saint of Ireland, banished them from the island.

Komodo Dragons Are Cannibals
The Komodo dragon is an enormous lizard that looks like a prehistoric dinosaur. It can be as much as 3 m (10 ft) long and weigh some 90 kg (199 lb). It lives on the island of Komodo and a few other Indonesian islands, and was first discovered in 1912. The Komodo dragon feeds mostly on young deer and wild pigs. It is so greedy that it will also attack and eat wild horses and even other Komodo dragons!

Did You Know?

The flying lizards of South-east Asia are the first reptiles to take to the air since the age of dinosaurs.

There are no reptiles in Antarctica, Greenland, Iceland or the Arctic Circle. Too cold!

Many reptiles shed their skin several times a year.

The tuatara of New Zealand looks like a lizard, but is more closely related to a dinosaur.

In medieval times, people believed in a reptile called Draco the Dragon which suffocated elephants with its tail.

Dragons are evil creatures in European tales such as George and the Dragon, but symbols of good luck in Asia.

Komodo dragon

Snakes

All snakes have bodies covered with waterproof scales. They have no eyelids or legs. Their forked tongues smell and taste the air, and they are flesh eaters. A lot of snakes have poison glands in their head. When the snake opens its jaws, the poison is forced into the fangs which inject it into the enemy's flesh. Some snakes, such as cobras, spit venom at prey. Constrictors wrap their body around a victim and then squeeze it to death. The biggest member of this family is the anaconda, which lives in rivers and swamps in South America.

Snakes Are Concertinas

Many snakes draw themselves up into a concertina shape, then move their head forward, bringing the tail up to form a another concertina. Some snakes wriggle from side to side, while others grip the ground with their tough scales.

Boa constrictor

Snakes Swallow Their Prey Whole

A snake's jaws are specially hinged so that they can open extremely wide, which allows them to eat their prey whole. By moving its jaws alternately, a snake gradually works its prey down into its throat, where the prey is swallowed. After its meal, the snake rests until the food has been digested which can take several days if the prey is large. At the end of this time, the snake disgorges a ball of fur — the only part of the prey that it cannot digest!

Rattlesnake

A Snake Can't Shut Its Eyes

Unlike most other reptiles, snakes have no membrane to cover their eyes — so their eyes are always wide open. Most snakes have extremely good eyesight but some, such as the burrowing snake, are almost blind.

Reticulated python

Smallest Snake

The smallest snake is a thread snake from the West Indies which is only about 10 cm (4 in) long. They have rigid skulls for burrowing underground. Thread snakes have a very specialized diet, eating only slugs and snails.

The Deadliest Snake

The deadliest of all snakes is the olive sea snake, which lives in the Pacific Ocean. Its venom is said to be a hundred times more poisonous than any other snake. Fortunately, it is shy and rarely seen. The other most dangerous snakes are the kraits and cobras of Asia, the saw-scaled viper of Africa and Asia, the diamond-back rattlesnake of North America and the tiger snake of Australia.

How A Rattlesnake Rattles

A rattlesnake's rattling noise is made by bony rings in its tail. When the snake shakes its tail rapidly the rings rattle together. These rings have formed from large scales that are left behind when the snake sheds its skin. Because a snake sheds its skin up to six times a year, you can tell roughly how old a rattlesnake is by counting the rings in its tail.

Did You Know?

Several snakes share the bright colours of the deadly poisonous coral snake. Presumably nothing stays around long enough to find out they don't share its poison!

American hog-nose snakes and European grass snakes roll belly-up and play dead when in danger.

The West Indian wood snake not only plays dead – its body releases the smell of rotting flesh, and blood vessels colour its eyes red!

Snakes have been Christian symbols of evil since the Serpent tempted Adam in the Garden of Eden.

An important Aztec god called Quetzalcoatl was a cross between a rattlesnake and a bird called a quetzal.

During the Snake Dance, Hopi Indians of Arizona dance with rattlesnakes in their mouths.

Alligators and Crocodiles

There are 22 species of crocodilians — the family of reptiles that includes alligators, crocodiles, gavials and caimans. All are armour plated, have powerful tails and deadly fangs. Crocodilians eat fish and other creatures, which they catch in their strong jaws. Being good swimmers, they move very fast in the water.

Biggest And Smallest Crocodile

The largest member of the crocodile family is the saltwater crocodile of Asia and Australasia. The male averages almost 5 m (16 ft) long and weighs about 520 kg (1,150 lb). The smallest crocodilian is the dwarf crocodile found in the Congo River of western Africa. This creature is only 1 m (3 ft) long.

Crocodiles Are Good Mothers

A mother crocodile lays her eggs in a hole, which she then covers with mud. When the babies hatch out, the mother guards them carefully from predators. She picks the babies up gently in her jaws and carries them to the water.

Plovers Clean Crocodiles' Teeth

Most creatures keep well away from crocodiles, but plovers have quite a friendly relationship with them. The bird walks all over the crocodile's body, feeding off the leeches that have attached themselves to it. The birds will even go into the crocodile's mouth and peck at food particles on the teeth. Crocodiles benefit from this service and never harm the plovers.

Plover and crocodile

Did You Know?

★

The best way to tell a crocodile from an alligator is from a distance! (Actually, the alligator has a broader, rounder snout.)

Crocodiles cannot seal their mouths underwater, because they have no lips. They have flaps in their throat instead.

The East Indian saltwater crocodile, the Nile crocodile and the Orinoco crocodile have been known to dine on humans.

Fossils have been found of 108 species of extinct crocodiles.

At Lake Itasy in Madagascar, a proclamation is read to the crocodiles each year warning them that any evil ones will be killed!

According to the famous historian Herodotus, ancient Egyptians kept tame crocodiles adorned with jewels!

Alligator

Caiman

Crocodile

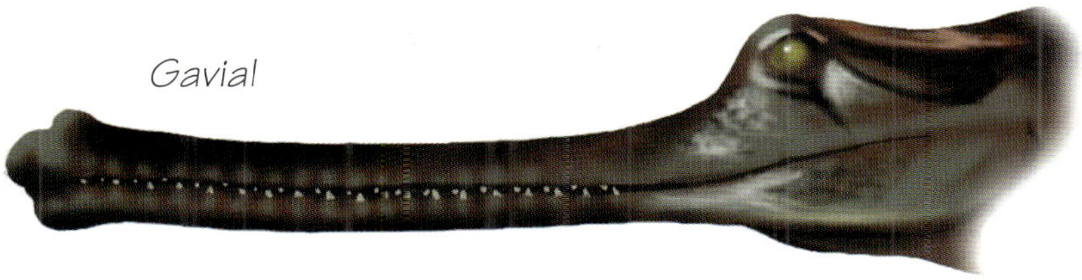

Gavial

Crocrodilians Have Different Heads

There are eight species of caiman living in South and Central America. They look like small alligators and feed on fish, birds and other animals. The gavial, which lives in the rivers of northern India, looks like a crocodile, but it has a long, narrow snout. It can grow up to 6 m (20 ft) long but is not generally dangerous to people. It feeds mainly on fish, which it catches by waving its snout from side to side in the water.

Where Crocodilians Live

There are two species of alligator, both of which are found in North America and China. American alligators are larger than their Chinese cousins and can grow to over 5 m (16 ft) long. Crocodiles live in Africa, Asia, South America and Australia. The esturine crocodile is the only member of the family to live in salt water, so it is also called the saltwater crocodile — and has often also been spotted well out to sea. It is the most fearsome man-eater of the whole family, although the Nile crocodile also has a bad reputation for killing people.

Tortoises, Turtles and Terrapins

There are about 240 species of chelonian (the family of reptiles that includes tortoises, turtles and terrapins). Most chelonians have a leathery skin and a shell to protect their bodies. They have no teeth — just a horny beak — with which they tear their food. Tortoises live on land, but turtles and terrapins are water creatures. Turtles live in the sea, while the smaller terrapin is a freshwater animal.

Galapagos tortoise

Biggest Turtle And Tortoise

The largest turtle is the leatherback turtle of the Pacific Ocean, which measures over 2 m (6 ft) from the tip of its beak to the end of its tail, and weighs up to 453 kg (1,000 lb). The leatherback is a giant when compared to the smallest marine turtle, the ridley turtle, which has a shell length of only 70 cm (27 in) and weighs just 36 kg (80 lb).

Some Tortoises Live More Than A Century

The largest tortoise is the appropriately named giant tortoise. It lives on islands in the Indian Ocean and the Galapagos islands in the Pacific. They normally live for a hundred years or more.

Did You Know?

Musk turtles defend themselves by emitting a foul-smelling odour!

The Hindu god Vishnu turns into a sea turtle in one famous tale.

The Tortoise and the Hare, the story in which the steady tortoise beats the sprinting hare, is the most famous of Aesop's Fables.

Green turtles travel over 2,000 km (1,243 mi) to lay their eggs on Ascension Island.

The African pancake tortoise has such a flat shell it can crawl into crevices to escape danger.

The snapping turtle has a tongue like a pink worm to tempt prey towards its snapping jaws!

Terrific Turtles

Snapping turtles spend most of their time in the water, just coming up every so often to breathe. There are two species, the common snapping turtle and the alligator snapping turtle, both of which live in North America. They are very aggressive creatures, and their sharp jaws can cause a nasty injury.

Alligator snapping turtle

Turtles climb trees

The Chinese big-headed turtle has long claws and a long tail. When it is out of the water it sometimes uses its sharp claws to climb up trees for safety. The box turtle of America has an even more amazing form of protection. It has a hinged bony plate on its belly, called a plastron, which it can close so that its body is completely inside and fully protected. The hinge-back tortoise of West Africa can perform the same trick.

Chinese big-headed turtle

The Starred Tortoise Resembles A Spider

The part of the shell that covers a chelonian's back is called the carapace, and is patterned. Some tortoises have amazingly colourful carapaces. For example, the starred tortoise of India has a black and yellow pattern of spider-like markings, the South American tortoise has a yellow or orange spot on its shell, while the rayed tortoise of Madagascar has a yellow spot with yellow lines radiating from it.

The Shoulders Are On The Inside

The backbone and the ribs are joined to the inside of a chelonian's shell. Because of this, the shoulder blades are inside the ribs, not outside as in other animals with backbones.

Lizards

There are about 3,750 species of lizard ranging in length from small geckos just a few millimetres long, to the Salvadori monitor of Papua New Guinea, which can be up to 4.75 m (15ft 7in) in length. Lizards are found in most parts of the world. Many live in deserts but some live near water, and are excellent swimmers. Most lizards have legs, but there are some that have no legs and look like snakes.

Skinks Are The Commonest Lizards

With some 600 different species, skinks are the commonest of all the lizards in the world. Most skinks are found in tropical Africa and Asia, although there are others to be found in Australia, Europe and North and South America.

Lizards' Tails Can Grow Again

If a predator grabs a lizard by its tail, the tail snaps off and the lizard makes its escape. A new tail grows in the old one's place.

A Lizard Can Have A Ruff

The frilled lizard of Australia and New Guinea runs away on its hind legs when threatened. If is cornered, it raises a large ruff around its neck to make it look bigger. Then it opens its mouth wide and hisses to make it appear frightening. The bearded lizard not only has a ruff, it also has a collar of scales at the sides of its throat which stand out when the lizard opens its mouth. It does this when frightened, turning bright yellow with orange bands.

Frilled lizard

Lizards Perform Tricks

The chameleon can change its colour to merge with its surroundings. The gecko has special pads on its feet which enable it to walk up walls and even upside-down on ceilings. Some lizards, such as the flying dragon of South-east Asia, appear to be able to fly. The flying dragon does not really fly but it can glide for 20 m (66 ft) or more to escape danger. It has a flap of loose skin on each side of its body, which can be opened out to form a pair of 'wings'.

Basilisk lizard

Lizards Can Run On Tiptoe

Several lizards can raise themselves up on their hind legs to run for short distances. The sand monitor, or goanna, of Australia can run so fast on its toes that it is nicknamed the racehorse goanna. The basilisk lizard of South America can even run across the surface of water for short distances, at a top speed of around 8 kph (5 mph), to escape from predators.

Birds

The Perfect Flying Machine

Birds are superbly built for flight. Their light, strong bodies give them the lift they need to fly. Even their feathers are designed to help them fly. Flying uses lots of energy, so birds spend much of their time eating to keep their energy level up. Birds' skeletons are all basically the same — one that is best adapted to the stresses of flying.

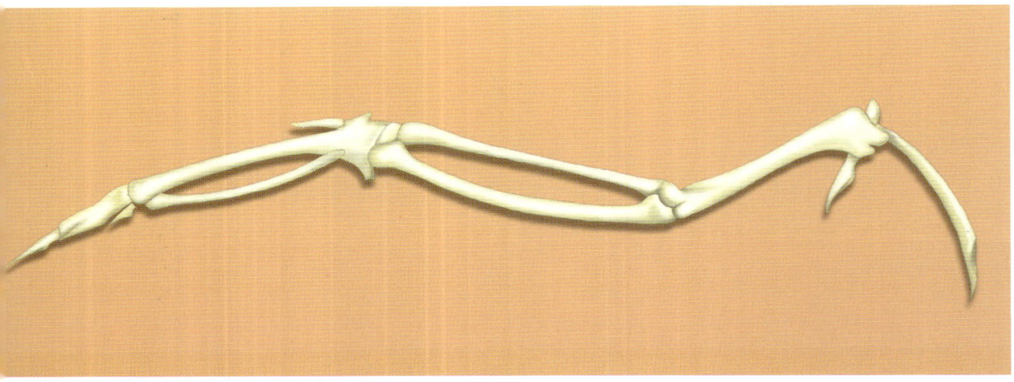

Bird's wing skeleton

Birds Have Hollow Bones

A bird's bones are light but strong. They are light because they are hollow. The larger bones are strengthened with a honeycomb of crossing struts, rather like the struts inside an aeroplane wing. A bird has about 175 different muscles, the biggest being those that work the wings. More than half of a bird's weight is in its muscles.

People birdwatching

Albatross

Did You Know?

A hummingbird may have only 940 feathers but a mute swan could have over 25,000!

The Romans used to use the flight patterns of birds to predict the future!

Birds developed from reptiles!

Not all birds can fly! The kiwi, ostrich, rheas, emus and cassowaries are flightless birds.

Every year, scientists and explorers discover at least two new species of bird.

The ancient Egyptians bred pigeons for food and to carry messages.

Flights Of Fancy

Wings are designed for different types of flight. An owl has especially soft wings so that its prey does not hear it approaching. Most sea birds have wings that are long and narrow, which are excellent for gliding. The wandering albatross has the largest wing-span of any living bird. From tip to tip the average span is 3.15 m (10 ft 3 in), which enables it to glide for long periods without flapping its wings.

Fastest And Slowest Fliers

Most small birds fly at about 30 to 50 kph (20 to 30 mph) but the fastest bird, the peregrine falcon, can reach 270 kph (168 mph) in a dive. Ducks and geese are the fastest fliers in level flight with speeds of up to 104 kph (65 mph). The slowest flying bird is probably the American woodcock which only achieves a top speed of 8 kph (5 mph), which is roughly the same as an adult human walking briskly.

Feather Facts

The number of feathers on a bird varies at different times of the year and from species to species. Feathers get battered and worn by wind and rain, but luckily they are replaceable. This process is called moulting. In most birds the new feathers simply push out the old ones. Birds that live in very cold areas cannot afford to be without the insulation that feathers provide. Because of this, the old feathers are not discarded until the new ones are fully formed. The new feathers fuse themselves onto the old ones so that the bird always has a warm coat.

Beaks, Feet and Eggs

A bird does not have any teeth. It uses its beak for catching and cutting up its food. Birds' beaks are different shapes depending on what type of food they eat. Birds with long, thin bills use them for probing. Birds with short, strong beaks, such as finches, are usually nut eaters. Beaks that are flattened tend to be used for dabbling through mud. Birds of prey, such as the bald eagle, have strong, hooked beaks for tearing at flesh. Wading birds, such as the avocet have long beaks to probe mud on river beds and beaches. A hummingbird's long beak is ideal for reaching right into tube-shaped flowers. The toucan's colourful beak plays an important part in attracting a mate. The beak is about as long as the toucan's body, but it is not heavy because it is hollow.

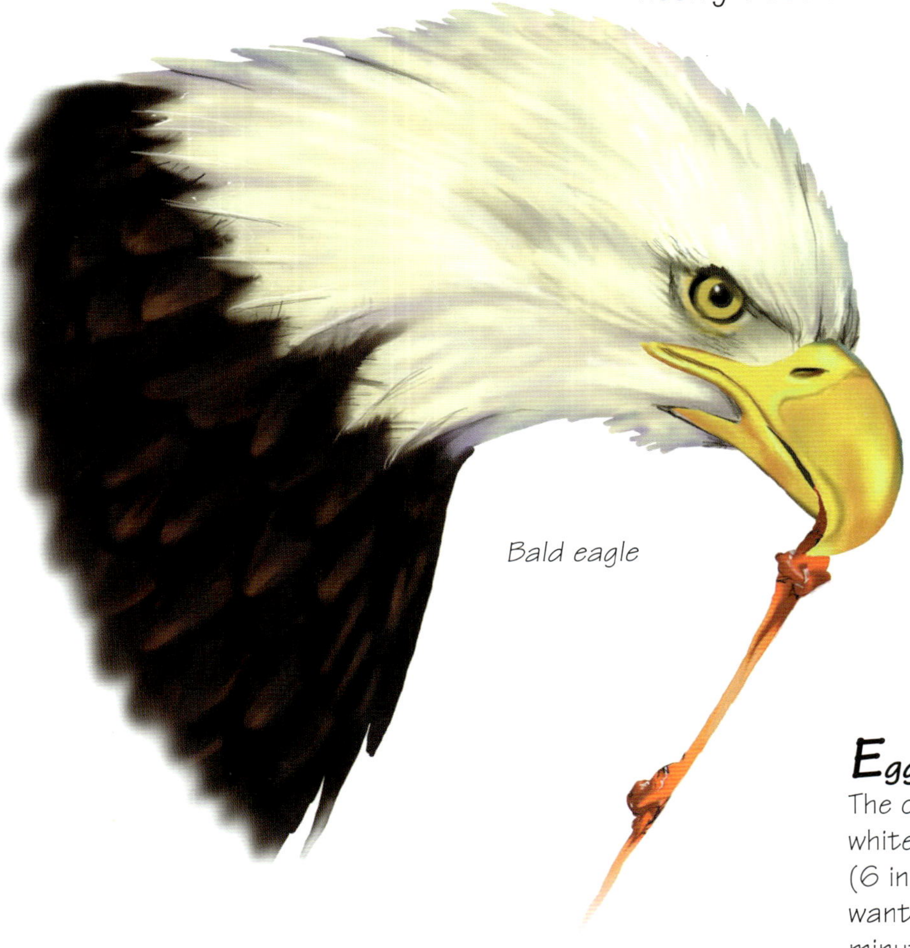

Bald eagle

Toucan

Coming In To Land

As it comes in to land a bird spreads its tail feathers to act as an air brake. It then stretches its legs forwards towards the ground or a perch. Once landed it closes its tail feathers to help it to balance.

Eggs Large And Small

The ostrich lays the biggest egg of all. They are a creamy white, measure about 20 cm (8 in) long, up to 15 cm (6 in) in diameter, and weigh about 1 kg (2.2 lb). If you wanted to boil one for breakfast it would take about 40 minutes to do.

The smallest bird is the bee hummingbird of South America. It measures just 57 mm (2 in) from the tip of its beak to the end of its tail — and half of that is the bill and the tail! Hummingbirds lay the smallest eggs, just 1 cm (1/3 in) long.

Feet Facts

Birds do not walk on the whole area of the foot like humans do — they walk on their toes. This is because the lower joint of the leg is not a knee but more like a heel. Most birds have four toes, three of which point forward and the other points backwards. There are lots of differences between birds' feet according to where and how they live. An ostrich, for instance, has just two toes. The jacana's long toes enable it to walk on floating plants in the marshy areas where it lives.

Jacana

A Colourful Beak

The toucan's colourful beak plays an important part in attracting a mate. The beak is about as long as the toucan's body, but it is not heavy because it is hollow. The bird does not need such an elaborate beak for eating, although it does help in reaching the fruits that it eats.

Did You Know?

The smallest living bird, the bee hummingbird of Cuba is smaller than a dragonfly and weighs less than 3 g (0.1 oz).

The albatross has a wingspan as wide as an elephant is tall.

All domestic chickens are descended from red jungle fowl!

The turkey was first domesticated by the Native Americans.

The study of finches on the Galapagos Islands enabled Charles Darwin to develop his theory of natural selection.

Feathers were made into spectacular cloaks by the Polynesians and the Eskimos.

The Nest Builders

A bird does not have to learn how to build a nest. It is instinctive. However, birds do get better at nest-building with practice. The variety of nests is enormous, from the simplest scrape in the mud to elaborately woven masterpieces. Some birds build mounds of debris up to 2 m (6.5 ft) high, puffins nest in rabbit burrows and other birds nest in holes in trees. The biggest nests are built by the bald eagle of America, the golden eagle in Scotland and the mallee fowl of Australia

Quetzal

Homes In Trees

The quetzal of the rainforests of Central and South America nests in holes in trees. It feeds mainly on fruit. With its yellow beak, bright greenish-gold plumage, red belly and tail feathers up to 105 cm (42 in) long the male quetzal is a spectacular sight. The ancient Mayan and Aztec peoples regarded the quetzal as a sacred bird. The quetzal is the emblem of Guatemala and the name of its currency.

Hornbills Live In Mud Nests

Female hornbills of Africa and Asia nest in a hole in a tree, but then block up the entrance. The male brings dollops of mud which the female mixes with her own droppings before plastering it around the hole, leaving an opening just big enough for the male to pass food in.

Most Intricate Nests

The most intricate nests of the bird kingdom are those of the weaver birds. They weave a nest using hundreds of long strands of grass. The male bird builds the nest, first tying lengths of grass to a branch and then using them as the skeleton on which to attach more grass. The entrance to the nest is at the bottom, and the eggs are laid on a platform built inside.

Using The Nests Of Others

Some birds do not bother to build a nest. They use those belonging to other birds. The female cuckoo picks a nest which already contains eggs and then lays one of her own in it. When the cuckoo hatches the young bird throws out all the other eggs and any birds that are hatched, so that it has all the food to itself. Small birds of Asia and Africa, called honey-guides, also lay their eggs in the nest of other birds, as do the widow-birds of Africa and the brown-headed cowbird of North America and Canada.

Did You Know?

You have heard of a gaggle of geese, but how about a watch of nightingales, a cast of hawks, and a murmuration of starlings!

Some birds build their nests near to hornets' nests to keep away unwelcome intruders!

Weaver birds in Africa use up to 300 strands of grass in their beautifully woven nest.

Australian megapodes keep their eggs warm in enormous piles of rotting compost.

The South American oven-bird is known as 'the baker' because it makes its nest from a dough of sand and cow dung which bakes solid in the sun.

The male emperor penguin keeps his egg not in a nest, but balanced on top of his feet!

The droppings of the guanay cormorant in Peru make such good fertilizer they created a major industry.

Cuckoo

Not All Birds Can Fly

There are several birds that cannot fly even though they have wings. Flightless birds are descended from birds that flew. Many lived where there was no need for flight. Their wings got smaller and they lost the power to fly. There are now fewer flightless bird. They are easier to catch, so many have been hunted to extinction.

Relatives Of The Ostrich

The male rhea, the South American cousin of the ostrich, is very busy during the breeding season. First he hollows out a nest in the ground and lines it with grass, whiile fighting off other males for the territory. Then he courts several females to the nest and when the eggs are laid — perhaps as many as 20 — it is the male's job to look after them. There are two species of rhea. The common rhea is found in Brazil and the smaller, Darwin's rhea, lives in Argentina and the Andes.

The emu, the second largest bird in the world, stands about 1.5 m (5 ft) high and can weigh up to 160 kg (353 lb). The adult emu is brown or blackish-brown but the chicks are grey with black stripes. The female lays up to ten greenish eggs in a nest of trampled-down grass, and these are incubated by the father. Closely related to the emu is the cassowary which lives in north-east Australia and New Guinea. The most distinctive thing about the cassowary is the large bony helmet, or casque, on its head. This helmet protects the bird's head as it runs, head downwards, through the forests and bush.

Emu and chick

Did You Know?

★

Ostriches can reach a height of 2.5 m (8 ft 2 in), but the extinct moa of New Zealand was over 3 m (10 ft) tall!

Ostriches don't really bury their heads in the sand – but they do tuck them in and fluff out their feathers to camouflage themselves as bushes!

The ostrich is the only bird with two toes!

The kiwi's enormous egg weighs nearly one third as much as its mother!

The extinct elephant bird's egg held nearly 10 litres (2.5 gal) of yolk – 30,000 times more than that of the smallest hummingbird!

The cassowary has such sharp claws, it can disembowel a careless human.

The Largest Flightless Bird

The best known and largest flightless bird is the ostrich, which lives in Africa. It can grow to a height of 2..5 m (8 ft) and weighs up to 155 kg (345 lb). It is the fastest living thing on two legs, being able to run at speeds of up to 65 kph (40 mph). The young chicks are almost as fast as their parents with a speed of some 50 kph (30 mph).

Ostrich

Kiwi

Emblem Of New Zealand

The kiwi of New Zealand is almost blind but has a good sense of smell. It has a long beak with sensitive nostrils at its tip — a feature found in no other species of bird. During the day it lives in an underground burrow and normally only comes out at night to hunt for worms, insects and berries. The Maori people named the kiwi after its shrill cry of "kee-wi, kee-w".

Birds of Prey

Birds that hunt and kill other creatures are known as birds of prey. They include eagles, hawks, buzzards, vultures and owls. Some birds of prey also feed on carrion – the decaying flesh of dead animals. All birds of prey have excellent eyesight to spot their prey, strong feet with sharp claws to seize it, and hooked beaks to tear flesh apart.

Lanner falcon

Elegant Eagles

There are probably about 60 types of eagle around the world. The golden eagle lives in mountainous areas, whereas the bald eagle lives along sea coasts and rivers feeding mainly on fish. The snake eagle feeds, as its name suggests, mostly on snakes. Sea eagles and fish eagles live solely on fish.

Monkeys in the South American rainforest are prone to attack from the world's largest eagle, the harpy eagle. Most eagles have large wings, but the harpy's wings are quite short which makes it very fast and agile. Monkeys are not the only prey for the harpy. It will also swoop to the ground to snatch up coatis, opossums and sloths. Another eagle that eats monkeys is the monkey-eating eagle, which lives in the Philippines.

Condors

The Majestic Condor

The condor, a member of the vulture family, is the largest and heaviest bird of prey. The Andean condor lives in the Andes mountains of South America and has a wing span of 3 m (9 ft) and a weight of 10 kg (22 lb). Its large wings help it to glide effortlessly up to heights of 2,000 m (6,600 ft) using the thermals (rising air currents) that abound in the mountains. Like all birds of prey, the condor has excellent eyesight which it uses to spot prey from high above the ground. Normally it feeds on dead and dying animals, but it will also attack live creatures such as lambs, deer, and llamas.

Hunting With Falcons

Lanner falcons are fierce birds of prey that live and hunt in the Sahara Desert. They are about 42 cm (16 in) long with a wing span of 110 cm (44 in) and live on birds, small animals and insects.

Peregrine falcons are the birds most used in the sport of falconry (the training of falcons to hunt for sport or exhibition). It has been a popular pastime since the Middle Ages. Falconry originated in India and eventually spread to Europe and North Africa, becoming particularly popular with royalty.

Peregrine falcon

Did You Know?

When a peregrine falcon dives it reaches incredible speeds over 300 kph (186 mph)!

Perhaps the sparrowhawk should have been called the mousehawk – it eats about 290 mice each year!

The secretary bird quills dangling behind its ears that look like a secretary's pens!

The owl was first seen as wise by the ancient Greeks, who believed the owl was the companion of Athene, goddess of wisdom.

King Arthur's magician Merlin used to carry an owl perched on his shoulder.

Falconry began in Asia as long ago as 2000 BC.

The Mystery of Migration

Migrating birds probably find their way by using the Sun and stars as 'maps'. Young birds seem to know instinctively which direction to fly in. In older birds, memory probably also plays an important part. Ornithologists (people who study birds) find out about migration by ringing birds. A bird is caught and a light aluminium ring is attached to its leg before it is released. If the same bird is caught in another country, its ring is identified and this information is recorded.

Why Birds Migrate

One of the main reasons for migration is the need to keep warm, so birds move to warmer places in the winter months. There is also less food available in cold weather but when the spring returns, the blossoms attract insects, while summer brings a wealth of fruit and berries so the birds can return to their breeding grounds.

Steering By The Stars

It is generally believed that migratory birds steer by the positions of stars and the Sun. They also sense the Earth's magnetic field which tells them in which direction to travel. They also use local landmarks when they are close to their destination. Young birds seem to know instinctively which way they should go, but it is believed that in older birds memory also plays an important part.

Great Distances Are Covered

Some birds fly very long distance when they migrate. The Arctic tern flies the greatest distance, from north of the Arctic Circle southwards across the equator to the Antarctic. Often these birds will cover a distance of 35,000 km (22,000 miles) to make the round trip.

Perhaps even more remarkable is the journey from Alaska to Mexico made by the rufos hummingbird each year. The round trip is some 6,400 km (3,800 miles) and yet the bird is very tiny. Measuring less than 9 cm (4 in) long, it is the smallest of the migratory birds.

Not All Birds Migrate

Some mountain birds will migrate just a short distance to lower, warmer countryside and in some species, such as the European blackbird and the Swedish chaffinch, the males will stay behind when the rest of the flock migrate. It is thought that they do this to make sure they keep the best nesting places ready for when the females return in the spring.

Migrating pigeons

Jungle Animals

Apes

There are four types of ape: gorilla, chimpanzee, gibbon and orang-utan. The gorilla is about the same height as a man but has longer arms and is much heavier and stronger. When disturbed, they put on a ferocious-looking display of chest beating and charge forward. This behaviour is all bluff, and intended to frighten the intruder. Gibbons live in the forests of South-east Asia. They spend much of their time in the trees, using their long arms to swing from branch to branch. The shy orang-utan, whose name means 'man of the woods', lives in the rain forests of Borneo and Sumatra. This second largest member of the ape family is reddish-brown in colour and lives mainly on fruit.

Mountain gorilla

Chimpanzees Live In Family Groups

Most of the ape family are found in the forests and jungles of Africa, South America and Asia. Chimpanzees live in family groups in the rainforests of central and west Africa. They live on fruit, leaves and roots. They also enjoy ants, when they find an ants' nest.

Apes Use Sticks As Tools

Apes are very intelligent. They can work out simple problems, and they can use their hands and feet quite skilfully. A chimpanzee will use a stick to get to out-of-reach fruit or insects, spider monkeys use sticks as weapons, throwing them at any potential threat, and the orang-utan will often use a large leaf as an umbrella.

Black how'er monkey

Apes Are Very Noisy

Most apes and monkeys are noisy but the howler monkey, the largest South American monkey, beats them all. They start howling as soon as they wake up, the noise being a signal to others that this territory is taken. Both males and females howl but the male has a much louder and deeper sound which can be heard 3-5 km (2-3 miles) away. A series of bones in the throat form an echo chamber (giving the animal the appearance of having a double chin), which magnifies the sound. Another noisy monkey is the proboscis monkey of Borneo which makes loud trumpeting noises through its long, drooping nose.

Orang-utan

Did You Know?

A gorilla weighs 3,000 times more than its fellow primate the pen-tailed tree shrew.

Chimpanzees, gorillas and orang-utans have been taught to use sign language.

Chimpanzees in the wild chew medicinal plants when they are feeling poorly.

The ancient Greek philosopher Galen of Pergamum wrote: 'The ape is likest to man in viscera, muscles, arteries, veins, nerves and in the form of bones.'

The first ape to be dissected, a chimpanzee in 1699, is still in the British Museum.

People were outraged when Charles Darwin suggested in 1859 that humans were descended from apes.

Butterflies and Moths

There are over 100,000 species of butterflies and moths, some of the most beautiful insects in the world. Among those found in rainforests are the brilliant blue Morpho butterflies of South America. The Dardanus butterfly of Africa has a vast array of colours. Some of the most spectacular butterflies are the swallowtails of the African rainforest. Swallowtails are also found in other areas of rainforest, such as in South America.

Some Butterflies Have Eyes On Their Wings

Some butterflies escape predators with 'flash colours'. The uppersides of their wings are brightly coloured, but they appear quite dull at rest, with their wings closed. When they open their wings, the sudden flash of colour is often enough to startle their enemy. Often this flash is backed up by large 'eye-spots' on the wings, to frighten the predator.

Birdwing butterfly

The Smallest Butterfly Lives In South Africa

The Queen Alexandra birdwing of New Guinea is the largest butterfly. It can have a wing span of over 280 mm (11 in). The smallest butterfly is the dwarf blue of South Africa with a wing span of just 14 mm (1/2 in).

The Smallest Moth Lives In The Canary Islands

The largest moth is the Hercules emperor moth which is found in New Guinea and Australia, with a similar wing span to that of the biggest butterfly. To see the smallest moth, you would have to go to the Canary Islands where there is one with a wing span of only 2mm (1/8 in).

Emperor moth

Not All Moths Are Dull

Morpho moths have brilliant metallic colours that sparkle in the light, as they soar among the trees in the tropical forests of Central and South America.

Birth Of A Butterfly

Butterflies and moths lay eggs that hatch into larvae, called caterpillars. When the caterpillar is fully grown it attaches itself to a twig and its skin changes into a hard chrysalis. The chrysalis looks inactive, but inside it the caterpillar undergoes a transformation, gradually changing into a butterfly or moth. Eventually, the adult insect breaks free of the chrysalis and is ready to fly away once its wings have dried.

Did You Know?

A butterfly's wings are covered with tiny scales.

Monarch butterflies migrate over 3,000 km (1,864 mi) from Canada to Mexico!

Silkworms are the caterpillars of a moth called Bombyx mori. It takes 2,500 of their cocoons to make 500 g (1 lb 2 oz) of silk.

Tiger moths defend themselves against bats by making a loud 'popping' noise!

The ancient Greeks believed that the soul left a dead body in the form of a butterfly.

Mexican 'jumping beans' jump because they have the caterpillar of a moth inside them.

Shy Creatures

Although life is tough in a jungle, there are many creatures who are quite docile. Shyest of them all must be the okapi, which lives in the dense jungles of Africa, and is seldom seen. Local pygmy tribes had hunted the okapi for many years, but the animal was not known to the rest of the world until 1900, when the British naturalist Sir Harry Johnston discovered some opaki skins. Because it has stripes on its legs it was thought to be a relative of the zebra, but the okapi is, in fact, the only living relative of the giraffe.

Okapi

A Pygmy Is Named After A Giant

Because they have a long, trunk-like nose. the 16 species of elephant shrew are named after the elephant — the biggest creature on Earth. This is in spite of the fact that they are only 12 cm (5 in) long. Elephant shrews are found throughout Africa. They seldom venture far from their burrows. They eat termites and often burrow into termite mounds to find food. They also eat seeds and berries. They are often known as jumping shrews because their back legs are much longer than the front legs, making it easy for them to jump from branch to branch in search of fruit.

Did You Know?

The okapi is related to the giraffe – though you might not guess it from their collar sizes.

The jaguar was a powerful god among the ancient Maya people, associated with the night and the underworld.

The scaly anteater gets the name 'pangolin' from the Malayan for 'rolling over'.

A pangolin will not only curl up in a ball to defend itself, but also releases a nasty smell!

The American president Theodore Roosevelt joined a tapir hunt in 1913.

Tapirs are an elusive prey, and will escape predators by leaping into water.

Tapir

Anteaters Have Long, Sticky Tongues

Ant colonies are a great place to eat — if you are an anteater. The giant anteater of Central and South America rips open an ants' nest with its long claws. Then it thrusts its long, sticky tongue in to the nest to pick up lots of ants, grubs and pupae. The claws on the anteater's front feet are so big that it has to walk on the sides of its feet.

Pangolins Can Curl Up Into A Ball

Another ant eating animal is the pangolin of Africa and Asia. To stop it getting stung by the ants, the pangolin has extra thick skin on its head. It can also close its nose and ears to keep out the ants. Its body is covered with large, overlapping scales and because of this it is sometimes called the scaly anteater. If threatened, the pangolin will roll itself into a ball for protection.

Pangolin

A Tapir Is Related To A Rhinoceros

The black and white tapir of Asia and the blackish-brown tapir of South America look a bit like a large pig with a snout extending into a short trunk — but they are actually related to the horse and the rhinoceros. Being very timid, the tapir feeds mostly at night on leaves, buds and twigs and goes about its business very quietly. It has no defence against enemies, but it is a good swimmer and usually lives close to rivers.

Jungle Snakes

Hanging down from the trees in a jungle are long, trailing vines — but things are not always what they seem: those vines could be vine snakes. A vine snake has a long, slim, green body and looks exactly like a creeper hanging from a branch, so that it is hidden from its prey. The bushmaster of Central America is another snake that blends in with its surroundings. Although it is about 3 m (10 ft) long, its colouring is like dead leaves which makes it very difficult to see. Another snake to be wary of in the jungle is the python, which is found in Africa and Asia. Pythons are constrictors — they squeeze their prey to death. Pythons are the biggest snakes of all. The longest python is the reticulated python of Malaysia. A smaller member of the same species is the Indian python. Other pythons are found in Africa and Australia.

The Fer-De-Lance Attacks People

Although it lives mainly in the rainforests of the West Indies the fer-de-lance will attack people working in the sugar plantations. It is a member of the viper family. It stays in its lair during the day and comes out to hunt in the early evening.

Harmless Snakes Can Look Poisonous

The red, black and yellow bands on a coral snake warn potential predators that the snake is venomous and ought to be avoided. Some snakes that are completely harmless, such as the scarlet king snake, have copied this colouring. This trick makes predators think that these snakes, too, are poisonous, and keep well away.

Fer-de-lance

Anaconda

Anacondas Rest In Trees

The boa constrictor lives in the trees of Central and South America and the West Indies. It can grow up to 4 m (12 ft) long but is generally not a danger to humans. The largest member of the boa family is the anaconda which can be over 6 m (20 ft) long. It lives in swampy areas along the banks of pools and rivers in South America waiting to prey on animals and birds that come to drink. It will often climb trees to rest.

Did You Know?

A snake charmer's music cannot be heard by the snake!

The Braminy blind snake is only about the length of your pencil.

The spitting cobra squirts venom at its enemies' eyes!

Snakes can have over 400 vertebrae.

Egg-eating snakes use spikes in their throats which cut an egg open, so they can suck out the yolk, and spit out the shell!

Snakes can sometimes go for years without eating!

Emerald Boas Are Bright Green

The emerald boa, so named because of its brilliant green colouring, spends most of its life in the trees of South American rainforests. Its colouring acts as a form of camouflage so it catches many birds unawares. The rainbow boa is a smaller member of the boa family. It has a red body decorated with blue rings, and lives under ground.

Bats

There are almost 1,000 species of bats living all over the world except polar regions. The rainforests of India, Burma, Madagascar and other tropical and sub-tropical regions are home to many types of fruit bat. Species, such as the leaf-nosed bat and vampire bats are found in South American rainforests. Bats are the only mammals that can fly. A leathery membrane stretches over the bones of their arms and hands, which are adapted to form wings.

Vampires Curl Their Tongues To Drink Blood

The vampire bat lives in rainforests in South America. It lands on the ground near its victim — usually a cow or a horse — and then walks towards it on all fours. It cuts a piece of skin from the victim with its teeth and then curls its tongue into a U-shape, so that the blood runs into it. Sometimes the bats take so much blood that they have difficulty flying afterwards. The victim does not lose so much blood that it is weakened, but there could be a danger of infection from the wound.

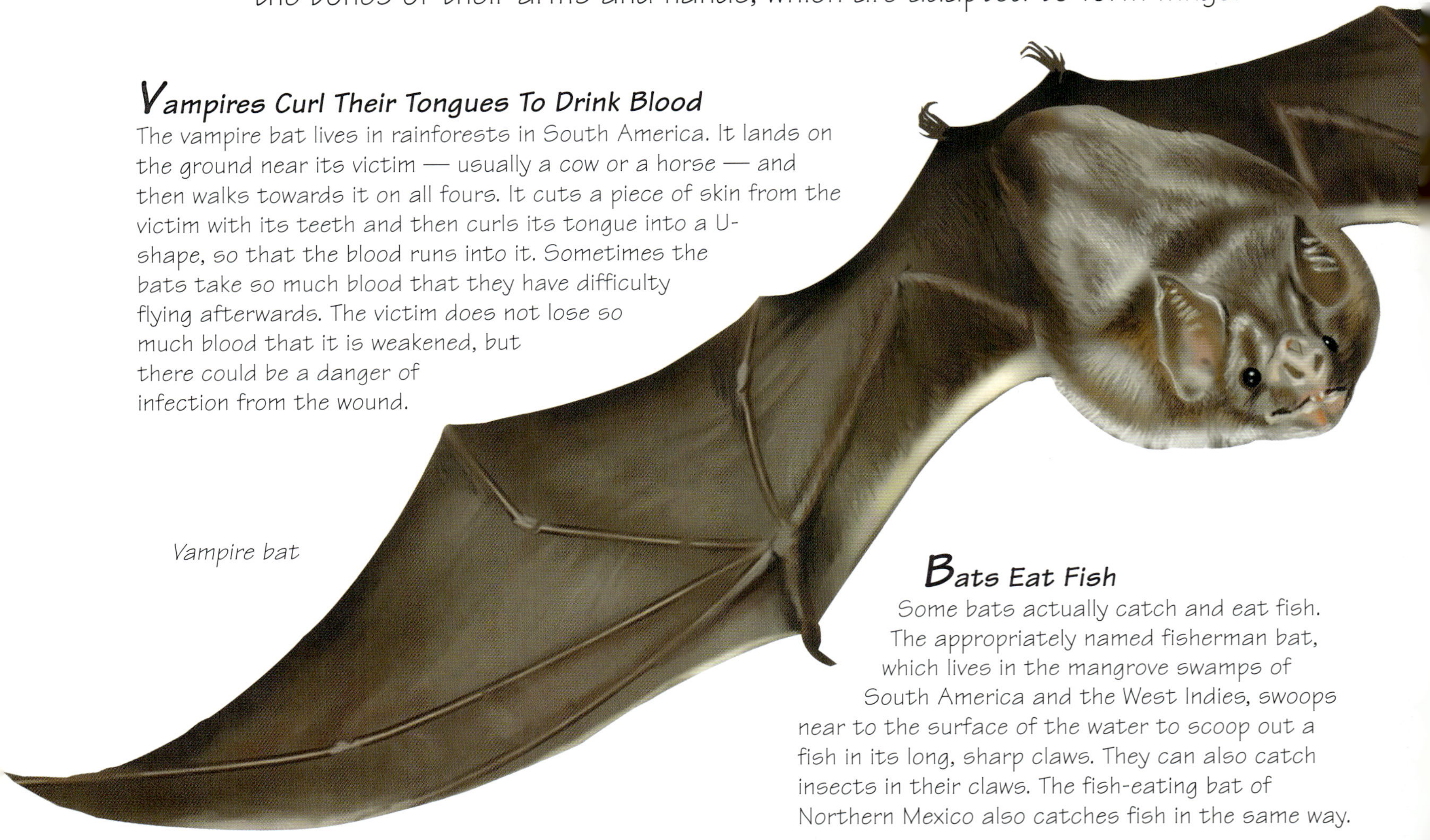

Vampire bat

Bats Eat Fish

Some bats actually catch and eat fish. The appropriately named fisherman bat, which lives in the mangrove swamps of South America and the West Indies, swoops near to the surface of the water to scoop out a fish in its long, sharp claws. They can also catch insects in their claws. The fish-eating bat of Northern Mexico also catches fish in the same way.

A Bat Can Build A Tent

Because it flies by day, the tent-building bat needs a way of sheltering from the sun. It does this by making a tent from fan-shaped palm leaves. It bites through a leaf until part of it collapses. The folded leaf provides an effective shelter from which the bat can fly to find food.

Tent-building bat

The World's Smallest Mammal Is A Bat

The world's smallest bat is also the smallest known mammal. It is the very rare Kitti's hog-nosed bat, or bumblebee bat, of southern Thailand. It has a wing span of about 16 cm (6 1/4 in) and a body length of around 3 cm (1 1/4 in).

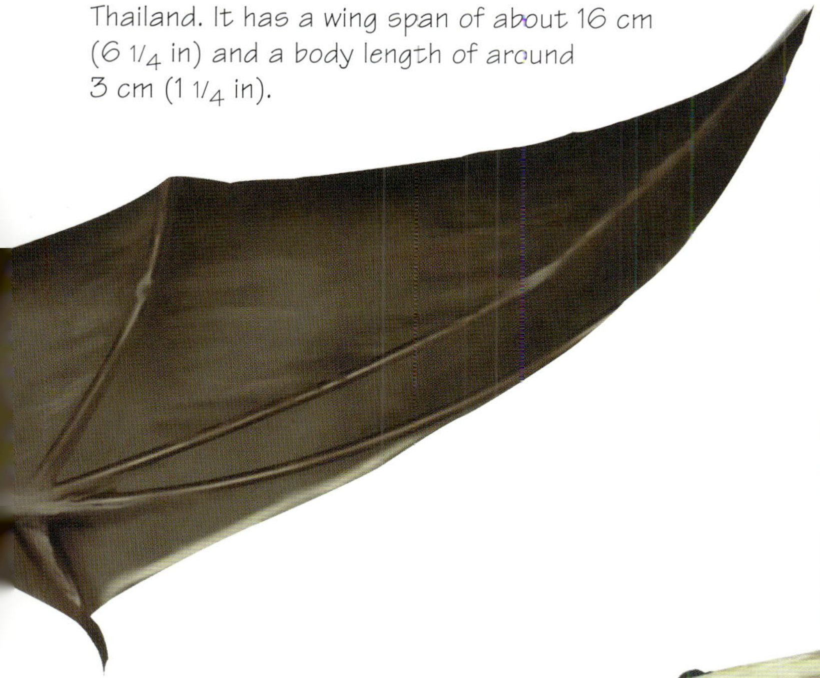

Did You Know?

The bat is the only mammal that can fly.

Bats have such good ears they can hear an insect's wings beating.

A bat may make up to 200 shrieks per second, so that it can guide itself by the echoes.

A vampire bat's teeth are so sharp it can bite and suck blood without its victim noticing.

In the seventeenth century, people in Europe dug up graves looking for vampires!

In the Far East, bats are symbols of good luck.

Flying fox

Flying Foxes Are Bats

There are about 130 species of fruit bat living in the tropical and sub-tropical regions of the world. They are often called flying foxes because the head is like that of a fox. The greater fruit bat, or kalong, found in the forests of Malaysia and Indonesia has a wing span of 1.5 m (5 ft) — the largest of any bat. The smallest fruit bat is the Queensland blossom bat which lives in eucalyptus and acacia forests in New Guinea and Australia. Its body is 6 cm (2 1/2 in) long and it has a wing span of up to 15 cm (6 in). It lives on pollen and nectar by sticking its long tongue into flowers.

Colourful Birds

Rainforests are full of vividly coloured birds. There over 300 species of parrots in the tropical and sub-tropical forests of the Americas, Africa, Asia and Australia. Parrots, believed to be the most intelligent of birds, include macaws, cockatoos, lovebirds, parakeets and budgerigars. Fruit, nuts and seeds are the main foods of the parrot family because their strong beaks are specially suited to cracking open shells. The largest member of the parrot family is the hyacinth macaw. Many macaws eat clay. They probably do this to counteract the effect of poisons in some of the seeds that they eat.

Some Birds Dance To Impress A Mate

Mating displays are sometimes very elaborate and often appear rather strange. The palm cockatoo holds a stick in his claw and bangs it against a tree trunk, like a drummer hitting a drum. The orange cock-of-the-rock, which lives in Brazil and Guyana, dances to impress a mate. He spreads his wings, then leaps around, turning his head and tail from side to side, watched by other cocks and hens, until he is exhausted. Birds of paradise also perform dances to impress their mates. Most birds perform alone but the male raggianas dance together, each trying to outdo the performance of the others.

Bird of paradise

Budgerigars Live Only In Australia

Burgerigars are natives of Australia. They are members of the parakeet (small parrot) family. In the wild, they are mainly green and yellow in colour.

Hummingbirds Hum With Their Wings

The hummingbirds of North, Central and South America are so called because their wings beat so fast that they make a humming sound. The speed of their wing beat enables them to hover in front of flowers. As they hover, they insert their beak into the flower to gather the nectar, which is their principal food. The largest of the hummingbirds is the giant hummingbird of the Andes, which can be up to 22 cm (8 1/2 in) long. The male bee hummingbird is the smallest bird in the world, measuring just 5 cm (1/4 in) from the tip of its beak to the end of its tail.

Budgerigar

Desert Animals

Keeping Cool in the Desert

Many desert creatures avoid the extreme heat of the desert because they are nocturnal. Rats, mice, foxes, and some frogs and birds come out only at night when the air is cooler. During the day, they keep cool in burrows or hidden under rocks and stones.

A Ground Squirrel Uses Its Tail As A Sunshade

Ground squirrels live in extensive underground burrows in the deserts of North America and South Africa. Like all members of the squirrel family, the ground squirrel has a long, bushy tail. When it goes out in the sun to search for food the animal fluffs out its tail and holds it over its body to act as a sunshade. In fact, the name 'squirrel' comes from two Greek words skia, meaning 'shade', and oura, meaning 'tail'. Ground squirrels are very social animals, so when they meet one another they 'kiss' briefly and give a hearty flick of the tail.

Ground squirrel

Fennec fox

Huge Ears Keep The Fennec Fox Cool

One unusual burrowing creature is the fennec fox, the smallest member of the fox family. During the day it stays in burrows, which it digs in the sand, and comes out at night to hunt for small birds, rodents and lizards. The outstanding feature of the fennec fox is its ears which are huge compared to the rest of its body. Its ears are 10 cm (4 in) long whereas its body (excluding the tail) is only 41 cm (16 in). The ears radiate heat which helps to keep the fennec cool.

Did You Know?

About 5,000 species of animal live in the desert.

More than half of all desert animals keep cool by living underground.

When there is severe drought, some desert lizards do not reproduce.

Some deserts are growing steadily larger. This is known as desertification.

People in the deserts of Mexico often include grasshoppers in their diet.

The burrowing owl has learnt from the creatures around it, and is one of the few birds to nest in a burrow.

Lizards Move In And Out Of The Sun

Many reptiles, such as snakes and lizards, live in deserts. Because they are cold blooded (and cannot control their body temperature), they have to constantly move in and out of the sun, so that they don't get either too hot or too cold. A desert lizard will bask in the sun during the morning to warm up. At midday, when the sun is at its hottest, the lizard will find some shade to keep its temperature down. Towards evening, it goes out into the sun again.

Bearded Lizards Dance To Keep Cool

The bearded lizard of Australia has a weird way of keeping cool- it dances! When standing still it lifts each leg in turn, which makes it look as though it's dancing. It often stands up and runs on just its hind legs to keep its body away from the hot sand.

Drinking in the Desert

Deserts are hot and dry so there is little water for the animals and plants that live there. Desert creatures have different ways of overcoming this problem. Many get all the moisture they need from food, others have more clever survival tricks.

Thorny devil

The Thorny Devil's Spines Give It A Drink

The thorny devil is a lizard that lives in North American deserts. It has come up with a clever way of getting water Large, jagged spines on its body give it a fearsome appearance but the animal is actually quite harmless. At night, the lizard lets dew condense on its body. As the dew condenses into water, the spines trap the water, and pass it along to the lizard's mouth.

Darkling Beetles Drink Fog

The darkling beetle of south-west Africa gets water from fog! It lives in the Namid Desert, which is often covered with sea fog. When this happens, the beetle stands on its head so its rear is up in the air. Moisture from the fog condenses into water on the beetle's body, trickles down it back and into its mouth.

Darkling beetle

Water-holding frog

Frogs Carry Their Own Water Supply

Most frogs and toads live in damp places but there are some that can survive in desert conditions. Most burrow deep into the ground, where they can find damper conditions and where they can soak up the water they need from the sand. One group of frogs in Australia carry their own water supply with them. They retain water beneath their skin, then during the dry season they go deep underground living on their store of water until the rains return. Because of this they are known as water-holding frogs. When there is extreme drought, the Aboriginals may dig the frogs up and squeeze a drink from them.

Rats Drink From Cactii

The nocturnal pack rats of Central and North America get their water from the saguaro cactus by chewing the flesh of the plant, inspite of its sharp spines. Although the red fruits of this plant are edible, the flesh of the plant is poisonous to humans but it does not seem to bother the pack rats.

Sand Grouse Chicks Drink Water From Feathers

Desert birds have found a variety of ways to get a drink. Vultures do not have to worry about finding water because they get enough liquid from the blood of the dead animals they eat. Emus, however, follow rain clouds in their constant search for water. One bird with a clever trick is the sand grouse, which lives in the dry grasslands and deserts of South Africa. The male flies long distances to water and immerses his whole body in it. When he returns to the nest, his young take a drink of water from their father's feathers.

Did You Know?

In 1955, when the Bicycle Dry Lake in the Mojave Desert filled with water for the first time in 25 years, it was instantly filled with millions of hatching shrimp!

A camel can consume 100 litres (22 gal) of water in one sitting.

The desert tortoise converts its food into water which it stores in sacs beneath its shell.

The Roman writer Pliny believed camels stored water in a mysterious tank in their stomach!

Kangaroo rats live their lives without ever drinking.

The kangaroo rat preserves water by having no sweat glands and rarely passing urine!

Dangerous Desert Creatures

Deserts are dangerous and hostile places, but they are made even more dangerous by some of the creatures that inhabit them. Many desert animals run away if an enemy approaches, but a lot will stand and fight, and they have some unusual weapons in their armoury.

Green toad

Green Toads Taste Horrible

No matter how they defend themselves, creatures do get eaten by others. If this happens to the green toad of East Africa, it has an effective last minute defence available. The green toad is covered with poisonous warts that taste so bad that any would-be predator is put off.

Gila monster

Cobras Spit In Their Enemies' Eyes

Some snakes, especially vipers and rattlesnakes, have poison in their fangs. The snake bites its enemy and the venom flows down a canal in the fangs and into the victim. Among the most poisonous snakes are the cobras. A cobra gives warning of an impending attack by raising its head and flattening its neck. If the attacker does not retreat, the snake will spit poison into the enemy's eyes, causing temporary blindness.

There Are Only Two Poisonous Lizards

The gila monster is one of only two poisonous lizards in the world, and is found in the south-western United States and Mexico. It has no fangs to inject its poison. When it bites its victim, venom flows from glands in its lower jaw and is chewed into the wound.

Did You Know?

★

The sidewinder snake leaves a strange trail like the steps of a ladder because it moves sideways!

Baby scorpions hitch a ride on their mother's back, under the protection of her lethal sting.

Scorpions clasp each other's pincers and dance when they are mating.

Some stick insects arch their tails over their bodies, in the hope that predators will mistake them for scorpions!

American ground squirrels can tell how dangerous a rattlesnake is just from the sound of the rattle!

The chuckwalla lizard escapes danger by squeezing into a crevice then inflating itself like a football!

Skunks Spray Poison

The skunk has an unusual but powerful weapon. It either turns around, or stands on its forelegs and fires an evil smelling liquid at anyone who threatens. This foul liquid is contained in two glands at the base of the tail and although it can blind the enemy temporarily, and may also affect its breathing, it is the smell that puts most animals off. The only creature that will attack without worrying about the skunk's pungent spray is the great horned owl.

Bombadier Beetles Fire Chemicals

The bombardier beetle shoots a jet of boiling chemicals from its rear end, with a loud explosion. Chemical warfare of another kind is used by the scorpion. It is armed with strong pincers, and its tail, which arches up over its back, has a poisonous sting. Most scorpion stings are painful but harmless, but there are some members of the family whose sting can kill a human.

Scorpion

Two Types of Camel

The Arabian camel has just one hump and lives in Arabia and North Africa. The smaller Bactrian camel has two humps and comes from Central Asia. Arabian and Bactrian camels can interbreed. The offspring of a male Bactrian and a female Arabian are in great demand as they are especially strong animals. The offspring have only one hump.

Bactrian camel and Arabian camel

A Camel Is Protected From Sand And Sun

A camel's head is designed to protect the animal from the sand. The eyes are almost like slits, and protected with heavy eyelids and long eyelashes that interlock to keep grains of sand out. The nostrils are also like slits, and can even be closed to keep out the sand. A camel's ears are small for such a big animal, and protected by a thick covering of hair. Sand does not bother a camel and neither does the sun. The lower parts of the legs are covered with thick skin, which helps protect them from the sun's heat, and the roughness of the sand.

Llamas Are Bad Tempered

The llama is related to the camel, but it is much smaller and does not have a hump. It does, however, have the camel's bad temper! Like the camel, the llama is used as a pack animal. It has been used as a beast of burden in mountainous areas by the South American Indian people for over 1,000 years.

Camels Do Not Store Water In Their Humps

Many people think that a camel's hump contains water but that is not true. It actually contains reserves of fat, which the body uses when little food or water is available. As the reserves are used up, the hump gets smaller. Camels can go without water for long periods. Their bodies are adapted in several ways to enable them to do this. They have very few sweat glands, so little moisture is lost through perspiration, and they do not produce very much urine. Another adaptation that helps them is their ability to close their nostrils as this prevents water loss through evaporation. Camels do, of course, still lose water, but they can lose up to a quarter of their body weight without any harm. A person could not survive such a great amount of dehydration. A camel's body returns to its normal shape after just ten minutes drinking.

Did You Know?

Camel dung is so dry it can be burned as fuel almost immediately.

Camels originated in North America about 40,000,000 years ago!

Some ancient peoples made their living by camel-trading.

Among the Teda people of the Sahara, a young man traditionally has to prove he is fit for marriage by stealing a camel.

The Tuareg people of the Sahara used to ride into war on the back of fast camels.

In the Bible, Jesus says: 'It is easier for a camel to go through the eye of a needle than for a rich man to enter into the kingdom of God.' (Matthew 19:24)

Camel train leaving an oasis

Deadly Hunters of the Desert

The caracal, sometimes called the Persian lynx, lives in the deserts of North Africa and western Asia. One of the striking features of the caracal is its long, tufted ears. It hunts mainly at dusk, and its prey includes birds, reptiles, sheep, mice, goats and deer. It is a superb runner and can even outrun the swift gazelle for a while. The caracal has an unusual way of hunting birds. It springs high up into the air to catch a bird in flight. It can leap 2 m (6 ft) from the ground and can even kill a large bird, such as an eagle, with a swipe from its strong paw.

Cheetahs Are The Fastest Animals

From standing still a cheetah can reach a running speed of 70 kph (43 mph) within two seconds. It has a top speed of 96 kph (60 mph), making it the fastest animal in the world. The cheetah is also known as the hunting leopard, and it has been trained by people for hunting, for a very long time. Hunting with cheetahs was once a popular pastime of Indian princes.

The Cat That Uses Camouflage

The sand cat makes full use of camouflage when it is hunting. The cat's fur is a sandy colour with dark markings on its head, legs and tail. This makes it hard to be seen in the deserts of Africa and Asia that are its home. Keeping its body close to the ground, it can stalk animals, such as gerbils, without being seen, pouncing on its prey at the last minute.

Caracal

Jackals Steal Meat From Lions

Another fearsome desert hunter is the jackal. Jackals are members of the dog family, and work as a pack when hunting. Jackals are found throughout Asia and Africa. They spend much of their day hiding in the undergrowth. In addition to hunting for food, jackals will eat carrion or the remains of animals killed by the big cats. Jackals also steal meat from lions. One jackal will distract the lion while another quickly drags the meat away while the lion is not looking. The jackal pack then enjoys their stolen meal together later.

Polar Animals

Survival in the Cold

The area around the north and south poles, called the Arctic and the Antarctic, are the coldest places on Earth. In spite of this, many creatures have adapted to these inhospitable conditions of ice, cold and snow.

Arctic fox

Blubber Keeps Animals Warm

Seals, sea lions, whales and walruses each have a thick layer of fat, called blubber, beneath the skin. The purpose of blubber is to keep the animal from freezing in the icy waters in which it lives. Other creatures, such as polar bears, also have blubber to help keep them warm.

Fur Keeps The Cold Out

The Arctic fox has thick fur and a layer of body fat to keep it warm. At night the fox wraps its tail, which can be up to 40 cm (16 in) long around itself to cover even its head, to help keep out the cold. Musk oxen of north-east Canada and Greenland have two layers of hair. The outer layer can be up to 1 m (3 ft) long. Beneath this is a layer of short, woolly hair to provide extra protection from the cold. The musk ox is one of the hardiest creatures in the world, but even they feel the cold at times so they huddle together to keep warm.

Did You Know?

★

The populations of animals in the harsh poles go up and down dramatically.

Many lemmings drown when they migrate, but the belief that they commit suicide by leaping off cliffs is not true.

Reindeer are the only living deer in which both male and female have antlers.

Reindeer are used as pack animals by the Sami people, or Lapps, of Russia and northern Scandinavia.

Prehistoric civilizations sacrificed reindeer by drowning or burying them, to appeal to the hunting gods.

Just as the desert fox has big ears to keep cool, so the Arctic fox has tiny ears to keep warm.

Some Polar Animals Migrate

Some animals escape the coldest season of the polar year by migrating to warmer areas in the winter months. Reindeer move south in the winter and then return to their feeding grounds on the edge of the Arctic Ocean during the summer. They may travel as much as 2,000 km (1,240 mi) each year. Grey whales swim about 20,000 km (12,400 mi) to spend the winter in the warmer waters off the coast of Mexico.

Polar Bears Have Hair Between Their Toes

To protect their feet from the ice, polar bears and Arctic foxes have hair between their toes. The toes of the rock ptarmigan are covered with feathers, but they grow even more feathers on their toes during the winter months to keep them warm.

Icefish

Fish Have Anti-Freeze In Their Blood

Many fish in polar seas have special chemicals in their blood to keep them from freezing. The long, slender icefish overcomes the problem of freezing by not having any red blood cells in its blood. This causes another problem because red blood cells are used to carry oxygen round the body. To cope with this problem, the icefish absorbs oxygen direct from the sea water.

Birds that 'Fly' Under Water

There are about 18 species of penguin all of which live in the southern hemisphere. We think of penguins as living in the icy wastes of Antarctica, but in fact, only two species — the emperor and the king penguin — actually live there. Although they cannot fly, penguins make up for this by being excellent swimmers. To help them swim they have webbed toes, streamlined bodies and wings adapted to form strong flippers. They swim by 'porpoising' — they swim for a distance and then propel themselves into the air before submerging themselves again. By porpoising, they can reach speeds of up to 40 kph (25 mph).

Emperor Penguins Are The largest Sea Birds

The emperor penguin is the largest of the species and can grow up to 1.2 m (4 ft) tall, making it the largest sea bird in the world. It is the record diver of the penguin world, being capable of diving to depths of 260 m (850 ft).

Emperor Penguins Eggs Are Looked After By The Male

Emperor and king penguins lay only one egg, but they do not build a nest. It is the male bird that has the job of looking after this egg and protecting the young chick after birth. The egg is held on top of the father's feet and protected from the harsh conditions by a fold of skin hanging down from the father's abdomen. Before the egg hatches — a period of about two months — the father does not eat and gets very thin. The female bird has been away fishing during this incubation period and it is not until she returns, by which time the chick has usually hatched, that the male can go to sea to feed. The young chick continues to live on the father's feet for a while until it is able to fend for itself.

Emperor penguin

The Smallest Penguin Is A Fairy

The smallest member of the penguin family is the fairy, or little blue, penguin. It is about 30 cm (12 in) high and lives in New Zealand and along the southern coast of Australia. This bird nests in burrows or among the roots of trees. The rarest penguin is also the one that lives the furthest north. It is the Galapagos penguin and it is found only on the Galapagos Islands, which are on the equator 1,000 km (600 mi) west of Ecuador.

Did You Know?

King penguins line up in perfect formation, most facing in the same direction, when they incubate their eggs.

Emperor penguins huddle so close together that only one-sixth of the surface of each is exposed to blizzards.

Sick gentoo and king penguins on the island of South Georgia travel inland to small pools to die.

A penguin chick recognizes its mother among thousands of almost identical penguins – by her call.

In emergencies, male emperor penguins can produce milk to feed their chicks!

The penguin's dark back and white belly camouflage it when it is swimming.

Adélie Penguins Build Nests Of Stones

The French explorer Dumont d'Urville explored Antarctica in 1840. He gave the name Adélie penguins to the birds he saw, after his wife Adélie. Adélie penguins build a nest of stones. This can lead to arguments because the birds frequently steal stones from each others' nests.

Adélie penguins

King of the Polar Ice

The scientific name for a polar bear is *Ursus maritimus*. *Ursus* means bear and *maritimus* means sea, so the polar bear is really a sea bear. This is not surprising as polar bears are superb swimmers and have been seen as far as 320 km (200 mi) from land. The average adult male bear measures some 2.4 m (8 ft) from nose to tail. They can weigh as much as 408kg (900 lb), about the same as five adult people!

Baby Bears Are Born Under The Snow

Polar bear cubs are born in the depths of the Arctic winter. At the end of the year the mother gives birth to one or two cubs. To keep them warm, they are born in a den dug into the snow where they stay for about three months. At birth the cubs are no bigger than rabbits, weighing less then 1 kg (2 lb), and are very weak. By the time they emerge from the den they weigh about 10 kg (20 lb) and can fend for themselves.

Polar Bears' Favourite Food Is Seals

The food that polar bears mostly eat is seals, which live beneath the ice. The seals make breathing holes in the ice so they can come up for air. The polar bears sniff out these holes and wait until a seal emerges. A swift swipe of the bear's paw kills the seal outright. During the summer months, the polar bear will also eat voles, lemmings, fish, grass and berries.

Polar bear cubs

Gulls Stay Close To Polar Bears

As a general rule, a polar bear is an animal to be avoided. But there is one creature that makes a point of being close to polar bears. This is the ivory gull, a pure white bird that lives in the Arctic. It follows polar bears, so it can feed on any scraps of food left by the bear.

Adult polar bear

Did You Know?

The liver of the polar bear is poisonous!

Under international agreement, polar bears can only be hunted by local populations using traditional weapons.

Native Americans such as the Inuit have traditionally used the teeth and claws of polar bears as ornaments.

A polar bear can swim for over 150 km (90 mi).

A polar bear sometimes goes green, when algae gets inside its hollow hairs!

A Hungry Bear Will Eat Anything

In 1969, men on a coastguard ship spotted a polar bear on an ice floe and threw it some food. Offered black molasses, the bear spread it all over his body and then ate the jam, pork and salami the men had thrown. Looking for further food the bear boarded the vessel and the crew tried to ward it off by turning fire hoses on it. Unfortunately, the bear enjoyed this so much it even raised its paws so the water would wash its armpits! In the end they had to fire a distress rocket near the bear, to encourage it to go away.

Small Creatures of the Polar Regions

Insects and many other small creatures are cold blooded, so they are unable to live in cold climates. The small creatures of the polar regions overcome this by surviving in the ice or frozen soil as eggs or larvae (young) during the winter months. When the warmer weather comes in the spring they hatch out in large numbers to feed on the algae, mosses and lichens that are also plentiful at this time of year.

Many Arctic Animals Feed On Plankton

The Arctic seas are rich in plankton — small or microscopic plant and animal life that drifts in the sea, especially near the surface. The word 'plankton' comes from a Greek word meaning 'wandering' or 'drifting'. Most of the plankton consists of single-celled plants and animals but at times also includes the eggs and larvae of larger organisms. The biggest creature in the world, the blue whale, survives solely on plankton but plankton is also a vital food for many fish, seals and birds.

Clouded yellow butterfly

Some Butterflies Have Anti-Freeze

To protect them from the extreme cold some Arctic caterpillars and butterflies are hairy. Others retain heat by being dark, as dark colours absorb more heat from sunlight. The beautiful clouded yellow butterfly protects itself from the cold by having a special fluid that acts like anti-freeze, in its blood.

Krill Weigh More Than People

A large variety of small, shrimp-like creatures [illegible]e in the Antarctic seas and are known as 'krill' (from the Norwegian wor[illegible]or 'tiny fish'). They are so plentiful that their weight in the sea is greate[illegible]han that of all the people on Earth. Krill are eaten by whales, and ha[illegible]o been suggested as a source of food for humans.

Krill Make The [illegible] Turn Red

In the summer, the k[illegible]n such large numbers that t[illegible]e sea looks red. At night, [illegible] the sea a greenish hue [illegible] their bodies contain orga[illegible] that glow green in the dark.

A Tiny Fly Can Kill A Huge Caribou

The caribou is a large deer that lives in the Arctic. The tiny warble fly can prove deadly to the big caribou. The fly lays its eggs on the caribou's body and the maggots that hatch out mostly make their way to the back of the animal, where they puncture the skin and form swellings called warbles. If a lot of maggots go in the opposite direction and hatch out in the caribou's throat, it will die of suffocation. The caribou also has problems with the most dangerous of Arctic creatures, the tiny mosquito. In the spring, huge hoards of mosquitos bite any warm creature, including the caribou, and suck their blood.

Did You Know?

There are mosquitoes in the Arctic! They appear in their millions in the short summer.

44 of the 70 animal species below the Antarctic Circle are insects!

The largest land animal in the Antarctic is a one-centimetre-long wingless midge!

Bumble bees are found as far north as Greenland.

The only animals that can survive the iciest parts of the world are ice worms and a few insects.

Tiny zooplankton gather in shoals of so many billions that it took one ship five hours to pass through one.

Seals and Walruses

Seals are a large group of marine mammals made up of three families — earless seals, eared seals (which includes sea lions) and walruses. Earless seals get their name because they have no obvious external ears. You can easily tell a male walrus by its very large tusks.

Walruses Use Their Tusks As Claws

Walruses live in the Arctic. They feed on shellfish, which they rake up from the seabed with their tusks. Their tusks can be up to 1 m (39 in) long. Their strong teeth can break even the hardest of shells. They also use their tusks as claws to pull themselves up onto the ice. The name 'walrus' comes from the Dutch word walvish, which means 'whale fish'. The walrus is related to the seal.

Walruses Like Sun Bathing

Although walruses use their tusks when fighting, they are normally gentle animals — in spite of their formidable appearance. Walruses like to gather together in large groups on land. During warmer weather they enjoy basking in the sun, but when it gets cold they huddle together to keep warm. Herding together also helps to protect the weaker members of the group from any predators. They will not usually attack a person unless provoked, but they will band together to attack and kill a polar bear that is unwise enough to attack one of the herd.

Elephant Seals Can Bellow

The elephant seal is the largest seal in the Antarctic. It is about 5 m (16 ft) long and weighs a massive 2,267 kg (5,000 lbs). It gets its name from its unusual swollen nose. During the breeding season the largest male collects a group of females and bellows at other males that come near. Because of this habit, the large bulls are known as beachmasters. Fights between males are quite common and many of the older males bear scars from their battles.

Walrus

Elephant seals

Did You Know?

Some seals are able to dive to depths of over 250 m (800 ft), and can stay underwater for more than 30 minutes.

The walrus gets its name from a Swedish word meaning 'whale horse'!

The Inuit used the ivory tusks of the walrus to make tools.

An elephant seal weighs almost twice as much as a hippopotamus!

Each of a crab-eater seal's sensitive whiskers is connected to about 1,200 nerve endings!

Sailors, tales of mermaids – half-woman, half-fish – may have been started by sightings of seals.

Leopard Seals' Favourite Food Is Penguins

The leopard seal is a ferocious hunter that is particularly fond of eating penguins. It will wait beneath an ice floe upon which the penguins are standing, then dart forward when one enters the water. Although penguins are excellent swimmers the leopard seal, with a speed of up to 37 kmh (23 mph), is also very fast. Having caught its prey, the seal beats it against the water to kill it before removing the skin and eating it.

Leopard seal and penguin

Polar Birds

There are no land mammals in the Antarctic and very few plants, so the gulls, petrels and other birds that live there must rely upon the sea for food. Birds of the Arctic regions have a greater choice of food, as there are plenty of plants and insects, as well as food in the sea. The snowy owl and the raven remain during the winter months, but the other birds avoid the extreme cold by migrating south to warmer climates.

Puffin

Puffins Often Nest In Rabbit Burrows

Puffins build their nests in burrows, which can be up to 2 m (6 ft) deep on a cliff. Sometimes they dig these burrows themselves, using their beak and feet, but they often simply take over a rabbit burrow, after first scaring away the rabbits. The puffin (sometimes nicknamed the sea parrot) is usually pictured with a bright red, yellow and blue beak, but it has this only during the breeding season. After breeding the beak fades to dull yellow, as the outer sheath is shed.

Petrel Birds Are Stinkers

The giant petrel is a large seabird related to the albatross. It gets its food by scavenging (feeding on dead animals). If an enemy goes too close to its nest, the petrel squirts a putrid-smelling liquid at them. Because of this they have been nicknamed 'stinkers'.

The Albatross Is Good At Gliding

The largest of the polar birds is the wandering albatross. The long, narrow wings of the albatross are excellent for gliding, even in still air. When it glides near to the surface of the sea, the albatross makes use of wind currents from the waves. It can then stay in the air without beating its wings for up to six hours!

Arctic skua

Arctic Skuas Are Pirates

The Arctic skua gets its food by harassing other birds in flight, so that they let go of their catch. Because of this, the skua is often described as a pirate.

Arctic Loons Are Clumsy

The black-throated diver, or Arctic loon, is a web-footed bird that is well adapted to swimming. They spend much of their life in or on the water because they only have short wings which makes flight difficult. Their legs are set far back on their bodies, to help them swim. This makes them clumsy and awkward on land. It is thought that the name loon actually comes from the Icelandic word 'lomr', meaning clumsy.

Arctic loon

Did You Know?

The ptarmigan changes the colour of its plumage at least twice a year.

Petrels defend themselves by spitting out a jet of oil dragged up from their stomach!

The giant petrel is known as a stinker because it eats so much carrion that it has to vomit before it can take flight!

The male Arctic tern attracts a mate by bringing her gifts of fish.

The ptarmigan survives on a diet of twigs during the long Arctic winter.

The Arctic bird of prey called the gyrfalcon is the biggest of the world's falcons.

Amazing Arctic Animals

Many Arctic animals have a clever way to avoid being seen in the snow: they change colour. The ptarmigan is a grouse-like bird. During the winter months the plumage of most species is white, so it is well camouflaged in the snow. Around May the plumage changes to red and black. The Arctic stoat also changes its colour according to the season. During the summer months it is brown to match the rocky terrain in which it lives. In the winter months it grows a new thick coat of white fur. This helps protect it from the cold and also gives good camouflage.

The Wolverine Is Greedy

Although it looks like a bear cub, the wolverine is a member of the weasel family. It has dark brown fur with lighter bands along its sides and neck. It is also known as a glutton and it certainly lives up to this name because it is a ferocious animal that will attack and eat almost anything it can find. Lemmings, hares, birds, frogs and fish are its usual meals, but it will even attack larger animals, such as caribou.

Reindeer Play Follow The Leader

Many creatures migrate to avoid the cold. When reindeer migrate, they move in long columns that can stretch for as much as 300 km (185 mi). Each animal treads in the footprints of the animal in front, so that it does not have to plough through deep snow. This helps to save energy in the long trek.

Wolves Live In Packs

A predator that Arctic animals have to watch out for is the wolf. Wolves live throughout the Arctic in packs of between eight and twenty animals. Their eerie howls communicate with other members of their group and to warn other wolf packs to keep their distance.

Wolves Are Cunning Hunters

Wolves are good at teamwork when attacking their prey. However, musk oxen, have an effective defence. They form themselves into a circle with the young calves protected in the centre. As the oxen face outwards with their long, curving horns pointing at the wolves, the wolves are clever enough to abandon the attack.

Reindeer

Creepy Crawlies

Spiders

A spider's body consists of two parts and it has four pairs of legs. Most spiders, of which there are over 40,000 species, live on land but there are some that live in streams and ponds.

Tarantula

Biggest And Smallest

With a length of some 250 cms (10 ins), the Goliath bird-eating spider of South America is the largest spider in the world. At the other end of the spider scale is one found in Western Samoa which is about 0.43 mm (0.017 in). Tarantulas are among the largest spiders. Their legs and bodies are covered with thick fur to help them to pick up vibrations from their prey.

Spiders' Webs Are Made Of Silk

Near the tip of its abdomen, a spider has six cone-shaped spinnerets, which produce a fine silk thread. The spider uses its legs to draw out this thread, attach it to branches and gradually shape it into a web. The most familiar design is the orb web, a series of circles of silk attached to an outer frame. Some spiders make tubular webs, pirate spiders make a web shelter in which they wait for prey, and water spiders make a cup-shaped web which is filled with air so that the spider can breathe under water.

Camouflaged Killer

Crab spiders hide in flowers until a tasty morsel comes along. To help it conceal itself, the crab spider can change its colour to match its surroundings.

Trapdoor spider

Some Spiders Lay Traps

Not all spiders weave webs, so they have to catch their prey by other means. One of the most intriguing is the trapdoor spider which digs a small shaft in the ground. A hinged trapdoor is placed over the top of the shaft. The spider then waits in the shaft, with the trapdoor almost closed. When an insect passes by, the spider rushes out and grabs it.

Did You Know?

Spider webs from 45 million years ago have been perfectly preserved in amber.

The Australian bird-dropping spider disguises itself as a lump of bird excrement while it lies in wait for delicious moths!

Scorpions are related to spiders. They mate with great caution to avoid each others' sting!

The net-casting spider throws its web over insects to catch a meal!

The bolas spider weaves a sticky ball on the end of a thread, and whirls it about to catch moths!

Scientists developing bullet-proof vests have studied spider silk. One thread is twice as strong as steel, but 250 times finer than a human hair!

Female black widow spider

The Female Black Widow Eats Her Mate

All spiders can give a poisonous bite but usually this is only deadly to the spider's normal prey. Most poisonous are the wandering spiders of Brazil, which bite ferociously several times and can even kill a small child. The black widow spider can also kill a child, but is better known for the fact that the female eats the male after mating!

Ants and Termites

Ants and termites are insects that live in large colonies, each of which has a queen who lays all the eggs. Although both termites and ants look similar, and termites are often called 'white ants', they are from different classes of living things. Termites are, in fact, more closely related to cockroaches than to ants.

Termite mound

Termite Mounds Are As Strong As Concrete

Some termites build enormous nests on the ground. They take pieces of soil, and glue them together with their own droppings and saliva. Some termite mounds can be over 6 m (18 ft) high and 4 m (12 ft) in diameter, the outer structure of which is as strong as concrete. Inside the mound there is a complicated system of corridors and chambers, all of which have a form of air conditioning to keep them cool.

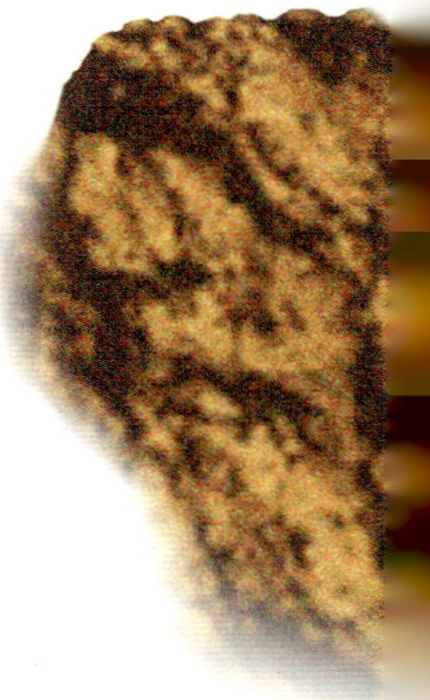

Leaf-cutter Ants Grow Their Own Food

In some parts of South America, leaf-cutter ants cause a lot of damage to crops. They cut small pieces from leaves, which they carry back to their nest. The leaves are chewed into a mulch, which is used to grow fungi. The ants love to eat the fungi.

Leaf-cutter ant

Some Ants Are Soldiers

Soldier ants, found in parts of India, Africa and South America, 'march' in long, wide columns feeding on small animals as they go. Even large animals will run away when the ants advance, and if they enter a house they will strip it clean of insects and vermin, which makes them quite welcome in some villages.

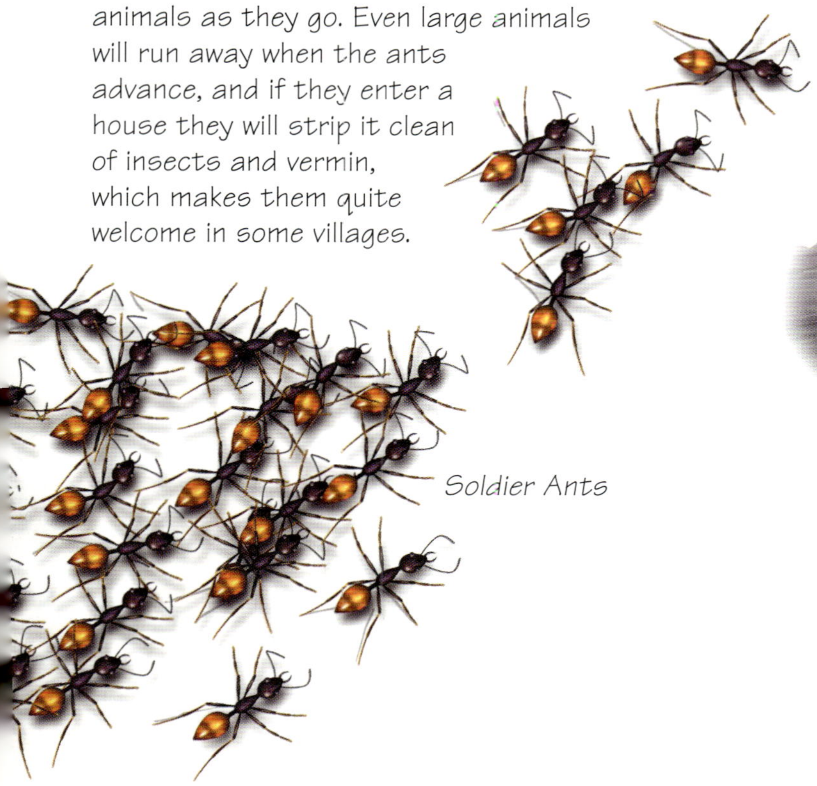

Soldier Ants

Soldiers Defend Termites' Nests

Many termite species keep 'soldiers' to defend the nest from ants who like eating the soft, juicy bodies of the termites. In some species the soldier termites have large heads and large, strong jaws and in others the soldiers have a hollow projection on the head which squirts a sticky fluid at the ants to disable them.

Termite

Did You Know?

The mighty ant can lift up 50 times its own weight!

Slave-maker ants steal the young of other ants and raise them as slaves!

Some honey pot ants are used as storage tanks by their comrades, who pour food into them until they are enormously swollen!

Compass termites build their gigantic mounds so that the long sides face perfectly to east and west!

In one of Aesop's Fables, called The Ant and the Grasshopper, the ant survives winter because it works so hard during the summer.

The Roman writer Pliny believed that in India there was an ant the size of a wolf, which mined gold!

Snails and Slugs

Snails belong to a group of animals called molluscs, which also includes oysters, squids and octopuses. There are over 35,000 types of slugs and snails, which have evolved as highly successful animals that can be found both on land and in the water. A snail shell, which is made mainly of chalk, is a hollow cone coiled around a central, hollow column. The snail's body is in a type of bag coiled up inside the shell with only the head and the bottom part (known as the foot) visible. To move, the snail slides along on its foot which gives off a slime to make movement easier, leaving behind a glistening trail as it does so. A slug is basically a snail without a shell, although some species do have tiny shells. Like snails, most slugs feed on living or decaying vegetation. The slugs with shells are meat-eaters. They eat worms, caterpillars — and the slugs without shells.

Giant African Snails Are Giant Pests

Minute snails, with a shell no bigger than a pin head, can be found in the hills of Malaysia and Borneo, but the giant African snail is the largest snail in the world, with a shell of up to 35 cm (13 in) long. Giant African snails are now found in other parts of the world besides Africa, and have become quite a pest. In the South Pacific Islands, for example, these giants were introduced by accident and almost wiped out the local and very rare Partula snail.

Giant African snail

Did You Know?

★

Some snails have gills. Others have lungs.

The Helix garden snail or 'escargot' is thought to be a great delicacy.

Sea snails called cone shells inject harpoons into their prey containing enough poison to kill a human.

Sea slugs eat anemones, then regrow the anemone's poisonous stings through their own skin and use them as 'second-hand' defences!

Some slugs can climb trees, then 'abseil' down on a rope of slime!

The Roman writer Pliny recommended using slugs as cures for sickness.

Snails And Slugs Have No Teeth

Instead of teeth, snails and slugs have rows of horny bumps on the tongue, known as a radula, which act like a file to break up the food. The number of bumps on the radula varies according to the species, and can be as few as 20, or as many as 10,000.

Slugs Mate In Mid-Air

Slugs mate by first circling one another and eating the slime from the other's body. Eventually they become twisted tightly together and they lower themselves on a thick string of slime and mate whilst suspended in mid-air. They then drop to the ground or climb back up the slime cord, eating it as they go.

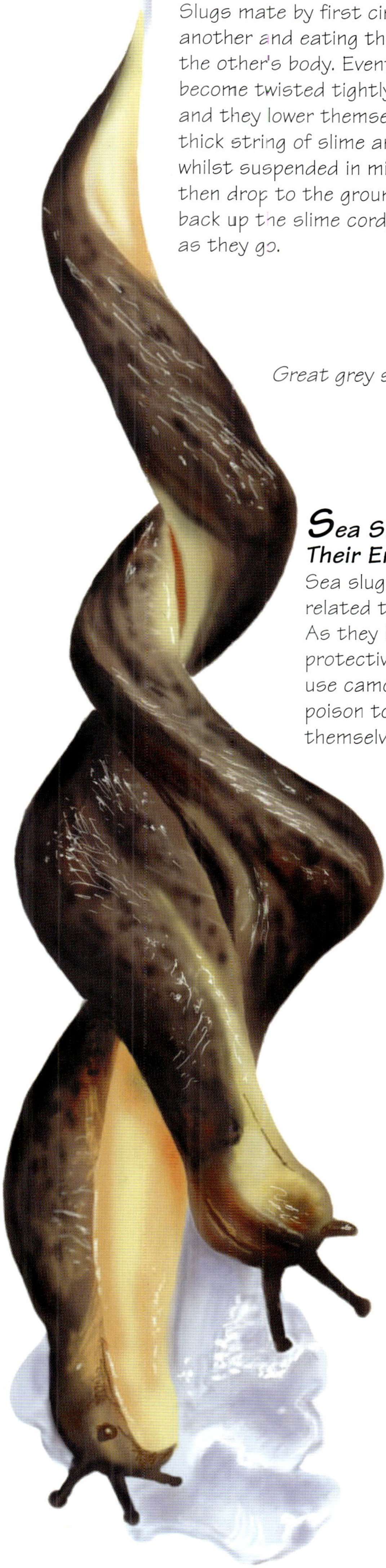

Great grey slugs mating

Sea Slugs Poison Their Enemies

Sea slugs are not related to land slugs. As they have no protective shell, they use camouflage or poison to defend themselves.

The Grasshopper Family

In the family of insects that includes grasshoppers, locusts and crickets there are over 20,000 different species. Most members of the grasshopper family have the hind legs specially modified for jumping. Grasshoppers are divided into two main groups, the short horned and the long horned, according to the length of their antennae.

Grasshoppers Sing By Rubbing Their Legs

Grasshoppers make sounds by rubbing their hind legs against their forewings. Inside the thigh of each leg are tiny pegs which make the wing vibrate when the leg is drawn over it. Crickets also 'sing" but they do so by rubbing their forewings together.

Grasshopper

Mole Crickets Live Underground

The mole cricket spends most of its life in underground burrows feeding on insects, worms and plants. They have large and powerful front legs with which they burrow through the soil, just like a mole. The entrance to its burrow often has two tunnels shaped like, and used as, amplifiers. The cricket sits near the entrance singing, and the sound is amplified so successfully it can be heard over 1 km (2/3 mi) away.

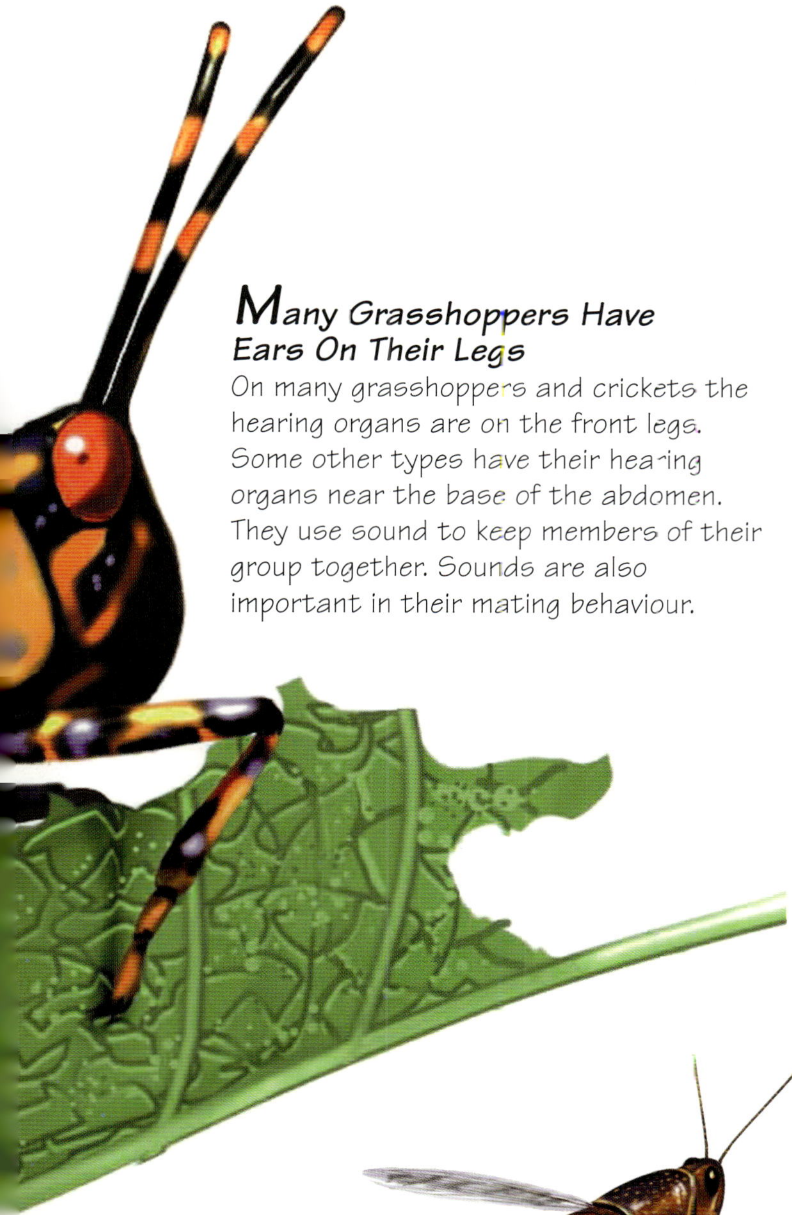

Many Grasshoppers Have Ears On Their Legs

On many grasshoppers and crickets the hearing organs are on the front legs. Some other types have their hearing organs near the base of the abdomen. They use sound to keep members of their group together. Sounds are also important in their mating behaviour.

Did You Know?

If humans had the grasshopper's jumping powers, they could leap one-third the length of a football pitch.

In the Bible, a plague of locusts was one of the ten plagues Jehovah sent against the Pharaoh.

A swarm of locusts can be so huge that it blocks out all sunlight!

Some crickets cut holes in leaves and use them as a megaphone to make their song louder!

Mormon crickets got their name in 1848, when a flock of gulls saved the Mormons' crops in Utah by eating all the crickets!

The South African grasshopper's poisonous defences are so effective it has forgotten how to jump or fly.

Swarm of locusts

There Can Be 50,000 Million Locusts In A Swarm

Locusts are short-horned grasshoppers that cause incredible damage to crops in Africa and Asia, devouring every leaf and blade of grass in sight when they group together to form enormous swarms. The most destructive are the migratory locust and the desert locust of Africa and the Middle East. Swarms of these locusts can contain 50,000 million individuals, covering an area of 1,000 sq km (386 sq mi).

Fleas and Lice

There are almost 2,000 different types of flea. Adult fleas feed on the blood of animals. They pierce the skin with their mouth and then suck up the blood. Because of this, several types of flea can transmit diseases. The most famous case of a disease being transmitted by rat fleas was the Black Death, or bubonic plague, which wiped out much of the population of Europe in medieval times.

Rat flea

Fleas Are Fussy Where They Live

A flea will lay some 300 to 500 eggs in the fur of the animal on which it lives. When the small, white, worm-like larvae hatch out they live on any bits and pieces they can find on the animal's body. When they are fully grown they spin themselves into cocoons from which they eventually emerge as adult fleas and live on the blood of the host animal. Fleas will move from one animal to another but most prefer just one particular type of host. The human flea has the Latin name *Pulex irritans*, meaning 'irritating flea', because its bite produces irritation. In hygienic conditions the flea is more likely to live on pigs rather than humans. Most people who are bitten by a flea are actually bitten by cat or dog fleas.

Fleas Are Champion Jumpers

Fleas have three pairs of very strong legs, which are used for jumping. A flea is capable of jumping over a hundred times its own height. The flea that lives on humans can jump up to 20 cm (7 in) high and a cat flea even higher, up to 34 cm (13 in).

Flea jumping

Some Fleas Lay Their Eggs In People's Feet

Most fleas do not stay for long on human skin, but the jigger flea, found in Africa, the West Indies and the southern United States, is an exception. The female jigger flea burrows into a person's foot to lay its eggs.

Did You Know?

★

A flea can jump 200 times the length of its own body!

In the 14th century, fleas helped wipe out a quarter of the human population of Europe – by spreading the plague known as the Black Death.

When a rabbit becomes pregnant, so do the fleas on its skin!

When Thomas à Becket's robe was removed after his murder in Canterbury Cathedral, England, the lice 'boiled over like water in a simmering cauldron'.

Victorian showmen ran flea circuses, in which tethered fleas rode chariots and bicycles, walked tightropes and fought sword-fights.

Soldiers in the trenches in the First World War were infested with lice, which spread a disease known as trench fever.

Lice Suck The Blood Of Humans

Lice are small, wingless insects that suck blood from their hosts. There are two main types, the chewing lice that live mainly on birds and the sucking lice that live on mammals. As well as causing irritation to humans, lice can also transmit typhoid and other diseases. There are two types of human lice. The body louse lives on clothing and the head louse lives in head hair on which it lays its eggs, which are known as nits.

Flies

There are many insects that look like flies, but a true fly has only one pair of wings, although some of the 60,000 different species have no wings at all. Flies range in size from tiny midges, just 1.5 mm (0.06 in) long, to robber flies, which can be over 8 cm (3 in) long.

Flies Lay Their Eggs In Rotting Food

The female fly lays 100 to 200 eggs in dung or rotting food. These hatch into a worm-like maggot, which feeds greedily for five or six days before entering a pupal, or resting, stage. About a week later the fully grown fly emerges from the pupal skin. Within ten days the fly has mated and the whole process begins again.

Hoverfly

Flies Spit On Food

A fly cannot eat solid food so it spits a digestive fluid on the food first to turn it into a liquid, which the fly can suck up.

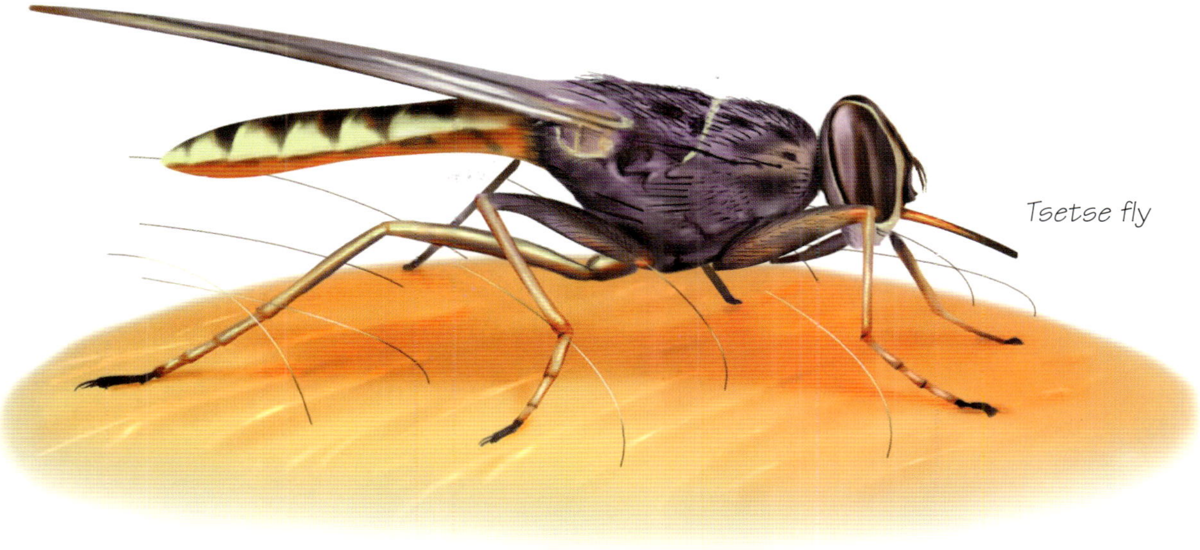

Tsetse Flies Spread Sleeping Sickness

When house flies and bluebottles lay their eggs on waste matter they pick up germs which can be carried onto food. When the food is eaten by humans, bacteria enter the body. The tsetse fly (which gets its name from the noise its wings make when it is flying), spreads a disease called sleeping sickness in which a person goes into a coma and eventually dies unless treated. The tsetse fly looks very much like a house fly but gives birth to grubs instead of laying eggs like the house fly. The tsetse fly is found only in Africa, where it lives on the blood of animals. Mosquitos also live on blood and because of this, some species are responsible for the spread of malaria and others for the disease called yellow fever. Mosquitos are found all over the world, even in the Arctic, where they cause disease among the caribou herds. However, many types of mosquito are harmless, apart from giving a very irritating bite.

Hoverflies Are Harmless

Hoverflies have black and yellow stripes that make them look like wasps, to scare off birds. In fact, they are harmless mimics, and do not have a sting.

Flies Can Walk Upside Down

On a fly's foot there are two fleshy pads covered in tube-like hairs. At the end of these are sticky, mushroom-shaped suckers which enable the fly to walk on walls and ceilings.

Did You Know?

As many as 500 million micro-organisms live on a house fly's body!

You will find plenty of house flies on a chicken farm – they find the birds' droppings delicious!

House flies like to lay their eggs in compost heaps.

The tsetse fly gives birth to just one baby at a time!

A house fly has a total of 8,000 lenses in its eyes – no wonder it's so hard to swat!

Fruit flies have been used by scientists studying genetics.

Beetles

Beetles make up the largest group of animals in the world with over 250,000 known species. Beetles have two pairs of wings but only the rear ones are used for flying, although there are many species that rarely fly at all.

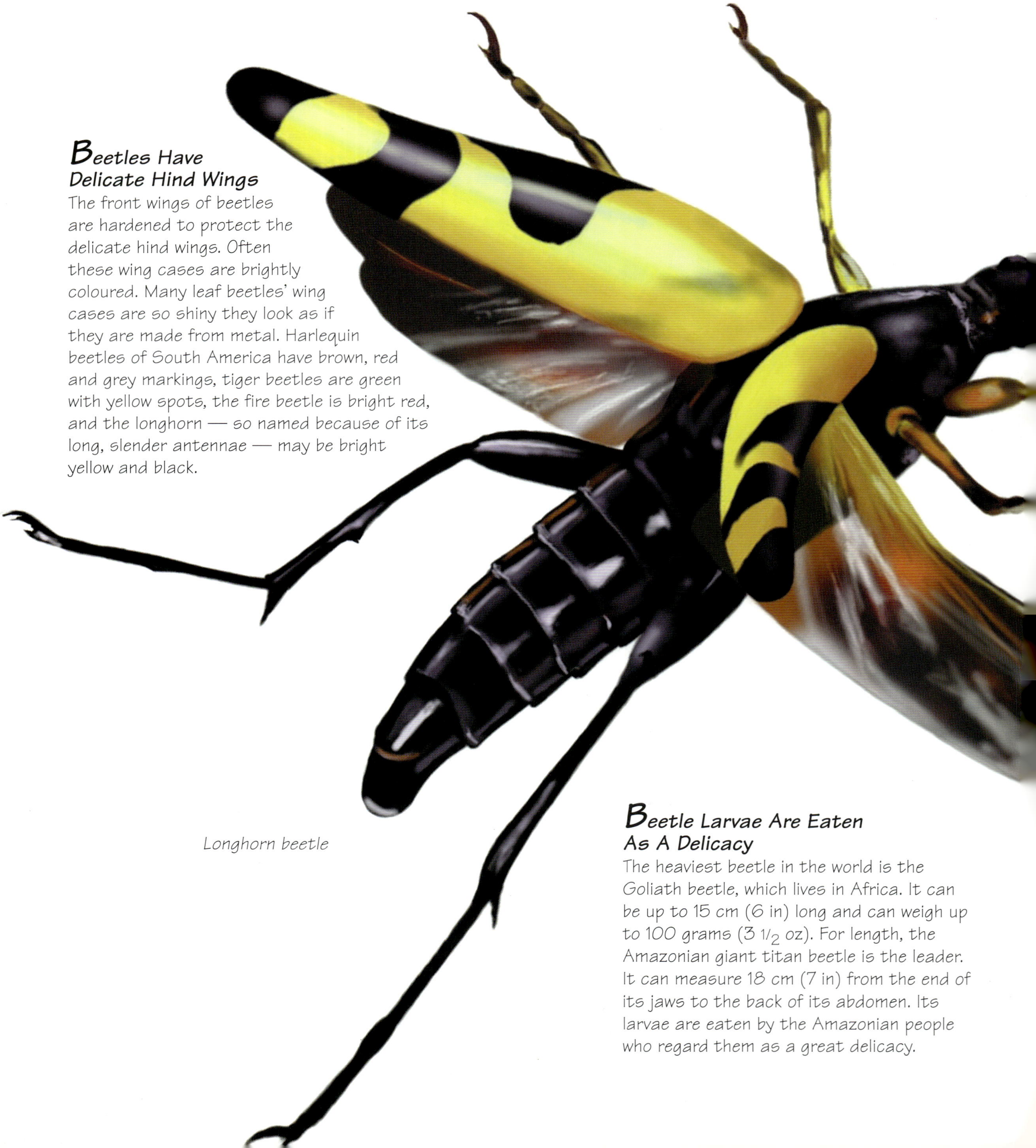

Beetles Have Delicate Hind Wings

The front wings of beetles are hardened to protect the delicate hind wings. Often these wing cases are brightly coloured. Many leaf beetles' wing cases are so shiny they look as if they are made from metal. Harlequin beetles of South America have brown, red and grey markings, tiger beetles are green with yellow spots, the fire beetle is bright red, and the longhorn — so named because of its long, slender antennae — may be bright yellow and black.

Longhorn beetle

Beetle Larvae Are Eaten As A Delicacy

The heaviest beetle in the world is the Goliath beetle, which lives in Africa. It can be up to 15 cm (6 in) long and can weigh up to 100 grams (3 1/2 oz). For length, the Amazonian giant titan beetle is the leader. It can measure 18 cm (7 in) from the end of its jaws to the back of its abdomen. Its larvae are eaten by the Amazonian people who regard them as a great delicacy.

Beetles Can Be Harmful

Beetles and their larvae can be harmful to crops and other plants. Woodworms, the larvae of the furniture beetle, bore holes in wood. The boll weevil destroys cotton crops, and the black and yellow striped Colorado beetle can cause immense damage to potato crops

Beetles Can Be Useful

Many beetles are useful. Some help to recycle dead animals by burying them and laying their eggs on them, so that their larvae can eat the flesh. Dung beetles, or tumblebugs, bury vast amounts of dung, which adds goodness to the soil. Ladybirds eat greenfly and so prove helpful to gardeners and farmers to whom greenfly are pests.

Did You Know?

There are seven times as many species of beetles as there are of vertebrates.

Some beetles are allowed to live in ants' nests, because the ants like their smell!

The champion of sprinting insects is the tiger beetle. It only moves at 2.5 kph ($1\frac{1}{2}$ mph), but if it were the size of a horse that would equal 400 kph (250 mph)!

If a click beetle lands on its back it does a somersault to right itself — making a loud clicking sound.

Light-producing beetles called fireflies are kept in containers by people in South America, and are used as lamps!

Ancient Egyptians used to cut out the heart of a corpse and replace it with a carving of a scarab beetle covered with jewels!

Scarab Beetles Were Sacred

Scarab beetles were very important in the religion of Ancient Egypt. The scarab is one of a family of beetles that are often called ball rolling, or dung, beetles because they roll up balls of animal dung and bury them. Some of these dung balls are used for food and others are used for egg laying — the female lays an egg in the ball and when it hatches the larva feeds on the dung.

Dung beetle

Worms

There are thought to be more than one million species of worm, living in a wide range of different habitats. Some, such as earthworms, live in burrows. Others live in the sea or in fresh water. There are three main groups of worms — the ringed worms, the flatworms and the roundworms.

Earthworms Eat Soil

Ringed worms include earthworms, marine worms and leeches. The best known to most people is the earthworm. The body of an earthworm consists of a series of rings, or segments, with an outer layer of muscle cells which the worm contracts and expands to move with the help of fine bristles along most of its body. Earthworms feed by swallowing soil and vegetation and passing it through their bodies. In doing this they help break down plant material in the soil. They also help make the soil light and airy. Most earthworms are only a few centimetres (inches) long but in some parts of the tropics there are worms that can be up to 6 m (20 ft) long and 20 mm (3/4 in) in diameter.

Leech

Some Leeches Live In Trees

Leeches are related to earthworms. Leeches mostly live in water, but there are some that live in trees. When a leech attaches itself to the body of an animal, its sharp teeth dig into the flesh and suck the blood. It injects a fluid into the wound that prevents the blood from clotting while the leech is feeding. When its body is swollen with blood, the leech drops off. In days gone by doctors thought many illnesses were caused by the patient having too much blood. They would put leeches on the patient's body to remove some of the blood.

Tapeworms Absorb Food Through Their Skin

Flatworms — worms with flattened bodies — are member of a group that includes threadworms, hookworms and roundworms. Some flatworms are parasitic, living inside the bodies of other creatures including humans. The worst of the parasitic flatworms is the tapeworm, of which there are several varieties. The tapeworm enters an animal's body as an egg which then hatches inside the creature's stomach. Tapeworms have no digestive organs — they absorb their food through the skin. They multiply rapidly and can grow quite long inside the animal's stomach. In a human they can be up to 10 m (30 ft) long. People can get a tapeworm through eating pork or beef that has not been cooked sufficiently to kill any worm eggs that may be in it.

Did You Know?

An earthworm is hermaphrodite — which means it is both male and female!

The Gippsland giant earthworm, found in Australia, can grow to 4 m (12 ft) in length!

When a tapeworm larva irritates the inside of an oyster, the oyster surrounds it with a substance called nacre. This hardens and forms a beautiful pearl!

Tapeworms can grow to over 10 m (30 ft) inside the intestines of animals including humans. Yuk!

Doctors became known as 'leeches' because of their enthusiastic use of the creature.

Earthworm

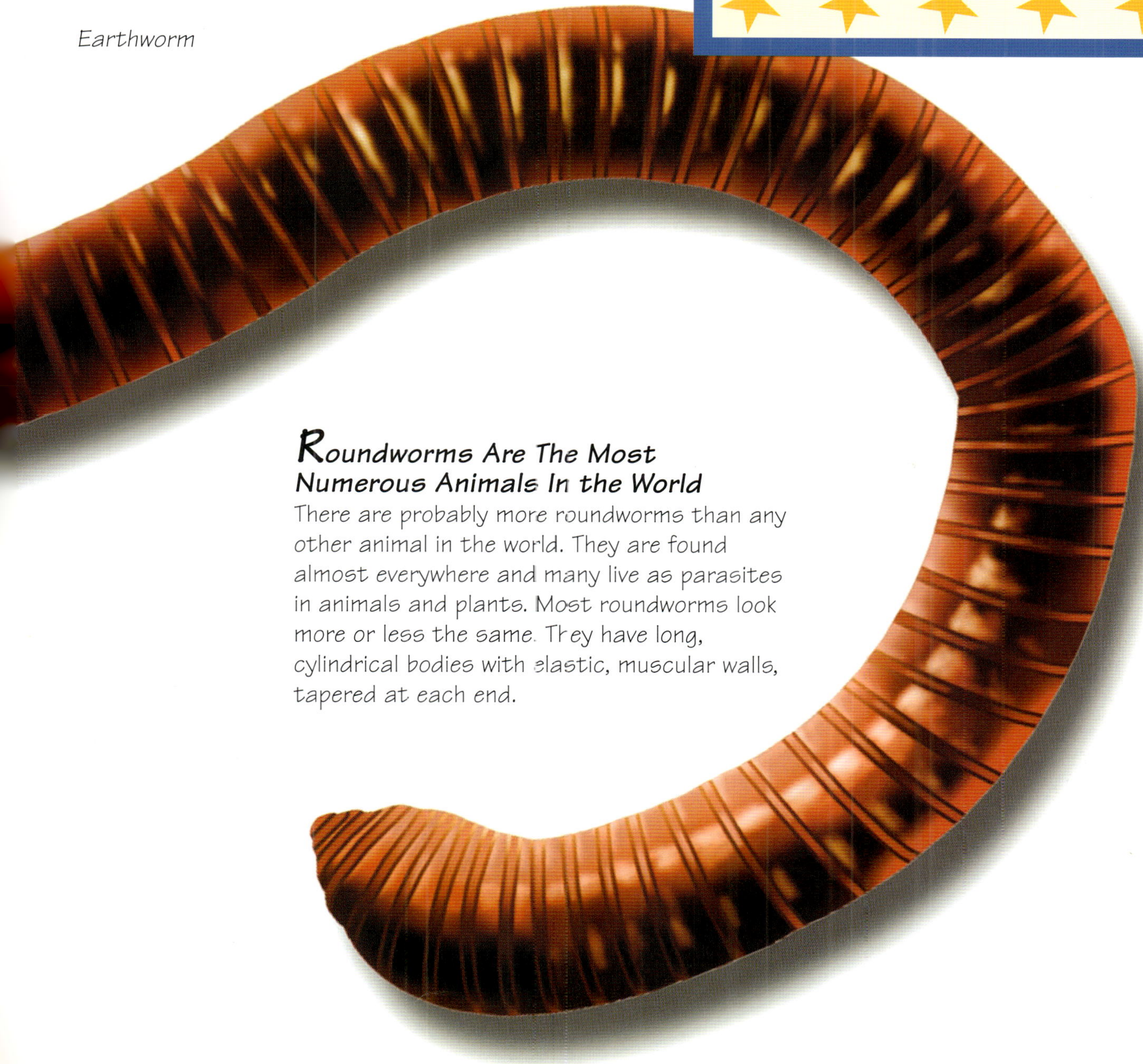

Roundworms Are The Most Numerous Animals In the World

There are probably more roundworms than any other animal in the world. They are found almost everywhere and many live as parasites in animals and plants. Most roundworms look more or less the same. They have long, cylindrical bodies with elastic, muscular walls, tapered at each end.

Bees

Most bees live in colonies of up to 75,000 insects, where they cooperate to build nests, gather food and rear their young. There are around 25,000 different types of bee.

The Qeen Bee Is Fed By Worker Bees

The main job of the queen bee is to lay eggs. The drones are male bees who live solely to mate with the queen. The queen does not have to search for food but is fed by small female bees called workers. Most of the bees in a colony are workers. They build the hive and maintain it, look after the growing grubs and visit flowers to drink nectar.

Honeybees Dance

Honeybees have a unique way of telling other members of the colony which flowers to visit to gather pollen. On returning to the hive, the worker bee performs a sequence of movements, known as a 'waggle dance', which tells the other bees which way to go in relation to the sun and what distance to travel, to find the best flowers.

Bees And Flowers Benefit One Another

Bees and some flowers depend upon one another for life. The bees get their food, in the form of nectar, from the flowers and in doing this they transfer pollen from one flower to another, so the flowers are pollinated and will reproduce. The pollen is caught on hairs on the bee's body and every so often the insect scrapes the pollen off into a small pouch on its legs, to carry it back to the hive for food. Some of the nectar is turned into honey and stored in the hive for the bees to feed on during the winter.

Bee collecting pollen

Endangered Animals

Threats to Wildlife

Animals become endangered partly because man is killing them faster than they can breed. Many are hunted for food, others for their skins, some to be kept as pets. For example, elephants are killed for their ivory tusks. The skins of crocodiles and snakes can be made into shoes, belts, handbags and other clothing. Animals with fur become coats for humans. Animals are also becoming endangered as humans destroy the places where they live. Pollution, and the chemicals used in farming are dangerous to animals, too.

What 'Endangered' Means

When an animal is said to be endangered, it means that its species is in danger of becoming extinct, with no individuals left in existence. For example, the white rhino is endangered. Soon there may be none left in the wild.

Black rhino

Did You Know?

By exterminating millions of buffalo from the American plains – there were 541 left by 1889 – hunters ended the traditional life of the Plains Indians who depended on them.

If global warming continues, the temperature of the planet will have increased by at least 2 °C (35.5 °F) by the end of the 21st century.

In the last century, gases creating the greenhouse effect have increased by a quarter.

The human population of the world is fast approaching 6 billion.

A quarter of the world's plants are facing threat of extinction.

Conservationists believe in the 'mosaic' theory – if you remove one piece, the whole picture is affected.

Human Expansion Poses A Threat

Animals die not just because they are hunted. It also happens if a creature's habitat is destroyed. Forests are cut down, wetlands are drained, while industrial chemicals and waste are gradually polluting the atmosphere, the rivers and the seas. As the human population of the world increases more and more land is needed for homes, roads, industrial buildings and farms. This expansion is using up land fast and leaving fewer areas for wildlife to live.

The Numbers Of Many Creatures Are Declining

Frogs, toads and other amphibians are dying out all over the world. The global population of such creatures has declined by 40 percent since 1970. The number of African elephants halved in the 1970s and 1980s and were only saved from extinction by a ban on the trade of ivory in 1989. The populations of many other creatures are also going down.

Rhino suffering the effects of drought

Rhino's Horn Is Made Of Keratin

Rhinos live in Africa and in Asia. It is not just hunting that is killing off the rhinos, the African savannah frequently suffers drought. Many rhinos are now protected by guards in the hope of keeping the hunters at bay. Some conservationists tranquillize rhinos in their care, and cut off their horns. They hope that without their valuable horns, the poachers will not want to kill the animals. Cutting off the horn is not painful — it is like cutting your fingernails. The horn is made of keratin, as are your hair and nails. It is the horn that gave the rhinoceros its name because 'rhino' means nose and 'ceros' means horn. It is estimated that there are fewer than 8,500 white rhinos, 2,600 black rhinos, 200 Indian rhinos, 400 Sumatran rhinos and only 70 Javan rhinos left in the world.

Rainforests

Jungle is an Indian word meaning 'wild place'. The correct term for those areas of thick forests, where the weather is always hot and rainy, is 'rainforest'. Plants grow quickly in the rainforest to form a thick canopy of vegetation. The forest floor is a carpet of plants, through which rivers wind. An amazing variety of wildlife lives in the rainforest, ranging from exotic butterflies and snakes to large mammals, such as jaguars. Unfortunately, much of this beautiful habitat is now endangered.

Rainforests Could Become Deserts

Many of the trees in the rainforests are being felled for timber, even more are being chopped down to provide new roads and vast areas have been burned to the ground to make way for farms and cities. Felling trees at such a rate does great harm to the environment. It can lead to soil erosion and changes in the local climate. What were once lush jungles could easily become arid deserts if nothing is done to curb the destruction. Such changes to the environment also affect the creatures that live there, even the microscopic ones. Many rainforest animals already struggle to survive and could become extinct as a direct result.

Felling trees in the rainforest

Giant panda

Did You Know?

There can be 200 different species of tree in one acre of rainforest.

One tree in the rainforest provides the home for 10,000 species of bug.

Click your fingers. In that moment, an acre of rainforest disappeared.

Since the 1940s, over half the world's rainforests have been destroyed.

One hundred species of invertebrate are lost every day due to deforestation!

In 1999, 50 million acres of rain forest were being destroyed each year.

Pandas Eat Mainly Bamboo Shoots And Leaves

Pandas look like bears and are often called bears, but they are really members of the racoon family. They live in the bamboo forests of China, where bamboo shoots and leaves are their main food. Unfortunately, bamboo dies after flowering. This makes the bamboo forests fragile because once the trees are cut down, there is little chance of the forest growing again. Added to this is the expansion of farm and for which many areas of bamboo have been cleared. Half of the forests disappeared in just 14 years, and as adult pandas eat up to 30 kg (66 lb) of bamboo a day, this has had a devastating effect on the numbers of pandas. Although conservationists try to preserve the panda's natural habitat — and it is now illegal in China to harm a panda in any way — there are only about 1,000 giant pandas left in the wild.

Efforts to Save Wildlife

People are beginning to realize that it is possible to live in harmony with wildlife, but it is proving to be a long, hard process. Even governments that agree that something should be done continue to allow hunting, pollution and habitat destruction. However, groups world-wide are working to prevent this.

Hawaiian Geese Were Saved From Extinction

About a hundred years ago there were some 25,000 néné (a type of goose) on the islands of Hawaii. The bird was killed for food and was also under attack from cats, dogs and pigs. By 1950 the number had fallen to around 50 and action had to be taken if the species was to survive. A pair of the birds were shipped to Slimbridge Wildfowl Trust, England. Within 12 years the project had proved so successful that 30 geese bred at Slimbridge were returned to Hawaii, where the néné continues to thrive.

Néné

The Oryx Was Bred In Captivity

The oryx, a type of antelope that lives in Arabia, was saved from extinction by taking a few animals to the USA, where they were bred in captivity. Numbers increased slowly until it was possible for some of the oryx to be returned to their natural habitat.

Did You Know?

★

The first textbook on conservation, Man and Nature, by George Perkins Marsh, was published in the 1860s.

By 1997, over 120 countries had agreed to protect wildlife by belonging to CITES (Convention on International Trade in Endangered Species of Wild Fauna and Flora).

There are over 7,000 protected areas of land around the world.

The kangaroo, gray whale and Arctic peregrine falcon were all once endangered, but have recovered enough to be removed from the World Endangered Species list.

In 1997, Dolly the sheep became the first mammal to be successfully cloned.

More than one hundred California condors have been bred in captivity and released into the wild since the last remaining one was captured in 1987.

Tigers Thrive In India

In recent years there have been many success stories of wildlife that has been saved from extinction. In the 1970s, there were only about 2,000 tigers in India. Wildlife reserves were set up to prctect the tigers and the number gradually increased. Because hunters were not allowed into these protected areas, other animals as well as the tiger also began to thrive again.

Turtles Are Being Saved

The hawksbill turtle has a beautiful, patterned shell which people use to make ornaments and jewellery. So many of these turtles have been hunted for this trade that they are in danger of extinction. Many other turtles have been hunted by people and are also in danger of being wiped out. Turtle meat is used for soup and the shells are made into beautiful objects. Now, however, some beaches where turtles lay their eggs have been closed to people during the breeding season, to help save the turtles.

Loggerhead turtle

Sea Creatures in Danger

Pollution and global warming are affecting life in the seas. Catching and killing creatures to make money is another major reason for the dwindling wildlife in many of the world's oceans. This is particularly noticeable with fish where large scale over fishing has resulted in a serious depletion of stocks. The seas are an important source of food for humans but excessive fishing and increasing pollution are causing fish stocks to deplete so rapidly they may never be replenished.

Manatees May Soon Be Extinct

Three species of manatee, a whale-like creature, are found in the coastal waters and rivers of South America, the West Indies and Africa. Steller's sea cow is a relative of the manatee that used to live on islands in the Bering Sea. In the 18th century, sailors on expeditions to North America used to spend winters on these islands. They killed the sea cows in order to stock up their meat supplies. Within 30 years, as a direct result of this slaughter, the species was extinct. Both manatees and their relatives, the dugongs, are still in danger. They could be completely extinct by the year 2020.

Manatee

Dolphin caught in a net

Dolphin Numbers Are Declining

Fishing with nets for fish, such as tuna, often results in dolphins being netted as well. This has had a devastating effect on their numbers. Some fishermen now use 'dolphin friendly' nets which allow the dolphins to swim over the top of them. (The tuna swim at a lower level and are caught.) This has not proved very effective, so responsible fisherman now catch tuna using just a rod and line.

Why Whales Are Hunted

Whales are hunted as a source of meat but also for their blubber, a fibrous tissue filled with oil. In some whales, the blubber can be as much as 40-50 cm (15-20 in) thick. The oil extracted from the blubber used to be made into soap and margarine and the bones of the whale are ground down for use as fertiliser. By the 20th century, whaling methods were so efficient that the number of whales was declining fast. They are now in danger of being completely wiped out. Although an International Whaling Commission has been set up to control the hunting of whales, many countries continue to catch more than they should because they can still sell whale meat and blubber.

Did You Know?

Steller's sea cow was named in 1741 by Georg Wilhelm Steller. By 1768, it was extinct.

Commercial whalers have slaughtered a total of about one million sperm whales.

Baleen from whales' mouths has been used by humans to make umbrellas, corsets and wig-curlers.

There were less than fifty Yanktzee River dolphins left alive in 1999.

In 1986, a ban on all whaling was announced by the International Whaling Commission.

In 1995, Japan insisted that their continued practice of whaling was for scientific purposes.

Endangered and Extinct Birds

Over the past one hundred years, many birds have become extinct, often through being hunted, but sometimes because people moved to the places where they lived and disturbed their habitats. Even though people are now aware of the dangers, it is too late for many species and many more are still in danger of extinction. Like other forms of wildlife, birds, too, face the dangers of pollution and modern chemicals.

The World's Rarest Bird Is A Parrot

The kakapo is a small, greenish-brown parrot found in New Zealand. It is the only nocturnal parrot that cannot fly. It is sometimes called the owl parrot and is the heaviest of all parrots. It used to be quite common but is now very rare because of the destruction of its habitat and the fact that people brought animals, such as dogs, which either kill the kakapo, or are in competition with it.

Kakapo

The Last Passenger Pigeon Died In 1914

At the beginning of the 20th century, enormous flocks of passenger pigeons were a common sight in North America. Because they flew together in such great numbers, they proved very easy to shoot and kill. They were also clubbed to death, and chicks were pushed from the nests. Within 25 years, the passenger pigeon was no longer seen in the skies. The last one died in Cincinnati Zoo in 1914.

Humans Are The Biggest Threat

Even though some birds are in danger of being wiped out, humans still collect their eggs as a hobby, which puts species in even more danger. There are laws protecting birds, but egg collecting still goes on and numerous birds are shot or trapped by hunters. A wide variety of habitats are being destroyed by humans as well. Marshlands are drained, forests are felled, hedgerows are destroyed to make larger areas for crops, and cities grow bigger — all of which deprives birds of places to live.

The Male And Female Huia Had Different Shaped Beaks

The huia was a black bird, about the size of a crow, that lived in the forests of New Zealand. It was unusual in that the beak of the male was completely different to that of the female. The male's beak was short and straight. He tapped trees with it to make the insects run out. The female's bill was curved and longer, shaped for catching the insects that the male had disturbed. Unfortunately, due to the destruction, during the 20th century, of the forests in which it lived, the huia exists no more.

Did You Know?

The enormous elephant bird of Madagascar had been wiped from the face of the Earth by 1650.

The dodo's name is Portuguese for stupid. It was friendly and could not fly, and by 1681 stupid people had hunted it to extinction.

There are 80 stuffed great auks in the world's museums. But a live one has not been seen since 1844.

Japanese scientists are trying to resurrect the world's tallest bird, the extinct moa, by injecting its DNA into chicken embryos.

The world's rarest wild bird is the Spix's macaw. There is one breeding pair left, because so many have been caught for private collectors.

Over 100,000 birds, of 90 different species, were killed in 1989 when the oil tanker Exxon Valdez spilt 42 million litres (over 9 million gal) of crude oil in Prince William Sound, Alaska.

Dodo

The Dodo Only Lived On One Island

The most famous of the extinct birds is the dodo, which once lived only on the island of Mauritius, in the Indian Ocean. It was killed off by humans in 1681. Today we still use the expression 'as dead as a dodo'.

Animals and People

Many creatures all over the world are in danger of dying out completely. Sometimes humans have done things to the environment without realizing that they are putting wildlife in danger. For example, dams that have been built in the Pyrenees Mountains to conserve water and produce electricity have affected the habitat of the desman, a small mammal that lives in fast flowing rivers. Its numbers have also declined because people hunt it for its fur, fishermen kill it because they claim that it eats fish —which it does not — and mink that have escaped from farms have taken over its territory.

Wolves' Bones Are Used To Make Medicine

All over the world many species of wolves are declining in numbers. They are hunted for their coats, for their bones (to make medicines), and because they are regarded as pests. The red wolf of North America is dying out because it has been cross-bred with other species. The maned wolf of South America is highly prized for its bones, and the Simien jackal of Ethiopia is hunted for its beautiful coat.

The Red Kneed Spider Is A Popular Pet

The handsome red kneed spider can eat creatures as large as a bird. It is in danger because of the demand for unusual pets. The spider is popular because of its huge size (it can grow up to 14 cm (5 $1/2$ in) diagonally across) and its attractive markings. This is In spite of the fact that it can inflict a painful — and poisonous — bite.

Red wolf

Sea Horse Fathers Give Birth

The sea horse has a stiff, bony body and a small horse-like head, from which it gets its name. It is unique because it is the only creature whose babies are born from the male and not the female. The female squirts her eggs into a special breeding pouch on the male's belly. The eggs develop in the pouch until they are hatched about a month later. Sea horses are endangered because people take them for aquariums.

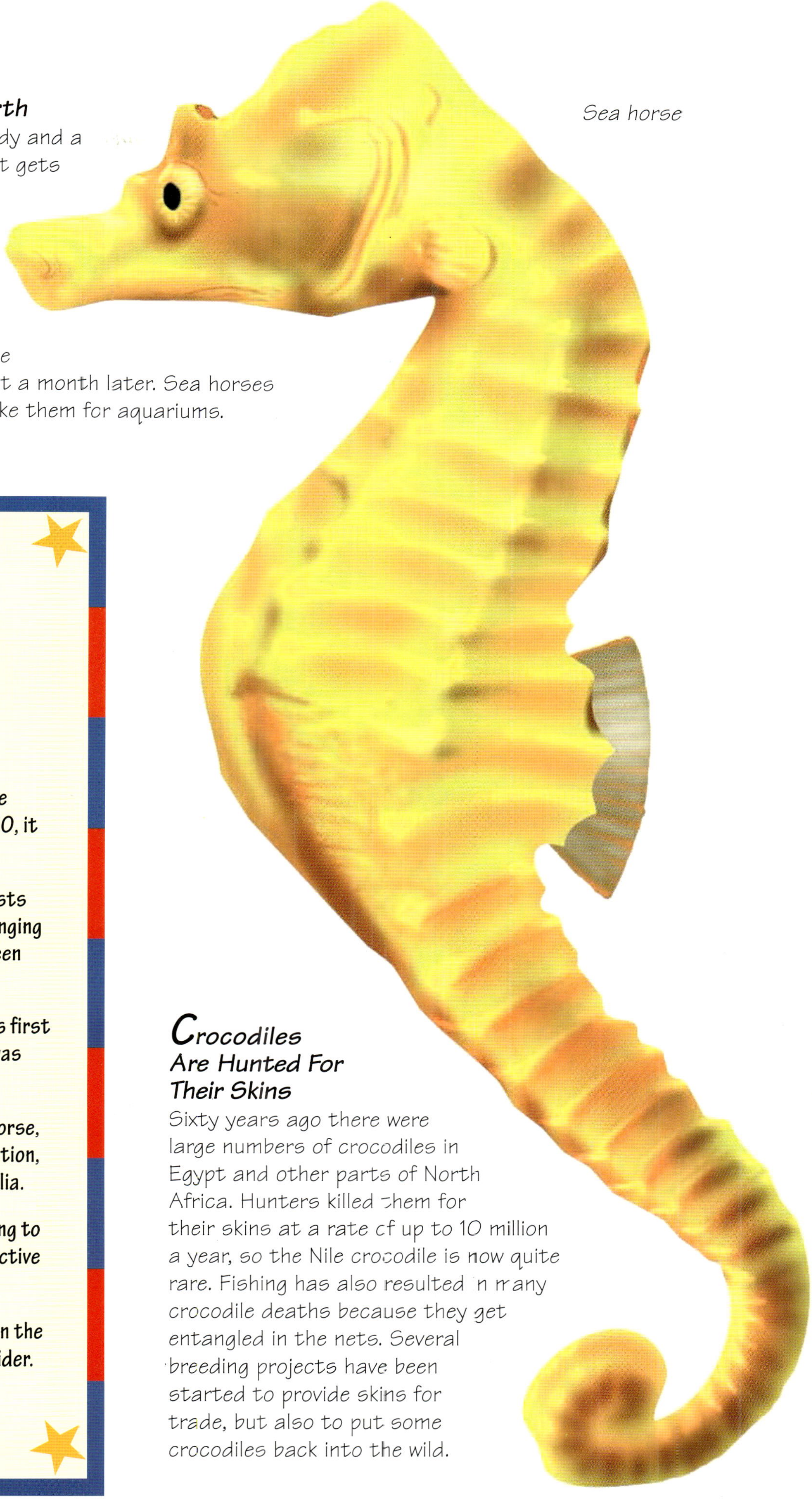

Sea horse

Did You Know?

Julius Caesar wrote about the magnificent giant wild ox. By 1630, it was extinct.

In May 1997, Australian scientists discovered a snapping turtle belonging to a species thought to have been extinct for 20,000 years!

A type of zebra called a quagga was first recorded in 1685. By 1883 it was extinct.

A wild horse called Przewalski's horse, once thought to be nearing extinction, has been rediscovered in Mongolia.

South African scientists are trying to recreate the quagga through selective breeding of zebras.

The Kauai Cave wolf spider, found in the USA, is the most endangered spider.

Crocodiles Are Hunted For Their Skins

Sixty years ago there were large numbers of crocodiles in Egypt and other parts of North Africa. Hunters killed them for their skins at a rate of up to 10 million a year, so the Nile crocodile is now quite rare. Fishing has also resulted in many crocodile deaths because they get entangled in the nets. Several breeding projects have been started to provide skins for trade, but also to put some crocodiles back into the wild.

Chinese Alligators Are Almost Extinct

A similar problem faces the Chinese alligator. It lives in part of the Yangtze River, but used to be more widely spread. This animal has been hunted for its skin to the brink of extinction. Pollution and the loss of its natural habitats are also to blame.

Apes and Monkeys in Danger

Because of the rapid destruction of the rainforests, many apes and monkeys are in danger of dying out. These include the magnificent mountain gorilla of Africa, the orang-utan in Asia, and numerous monkeys in South America.

Colobus monkey

Wars Endanger Gorillas

The mountain gorillas of Central Africa faced extinction because they were hunted, their forest home was being destroyed and wars in the area had also reduced their numbers. In 1979, a project was set up to protect the remaining forests and to educate local people about the importance of the animals and their environment.

Seeing Gorillas Helps To Save Them

One unusual way of saving gorillas has been to take people to see them in the wild. As a result, people become more aware of the plight of these magnificent animals, and want to help them.

Baby Orang-utans Are Popular Pets

Baby orang-utans are popular pets. To capture the babies, hunters first kill the mothers because without them, the babies become weak and easier to catch. Those babies that are captured may die from disease because the animals can easily catch human diseases. Trade in young orang-utans is now illegal, but it still goes on. This, and the destruction of their habitat, means that their number is probably going down by several thousand every year.

Gorillas In The Mist

The most famous person to help the mountain gorilla was an American conservationist called Dr Dian Fossey. She made friends with the gorillas and tried to stop them being captured or killed. She wrote a best selling book called *Gorillas In The Mist* about her work. The book was later made into a film. She was murdered in 1985, but her work is now being carried on by other conservationists.

Monkeys Are Hunted For Their Fur

The colobus monkey of Africa is rare because of the long, silky fur that hangs down its sides. The fur has attracted hunters who have killed the monkeys in their thousands. Another monkey hunted for its fur is the snow monkey of China. It used to be believed that it had the power to prevent rheumatism, a disease that causes painful muscles and joints. The snow monkey was hunted so much that the species was rare before the end of the 19th century. It is now protected by Chinese law, yet it is still possible to buy skins illegally.

Human Body

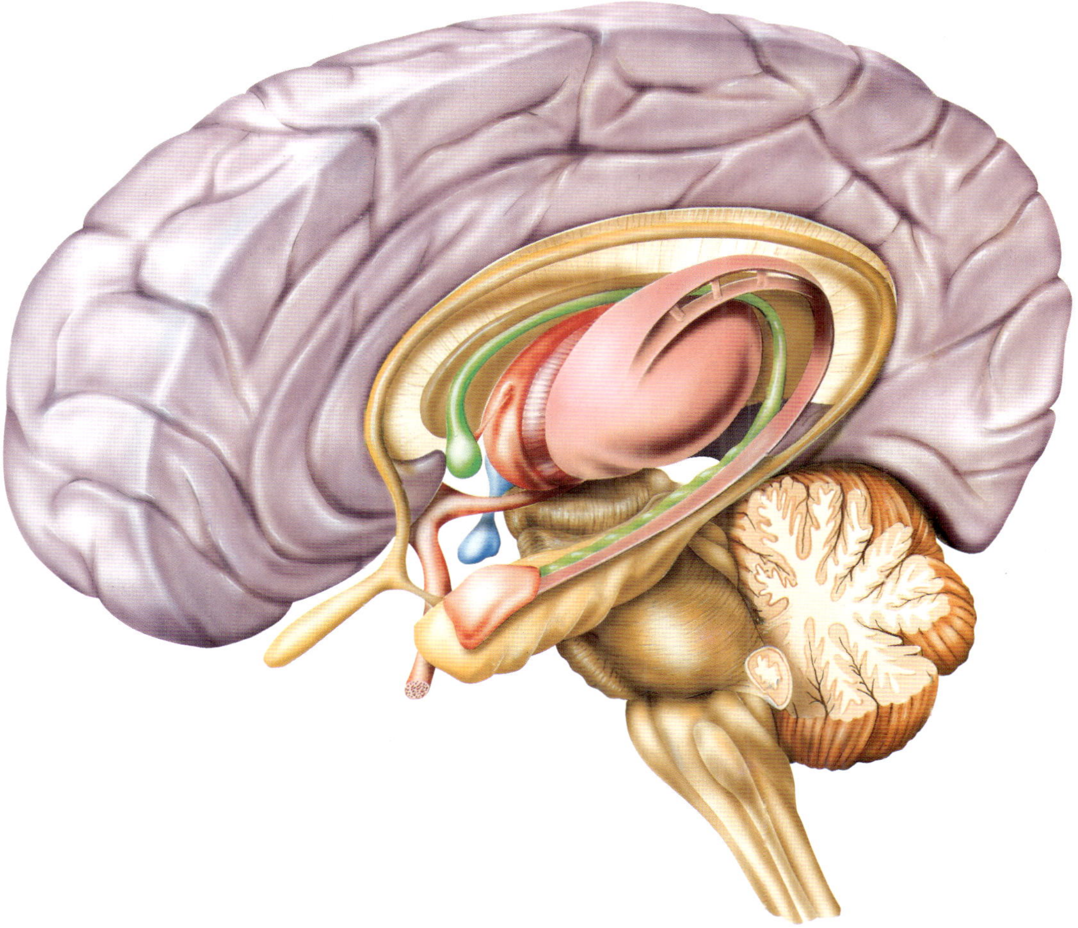

Bones and Muscles

The human body, in common with that of all animals, is supported by a number of bones. Together, the bones are known as the skeleton. In addition to providing support for the body, the skeleton also protects many vital organs, such as the heart and brain, and acts as a framework to which muscles are attached.

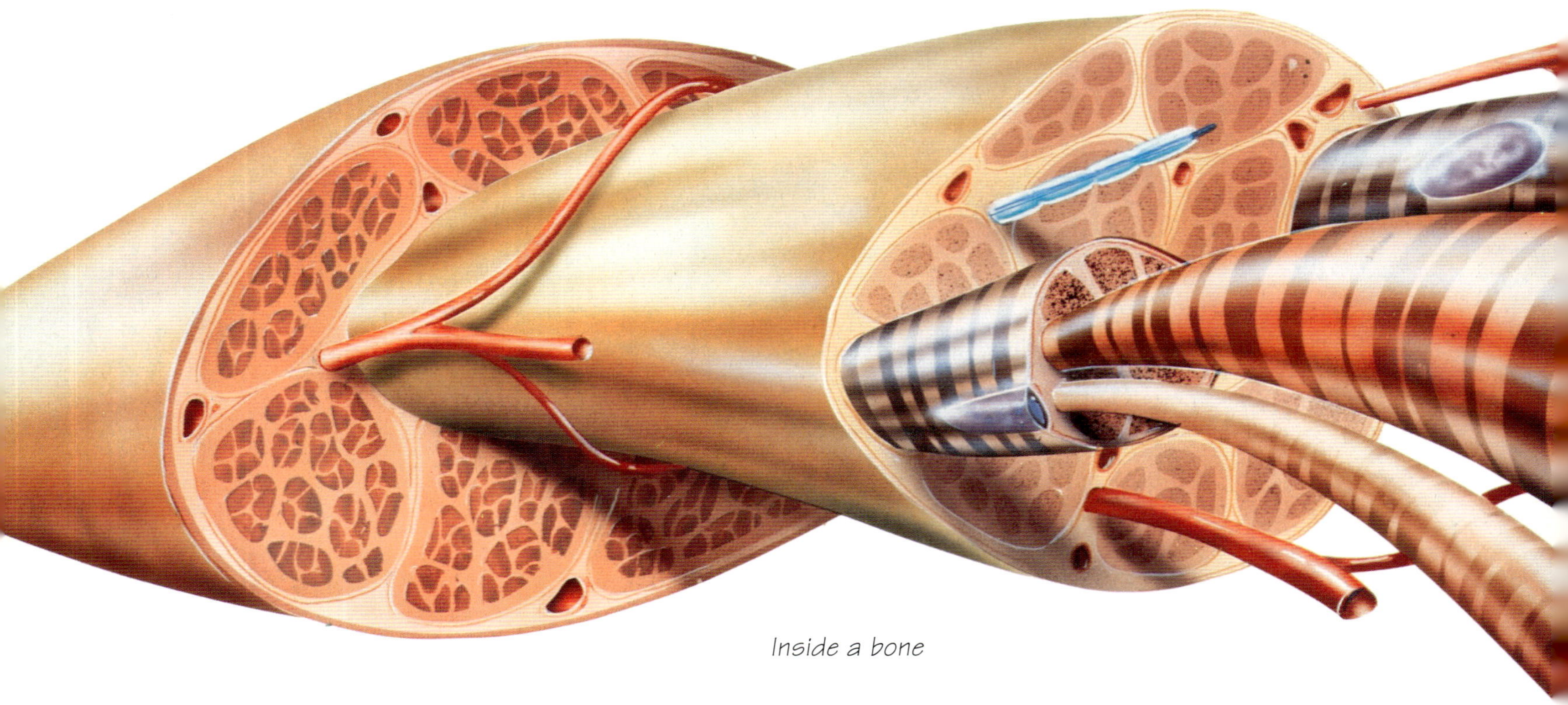

Inside a bone

Adults have Fewer Bones Than Children

The number of bones you have depends upon how old you are. A child has more bones than an adult because as the body grows older some bones fuse together. There are normally 206 bones in the adult human body — 32 in each arm, 31 in each leg, 29 in the skull, 26 in the spine and 25 in the chest.

There Are 26 Bones In Your Spine

The shortest bone, called the stapes, is in the ear. The stapes may be only 2.5 mm (1/10 in) long. The spine is not one long bone, but is made up of 26 small bones, called vertebrae. The thigh bone, or femur, is the longest bone being about 50 cm (20 in) in a man with a height of 1.83 m (6 ft).

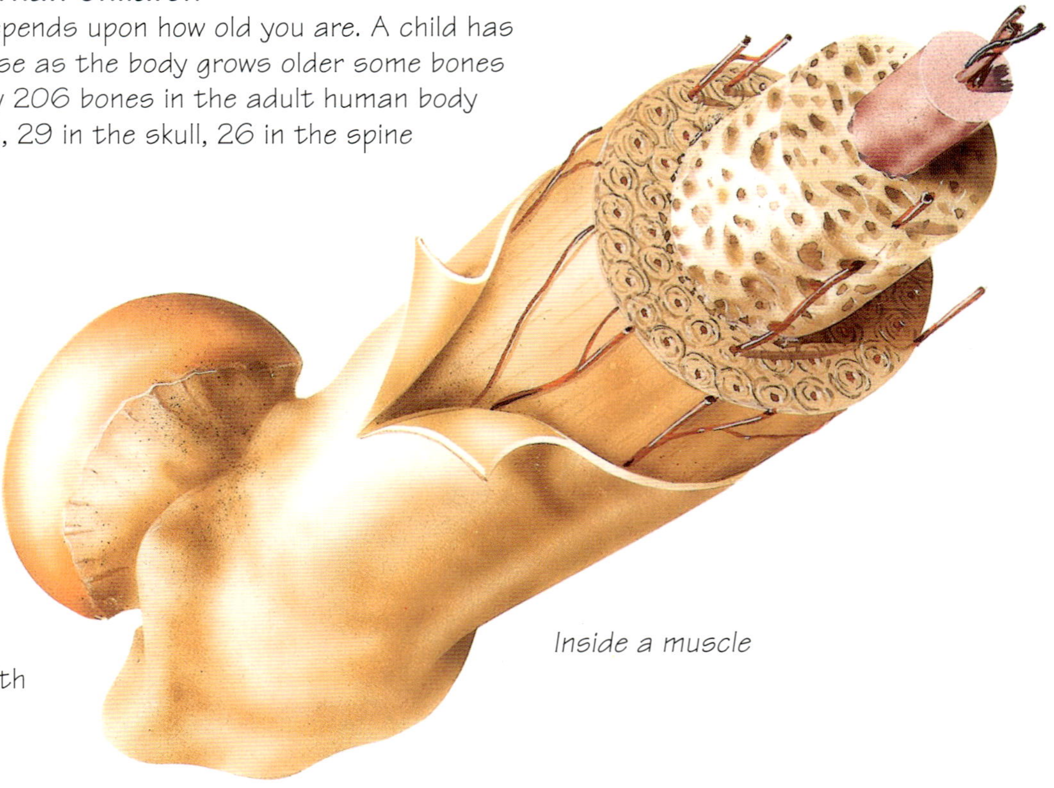

Inside a muscle

Bones Cannot Bend

Bones are fitted together in joints to allow movement because they cannot bend. There are several types of joint, each allowing a different type of movement. The knee, for example, is a hinge joint which can only move in one direction. The joint at the hip is a ball and socket joint, which allows you to move your pelvis in a circular movement. The shoulder joint is another example of a ball and socket joint. The saddle joint at the base of the thumb also allows a wide range of movement. Pivot joints, found in the forearm and in the neck, allow a turning movement. To prevent bones from grinding against each other, joints are cushioned by pads of soft but tough tissue, called cartilage.

Did You Know?

In about 450 BC, the ancient Greek doctor Hippocrates made the first detailed study of human anatomy.

The great artist and inventor Leonardo da Vinci produced beautiful and detailed drawings of dissected human parts!

Remains of prehistoric people show that they tried to set broken bones.

The biggest muscle in the human body is the gluteus maximus – or buttock!

In 1996, a dentist identified a new muscle in the human body – attached to the jaw, naturally!

An adult human has 206 bones, but a baby has more than 350!

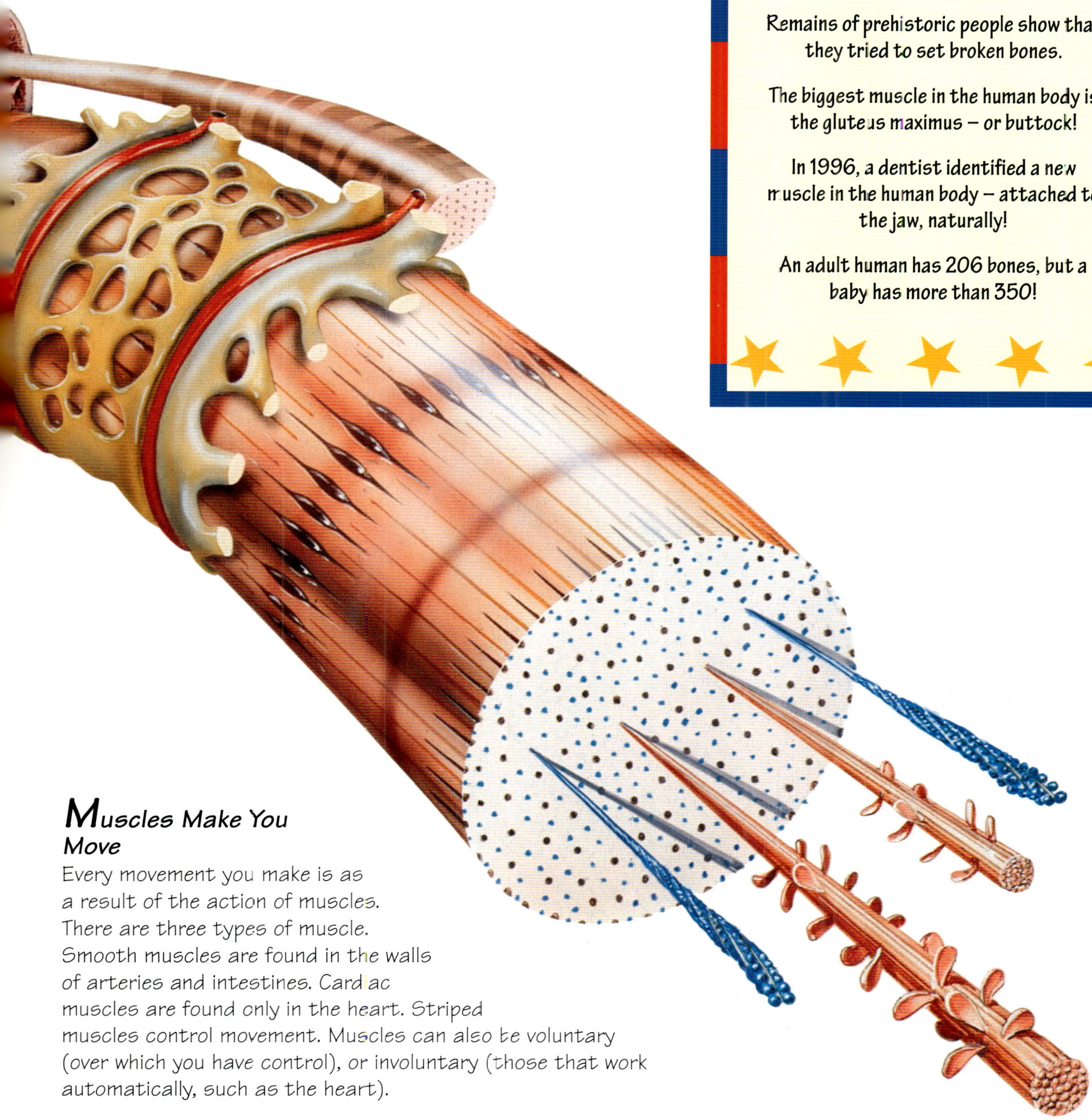

Muscles Make You Move

Every movement you make is as a result of the action of muscles. There are three types of muscle. Smooth muscles are found in the walls of arteries and intestines. Cardiac muscles are found only in the heart. Striped muscles control movement. Muscles can also be voluntary (over which you have control), or involuntary (those that work automatically, such as the heart).

Brains and Nerves

The brain is the control centre of the body. It is a complex organ. It receives messages from the senses, sends instructions to the muscles, regulates the bodily functions and, in fact, controls everything a person does. The main parts of the brain are the cortex, which controls thinking and the senses, the cerebellum, which coordinates movement and balance, and the medulla, which controls involuntary activities, such as breathing.

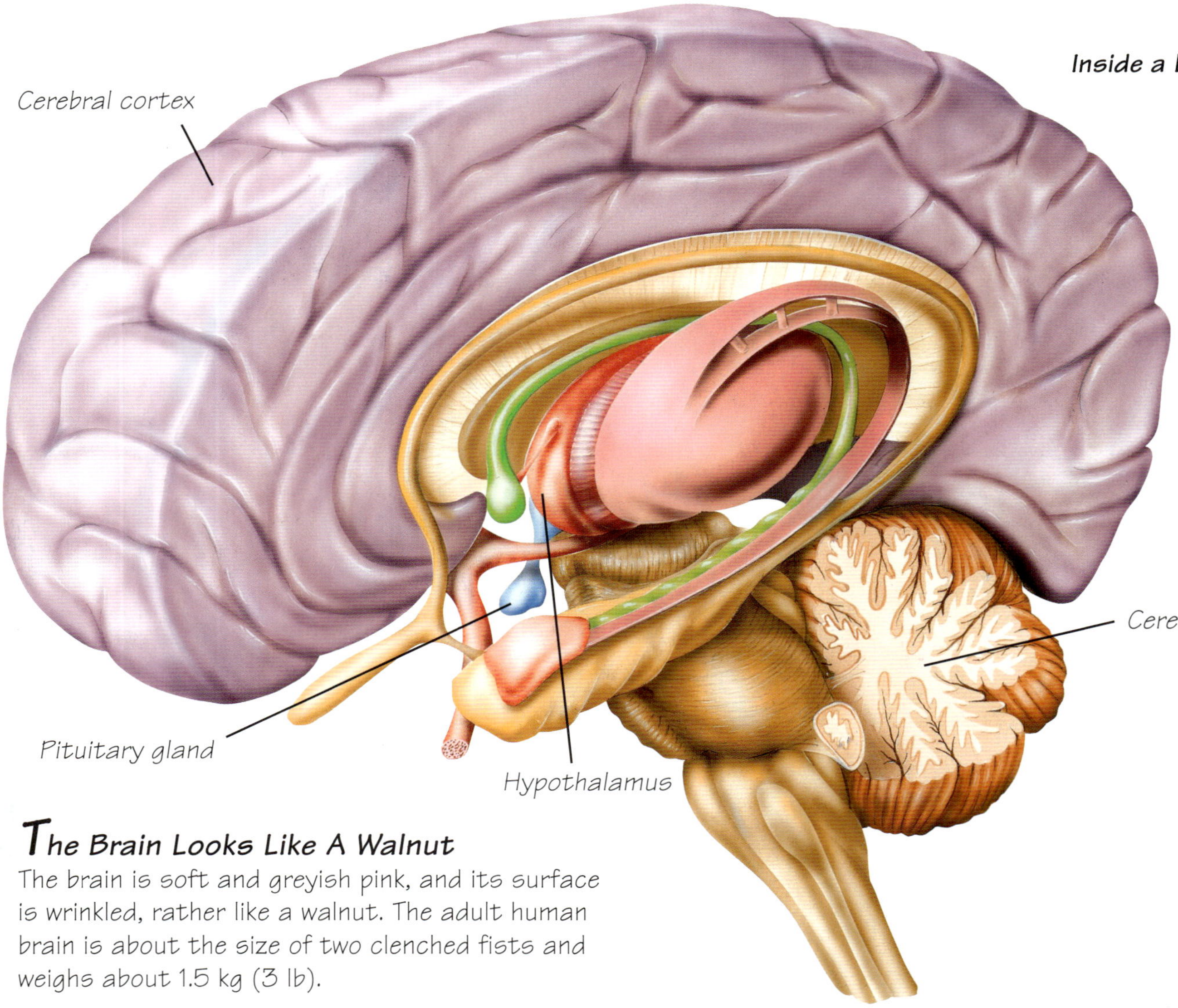

Inside a brain

The Brain Looks Like A Walnut

The brain is soft and greyish pink, and its surface is wrinkled, rather like a walnut. The adult human brain is about the size of two clenched fists and weighs about 1.5 kg (3 lb).

There Are Billions Of Nerves In Your Body

The brain and the spinal cord are known as the central nervous system. The spinal cord is made up of bundles of nerves, rather like wires forming a cable. From here, thousands of millions of nerves go out to all parts of the body, to form the outer nervous system. The purpose of the nerves is to transmit messages to and from the brain at a speed of around 320 kph (200 mph). None of the nerve cells are long enough to reach all parts of the body, so they are linked together in chains. Messages are transmitted electrically along the nerves, and then chemically from one nerve cell to the next.

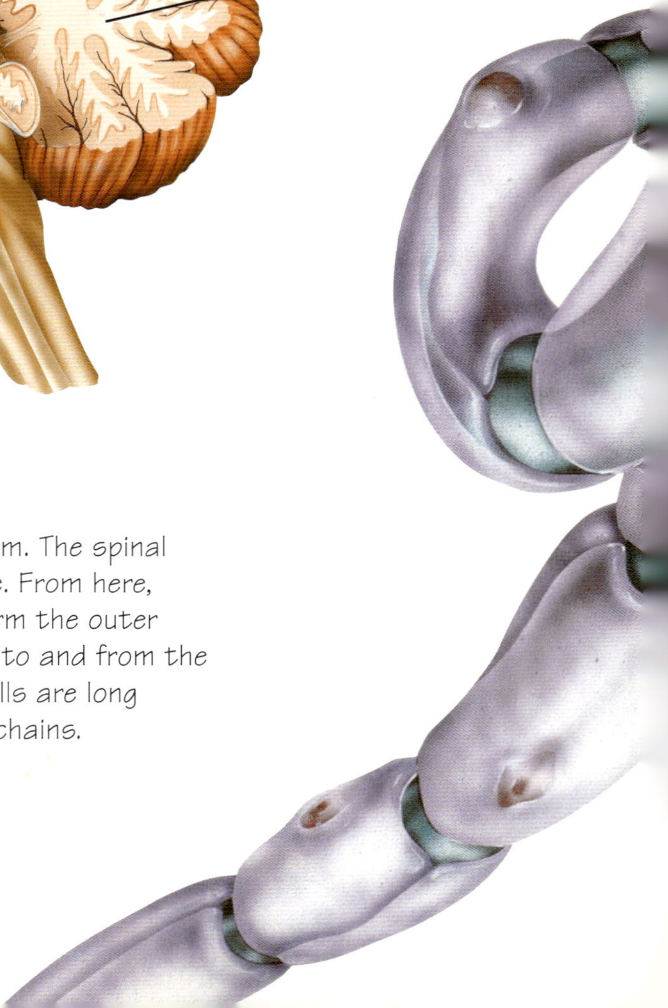

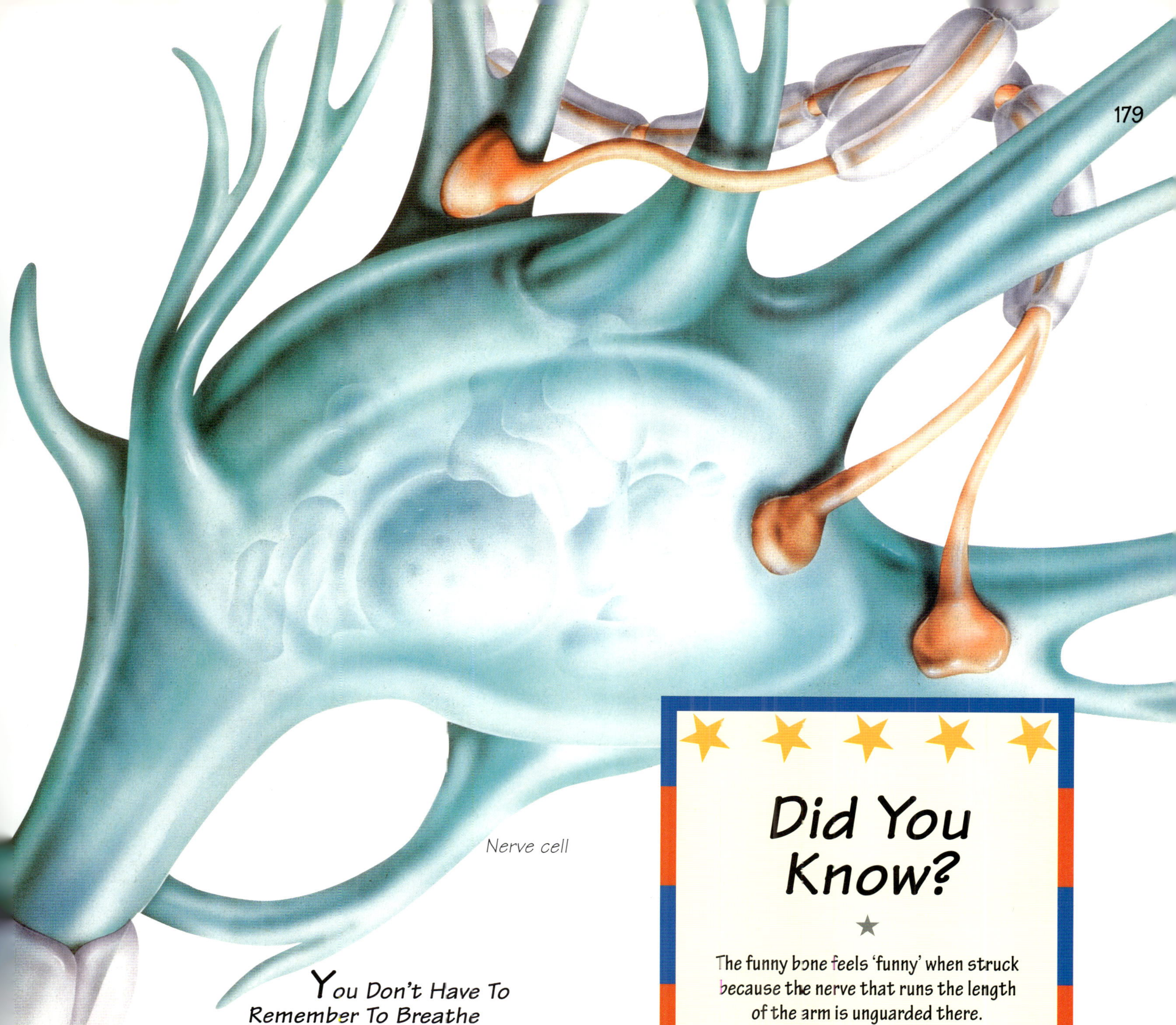

Nerve cell

You Don't Have To Remember To Breathe

The central nervous system controls actions that are done deliberately. There is a separate nervous system, called the autonomic system, that looks after all those actions that are not controlled by conscious thought. These include digestion, breathing and the pumping of the heart.

The Brain Does Not Control Reflex Actions

Although messages are sent very fast from the brain to the body, there may be times when action is needed even quicker. If you accidentally touch something hot, you whip your hand away from the heat instantly. In such a case the nerve messages take a short cut — they do not go to the brain but just to the spinal cord and back again. You respond automatically, without the brain telling you what to do. This is known as a reflex action — an automatic reaction. Blinking is a reflex action to protect the eye, and sneezing is another. It is an automatic response to something irritating the nose.

Did You Know?

The funny bone feels 'funny' when struck because the nerve that runs the length of the arm is unguarded there.

A human learns most during the first six years of life, when the brain is growing in size to three times the amount it weighed at birth.

A fifth of all oxygen taken into the body is used to supply the brain.

The brain of an adult human weighs about 1.4 kg (3 lb).

When embalming mummies, the ancient Egyptians used a special hook to remove the brain through the corpse's nostril!

Prehistoric doctors drilled holes in their patients' skulls to allow evil spirits to leave the brain!

The Senses

We gain our knowledge of the world around us through five main senses — sight, hearing, smell, touch and taste. From each of these senses, messages are sent to the brain to provide us with information. The brain may then issue commands to the body in response to the messages it receives. Without our senses, life would be dull indeed. An apple would have no taste or smell, we would not be able to see its colour, feel its smooth texture or hear our teeth crunch into it.

Our Sense Of Smell Helps Us Taste

Inside the nose are cells called olfactory cells that are sensitive to scent molecules in the air. Nerves from these cells transmit signals to the brain to give us our sense of smell. Humans can distinguish between several thousand different smells, but many animals have a much better sense of smell. The sense of smell is not very important to human survival, but it does play an important role in our sense of taste, working with the tongue.

Our Ears Control Our Sense Of Balance

The ear reacts to vibrations (movements of air caused by noise). Inside the ear, the eardrum also vibrates and through three tiny bones in the middle ear, these vibrations are transmitted along nerves to the brain. The brain interprets the vibrations as sounds. The ear also contains the semi-circular canals, small tubes filled with liquid that moves as the body moves. This controls the body's sense of balance. The movements are transmitted to the brain, which lets the person know which way the body is moving.

Inside the ear

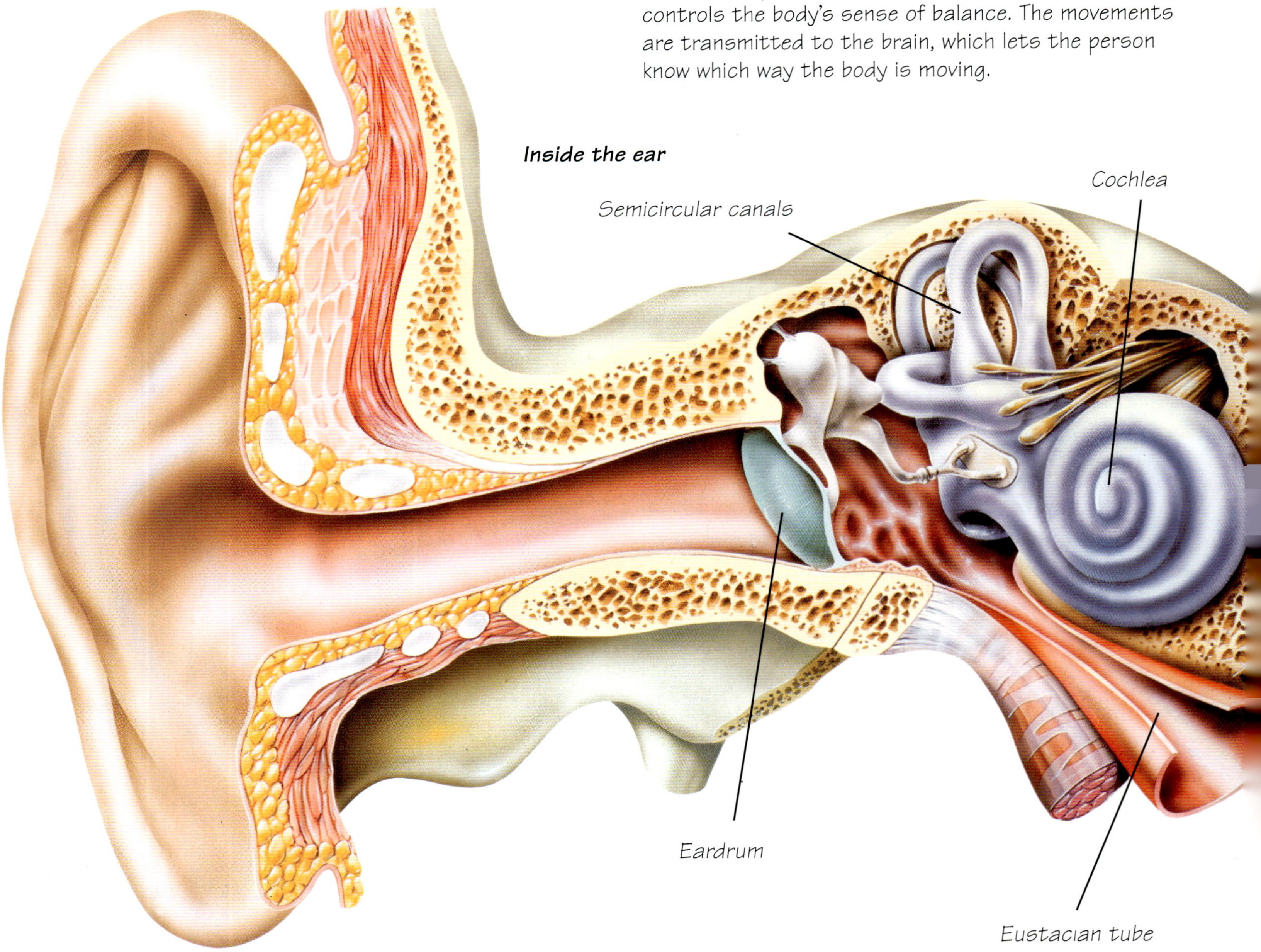

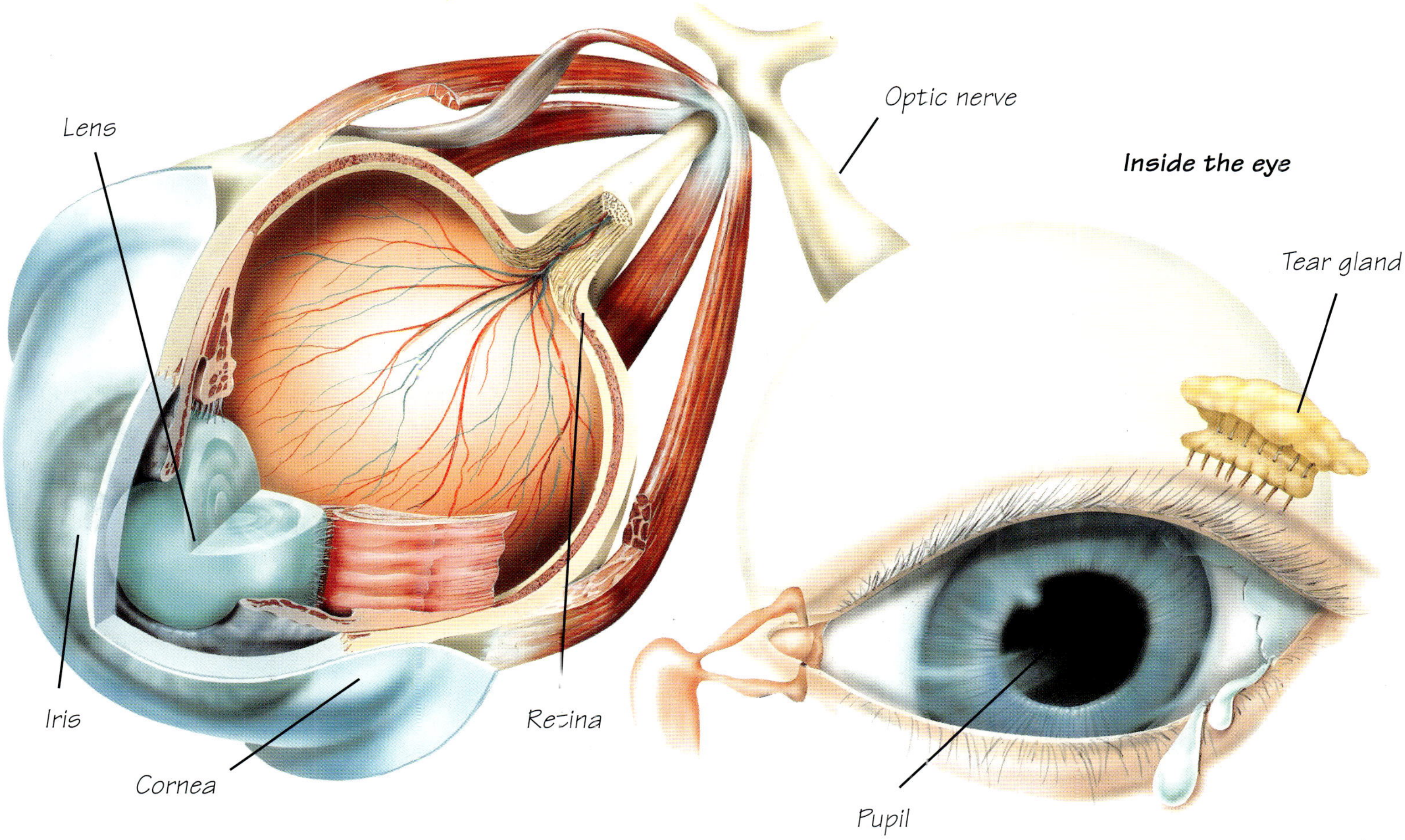

Inside the eye

Sight Is The Major Sense

Your eye works rather like a camera. Light passes through a lens that focuses the image of what you are looking at onto the back of the eye (the retina). Messages, picked up by 132 million light-sensitive cells in the retina, are transmitted to the brain along the optic nerve. The brain interprets what you see. The image formed on the retina is actually upside down, but the brain interprets the image the right way up.

Your Tongue Is Covered With Taste Buds

The tongue is covered with small projections, called papillae. Around these are groups of cells, known as taste buds, that send messages to the brain when stimulated. It is these messages that we interpret as taste and different areas of the tongue are particularly receptive to certain tastes. The tip of the tongue is sensitive to salt or sweet things, the back detects bitter tastes, and the sides respond to anything sour. All tastes are a combination of signals coming from these taste buds. As well as its taste, we are also affected by the smell, the appearance and the texture of the food we eat.

Itching Is A Pain

There are several different types of receptor cells in the skin that allow us to feel pressure, pain, texture and temperature. There are more pain receptors than the other types. Even itching is the result of these pain receptors being activated.

Did You Know?

A human can identify about 10,000 different smells!

The tongue contains over 8,000 taste buds.

A human can hear sounds when air molecules vibrating between 15 and 15,000 times a second strike the ear drum.

Cells in the human eye can detect 100 billionth of a watt of light!

The longer a human nose sniffs something, the less the brain will register the smell!

The lips, tongue and tip of the human nose are more sensitive to touch than the fingertips!

It's Got You Covered

The skin is the outer, waterproof, covering of your body. It contains nerves that respond to touch, pain and temperature. There are two layers of skin, the outer layer, the epidermis, grows continuously to replace dead skin cells. The thicker, under layer, called the dermis, contains the nerves and blood vessels. Beneath the dermis is a layer of fat which helps to keep the body warm. Skin is the largest of the human organs. In an adult, it can cover a surface area of 1.75 sq m (19 sq ft) and weighs about 2.25 kg (5 lb). It varies in thickness from about 1 mm (1/40 in) on the eyelids to 5mm (1/20 in) or more on the bottom of the feet.

Melanin Determins Skin Colour

Melanin is a brown substance contained in everyone's skin. The amount of melanin determines skin colour. Ultra-violet rays in sunlight cause the skin to produce more melanin, which is why people in hot climates have darker skins than those who live in cooler parts of the world. The purpose of the melanin is to protect the skin from the sun.

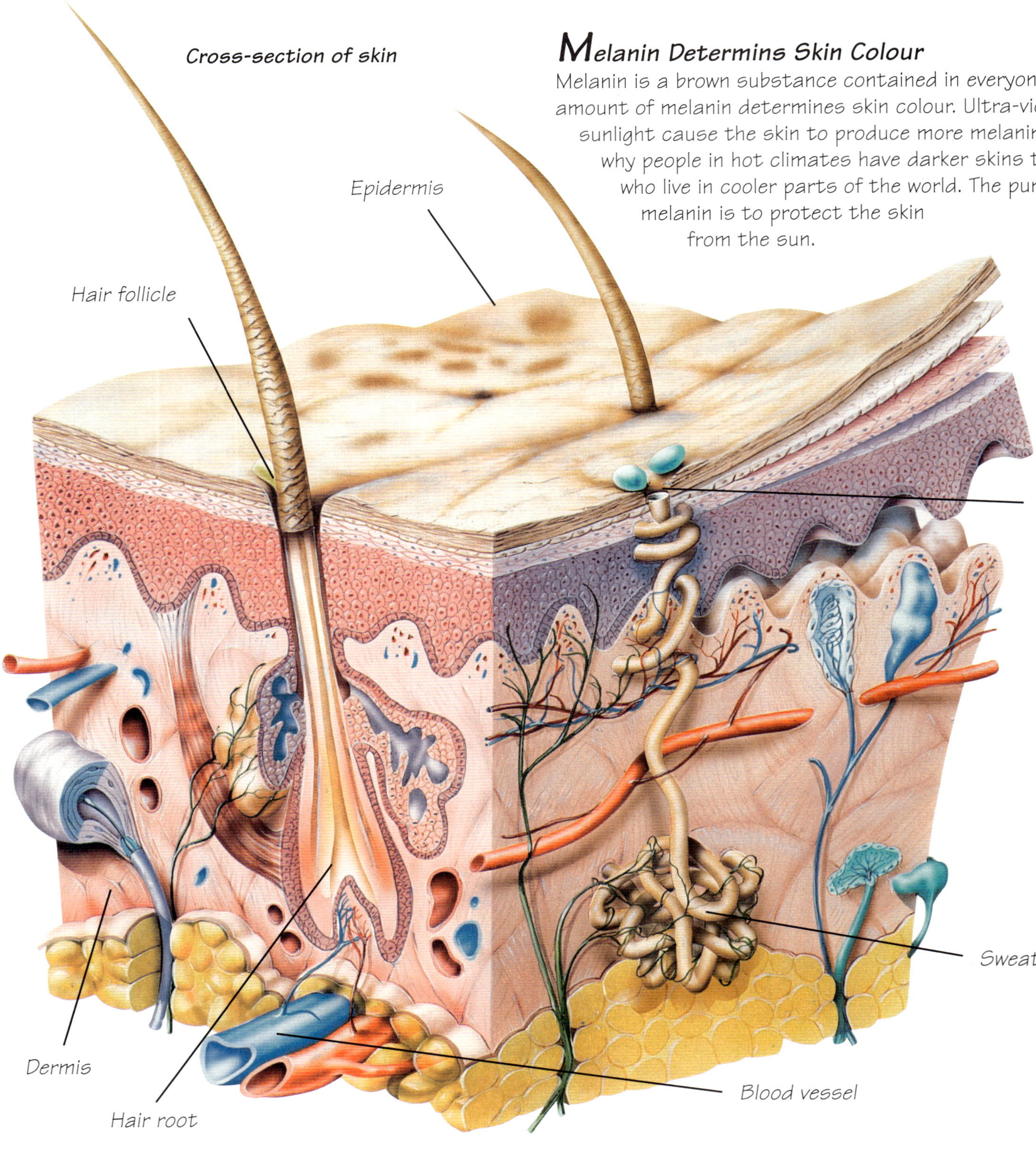

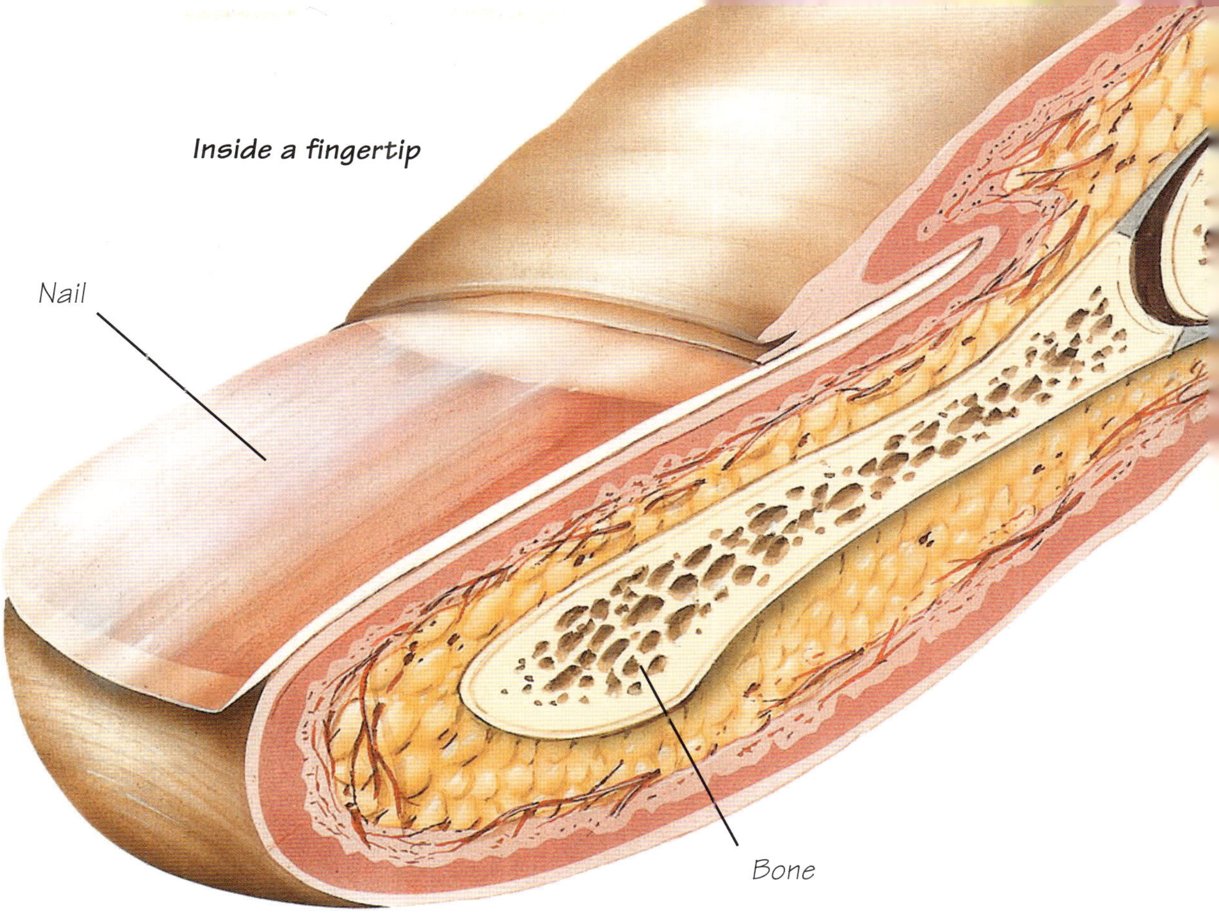

Nails Protect Your Fingers And Toes

Nails provide a protective covering for the ends of the fingers and toes. Each nail grows from a nail-bed at a rate of about 1 mm (1/40 in) every ten days. The new nail forms behind the cuticle, a fold of skin at the base of the nail. The new nail pushes the older nail along.

Did You Know?

★

There are 100 billion cells in the human body.

The human body is covered with 1.75 sq m (19 sq ft) of skin, which if removed and piled on some scales, would weigh about 4 kg (9 lb)!

Human hair and nails grow faster in the summer than in the winter.

Blondes have more hair! They have up to 140,000 hairs on their head, while redheads have as few as 90,000. But the hair colour has to be natural!

No two fingerprints are the same.

The human body is at its peak at the age of about twenty – then it starts to age!

Your Hair Is Dead

Hair is formed from keratin, the same substance that makes skin. The base of each hair is live material but the rest is dead, which is why hair can be cut without pain — just like the nails, which are also dead material. Each hair is a tube-shaped piece of keratin that is pushed up from a follicle, which houses the hair root.

You Lose 50 Hairs From Your Head Daily

Hair grows at a rate of about 12 mm (1/2 in) a month and can reach a length of 700 mm (28 in) before falling out. About 50 hairs fall from the head each day. After a resting period of some three months, a new hair grows from the follicle. The colour of your hair, which is determined by the amount of melanin in the body, is inherited from your parents.

Strands of hair

Bodies Need Food

Humans, like all animals, have to take in food to supply material for growth of the body, to help combat the normal wear and tear of body tissues and to provide energy. The food is converted into materials needed by the body through a process called digestion. Digestion changes the food you eat into a form that can be absorbed by the blood to be carried around the body.

Digestion Turns Food Into Molecules

Digestion is the process of breaking down foods into molecules that can be absorbed into the body.

Food, taken in through the mouth, is first ground into smaller pieces by the teeth. During this process saliva, a digestive juice secreted by glands in the mouth, starts the process of digestion.

The partially digested food is swallowed and passes through the oesophagus, a tube about 250 mm (10 in) long, to the stomach, where it breaks down further. Hydrochloric acid does part of this process. The stomach is protected from the acid by a coating of mucus on the stomach walls — otherwise the stomach would start to dissolve itself.

The processed food, which is now rather like a thick soup, goes into the small intestine, a long tube in which bile and other juices cause further digestion to take place. The digested material passes through the small intestine to the ileum where it is absorbed into the blood.

You Lose Water Through Breathing

The kidneys act as filters to remove waste and excess water from the blood as urine. About two thirds of the weight of a human body is water, but the level has to be regulated. Up to 2 litres (4 pints) of water can be lost from the body each day just through breathing and sweating. If the person drinks too much, there will be too much water so the kidneys produce more urine. If not enough liquid is taken in, or too much water is lost (perhaps through sweating on a hot day), the kidneys produce less urine.

The digestive system

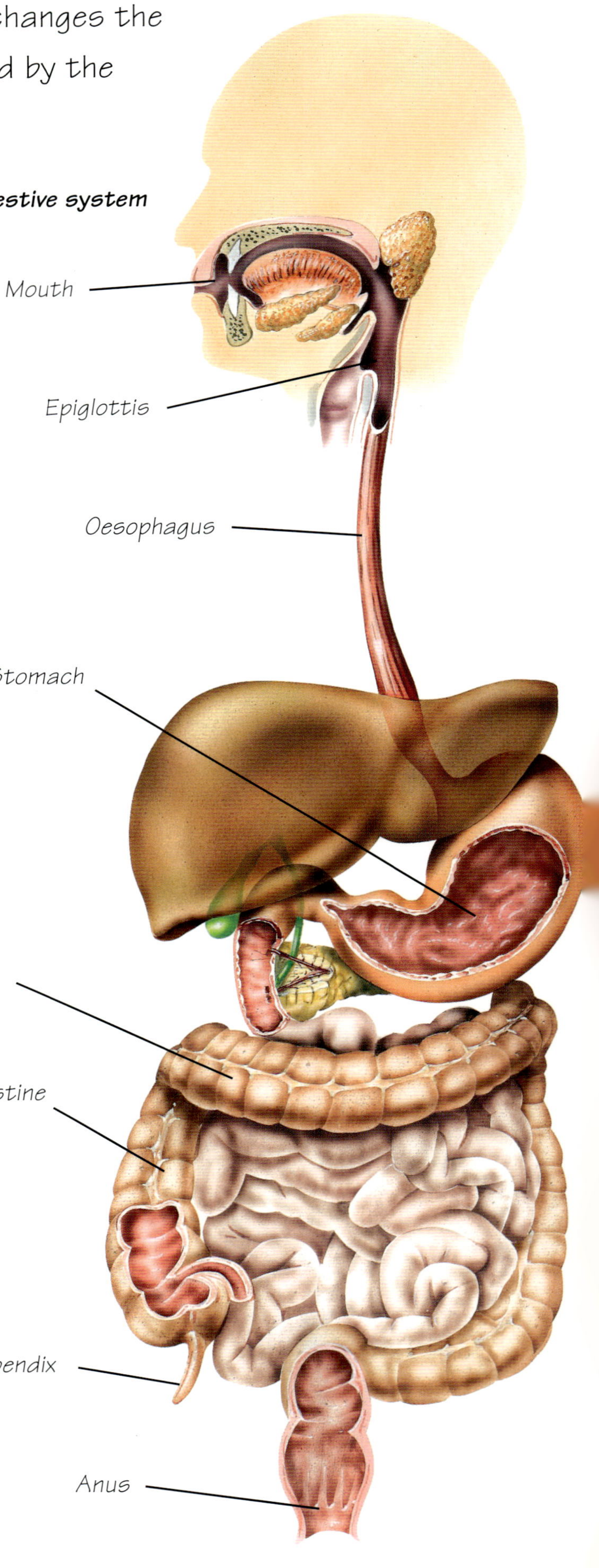

Did You Know?

The food a person swallows has to make a journey through 9 m (30 ft) of 'tubes'.

An adult produces an average of 1.5 litres (2.65 pints) of urine – every day!

Fresh saliva contains no bacteria or germs.

Ulcers are not new. In the seventh century AD, a Byzantine physician wrote: 'When there is an ulcer in the stomach... the patient must abstain from all acid food or drink.'

The muscle that controls how much food is allowed from the stomach into the small intestine is called the 'pylorus' – which means 'gate-keeper'!

'Butterflies' are caused because emotions like fear cause the stomach to produce too much acid.

Kidneys and bladder

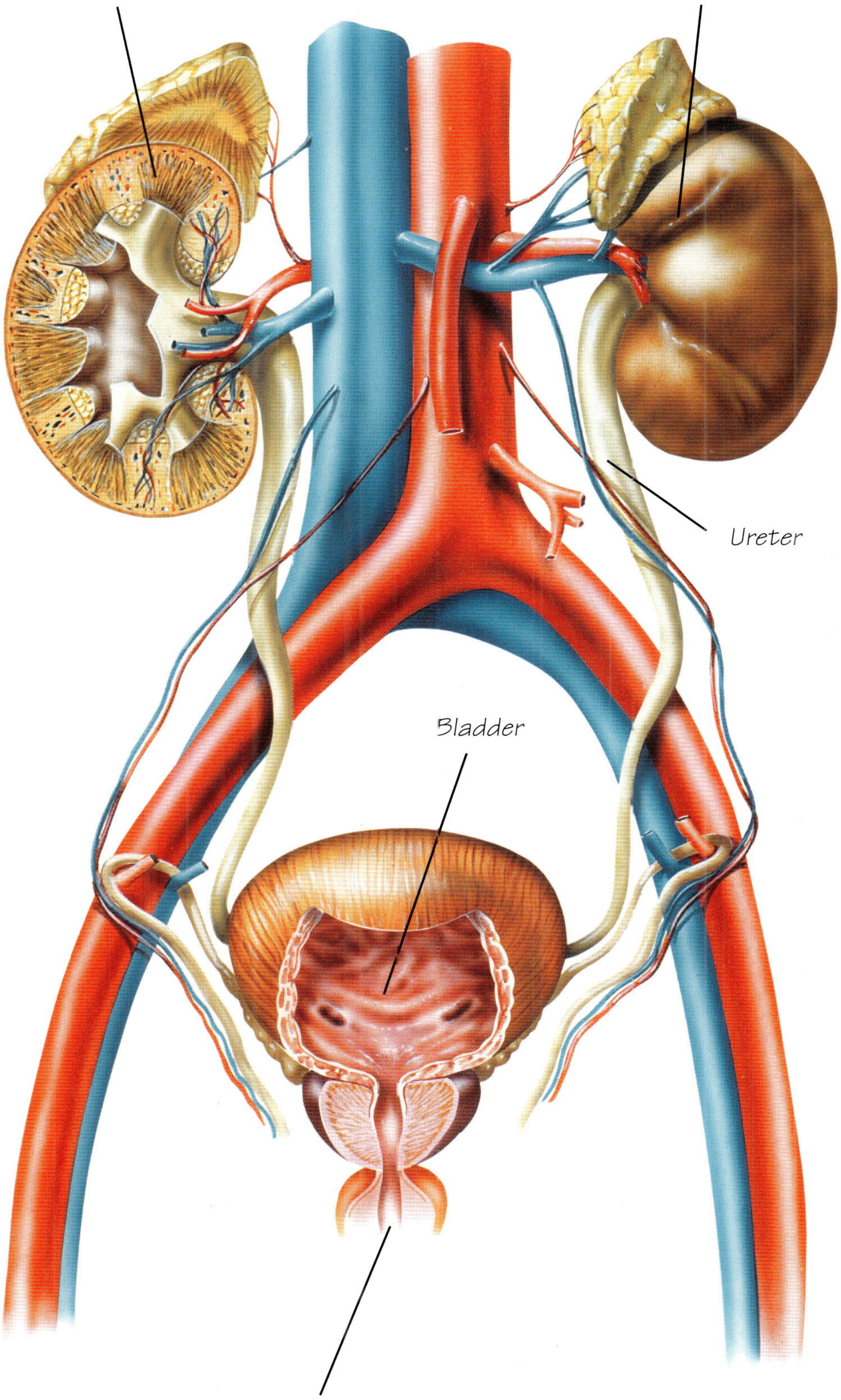

Your Body Gets Rid Of Waste

From the small intestine, water and waste is passed into the large intestine. Some of the water passes through the wall of part of the large intestine, called the colon, and into the bloodstream. What is left of the waste matter is now more or less solid. It passes into the rectum where it remains for a while. Waste matter is ejected out of the body as faeces, when you go to the toilet.

The Breath of Life

You need to breathe in order to take in oxygen (which is needed to burn food and produce energy), and to get rid of carbon dioxide from the blood. Oxygen is obtained from air, which is drawn in through the nose and through the trachea (windpipe), which divides into two tubes called bronchi. One bronchus goes to the left lung, the other to the right. The lungs are housed in a cavity formed by the ribs. Beneath the lungs is a domed sheet of muscular tissue called the diaphragm. To inhale air into the lungs, the diaphragm is flattened and the ribs expanded to enlarge the lungs and draw air in. To exhale, the muscles of the diaphragm and rib case relax so the lung cavity is made smaller, and air is forced out.

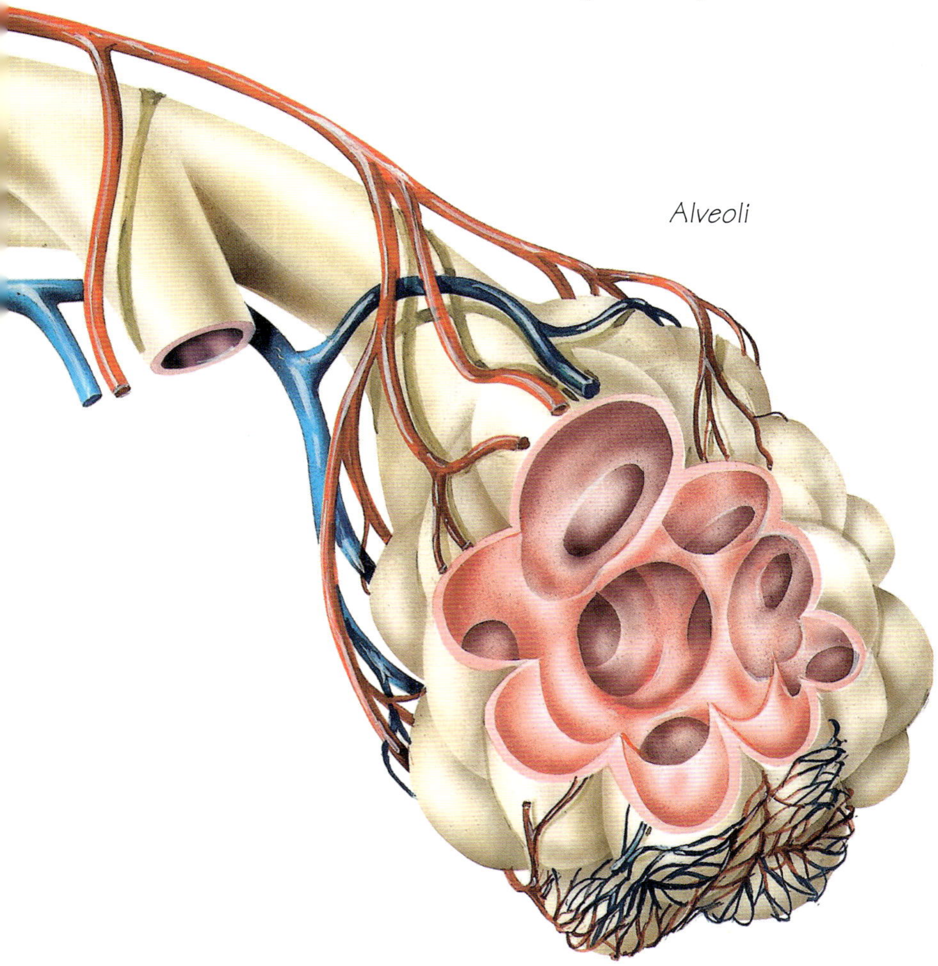

Blood Vessels Take Oxygen Into The Blood

Inside the lungs, the bronchi divide into smaller and smaller tubes, the smallest of which are called bronchioles. The bronchioles end in a cluster of air chambers called alveoli. There are over 600 million alveoli in the lungs. In the alveoli are microscopic blood vessels, and it is these that take oxygen into the blood. The reverse of this process takes waste carbon dioxide and exhales it from the body.

Did You Know?

In 1628, William Harvey explained how the heart acted as a pump to force blood around the body.

One drop of blood contains 5 million red blood cells and 15,000 white blood cells.

A person's lungs contain a total of 600 million tiny air chambers called alveoli.

The blood vessels in one human body would encircle the world twice if laid end to end.

The human body contains nearly 100,000 km (62,000 mi) of artery and vein to carry blood on its intricate journey.

A sneeze leaves the human nostrils at the speed of a fast car – about 180 kph (112 mph)!

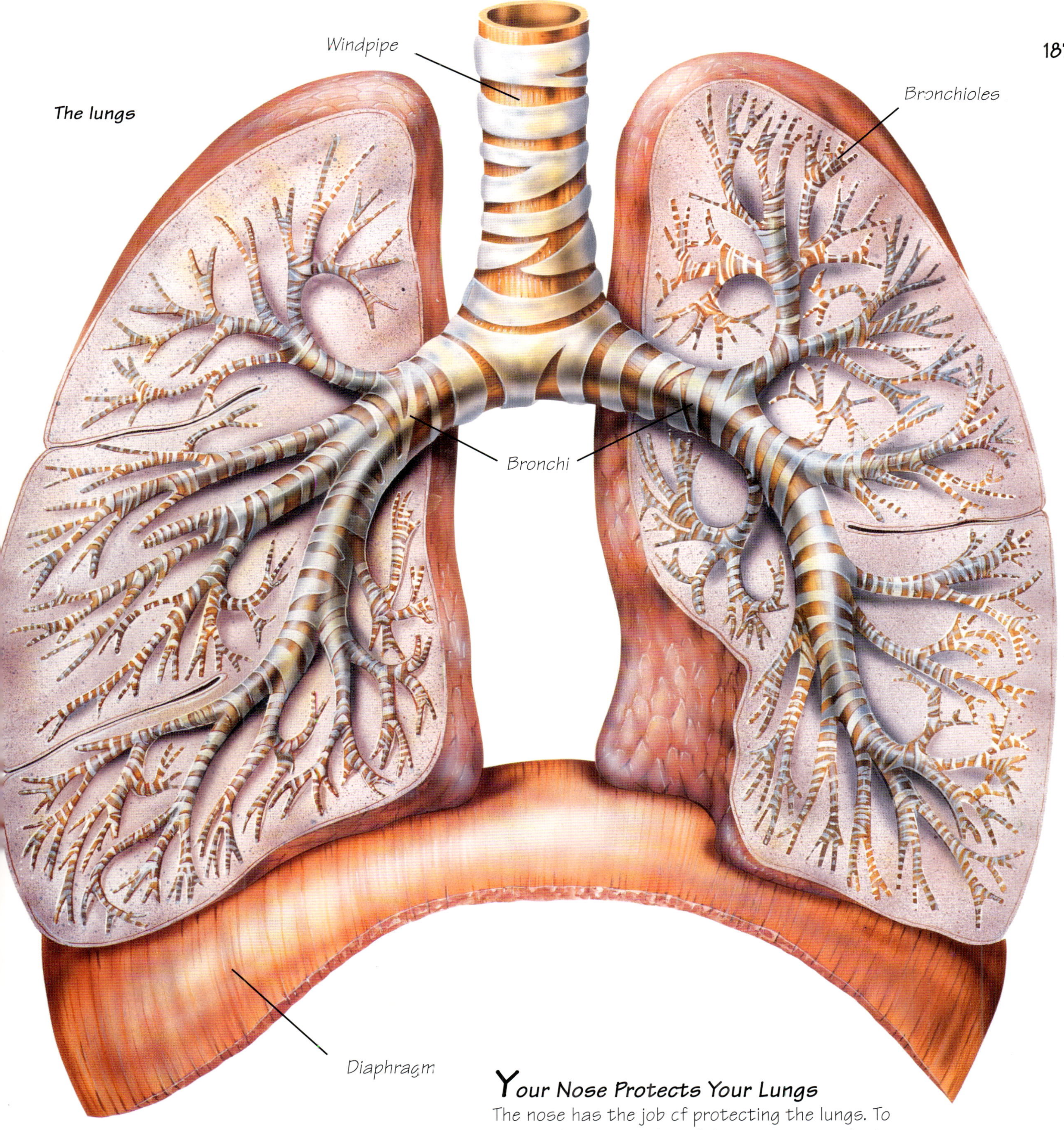

The lungs

Your Nose Protects Your Lungs

The nose has the job cf protecting the lungs. To prevent large particles of dust going into the lungs, the nose contains hairs which act as a dust screen. Smaller dust particles that can pass through the hairs are caught by a sticky mucus in the nose. This mucus is either expelled from the nose when you sneeze or when you blow your nose, or it is swa lowed. Air going into the lungs must be of a reasonable temperature and moistness. If the air is too cold, it is warmed up by blood vessels in the nasal cavity. If it is too dry, t is moistened in the nose before entering the windpipe.

Babies Breathe Faster

The rate at which a person breathes varies according to age and fitness, and the amount of activity taking place. A baby breathes about 65 time a minute but a person of around 40 years of age is breathing approximately 18 times a minute.

The Heart and Blood

The heart pumps blood around the body. The heart has four main parts — a left and a right auricle, and a left and a right ventricle. Blood carrying oxygen from the lungs enters the left auricle and is forced through a valve into the left ventricle. It is then pumped from there into the aorta, the body's main artery, to flow around the body. On the right side of the heart, blood that has been around the body and picked up waste products goes through the right auricle and the right ventricle to be pumped towards the lungs. In the lungs, the blood gets rid of carbon dioxide and takes on oxygen, ready to go back to the heart and start the journey all over again.

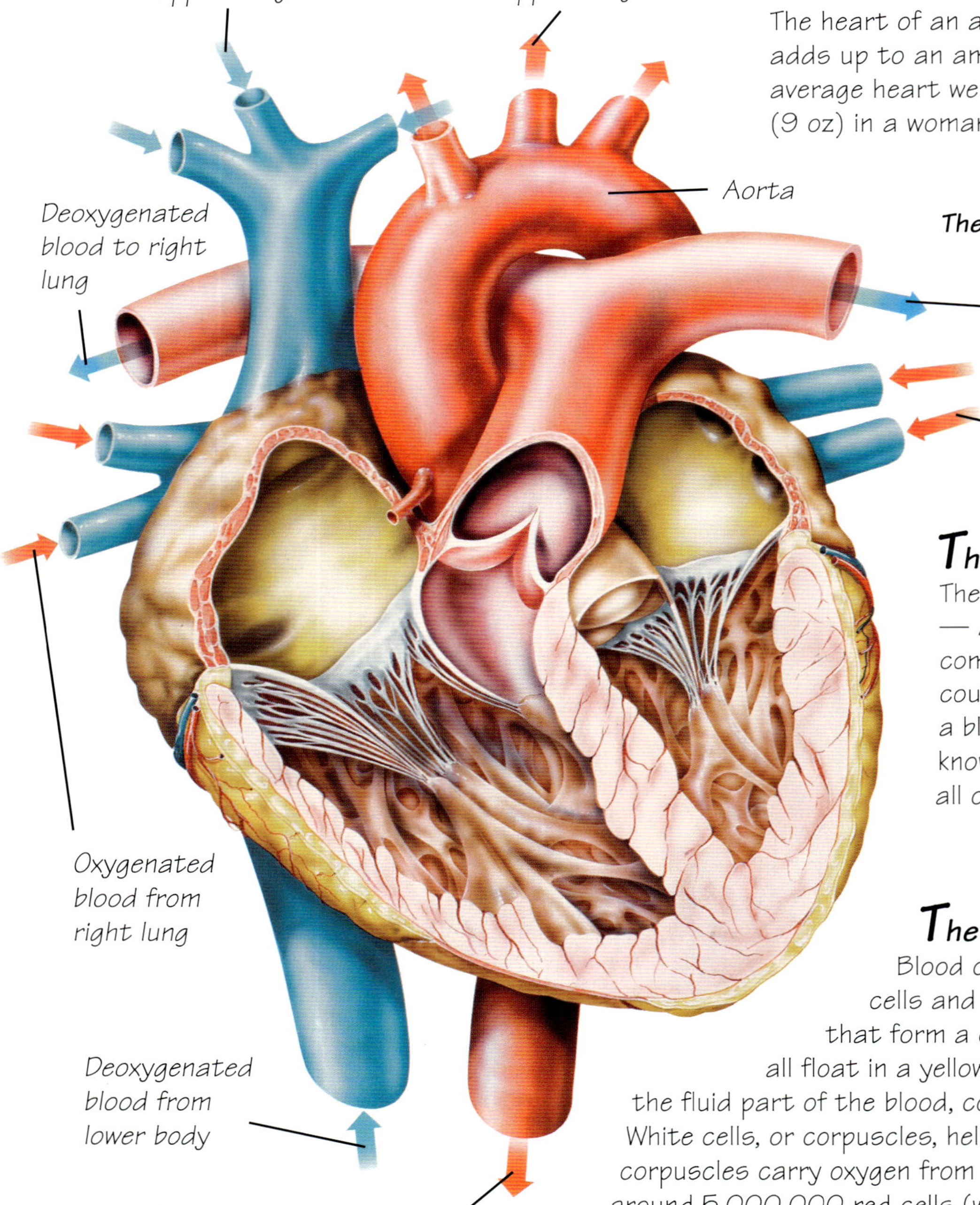

The heart

Your Heart Beats 37 Million Times A Year

The heart of an adult beats 70 times a minute, which adds up to an amazing 37 million beats in a year. The average heart weighs 310 g (11 oz) in a man and 260 g (9 oz) in a woman and is about the size of a clenched fist.

There Are Four Basic Blood Groups

There are four basic types, or groups, of blood — A, B, AB and O. Group O is the most common, but this varies from country to country. If a person is badly injured and needs a blood transfusion, the doctor needs to know the patient's blood group, because not all of them can mix with other groups.

The Make Up Of Blood

Blood consists of red blood cells, white blood cells and platelets. Platelets are tiny particles that form a clot when there is a cut to the skin. They all float in a yellow liquid called plasma. Plasma, which is the fluid part of the blood, contains the food required by the body. White cells, or corpuscles, help to fight infection and the red corpuscles carry oxygen from the lungs to the tissues. There are around 5,000,000 red cells (which give blood its red colour) and 8,000 white cells to each cubic centimetre (3/5 cubic inch) of blood.

Lands and People

The World's People

The people of the world are made up of many different nationalities, each with its own history, language, customs and culture. People are all essentially the same, but we have simply developed differently according to where we live. We may have different facial features, hair, skin, languages and different beliefs but we all belong to the same human species.

In Future, People May Live On Other Planets

People have made their homes wherever they could find food and water, and in places where the weather was suitable for living. Some people live in inhospitable places, but have adapted their way of life to survive. Originally, communities were small, but as trade and population increased more people began living in towns and cities. Nowadays, even the large cities are becoming so overcrowded that it is possible that at some time in the future people may have to live in towns in the polar regions, deserts and perhaps beneath the sea, or even on other planets. These towns would have to be specially built to protect people from harsh environments.

There Are Three Main Racial Groups

The peoples of the world form three main racial groups — caucasoid (white skinned), mongoloid (yellow skinned) and negroid (black skinned). At one time caucasoids lived mainly in Europe, mongoloids in Asia (although the group also includes Inuits and Native Americans) and negroids in Africa. Now people of all three groups live together and inter-relate all over the world.

Costumes Around The World

National flags

By 2030 World Population Could Reach Nine Billion

The population of the world is rising rapidly because the number of people being born is higher than the number of people dying. In the 1st century AD, the world population was 200,000,000. This figure had doubled by 1500 and that figure tripled by 1900 to over one billion people. During the 20th century the numbers increased at an alarming rate and by 1997 there were 5,840,000,000 people living on Earth. There are now almost 200 babies born every minute, so within the next 30 years there could be 9,000,000,000 people living on our very overcrowded planet.

Denmark Has The Oldest National Flag

Every country of the world has its own flag, a symbol that represents the country and its people. Often the flag incorporates something of the history of the country. For example, the flag of the USA has 13 stripes that stand for the 13 states that first formed the United States. The oldest national flag is that of Denmark, but other flags and banners have been flown ever since ancient times. According to legend, the Danish flag floated out of the sky to encourage Danish forces in a battle against the Estonians.

Did You Know?

The smallest country in the world is the Vatican City, which measures 0.4 sq km (0.15 sq mi)!

Antarctica is the only land area in the world not claimed by any country.

The entire world population could stand shoulder-to-shoulder on the island of Jamaica.

One fifth of the world's population lives in China.

Global population is rising by 77 million every year.

Britain's 'God Save the Queen (or King)' is the oldest national anthem in the world, and was first performed in 1745.

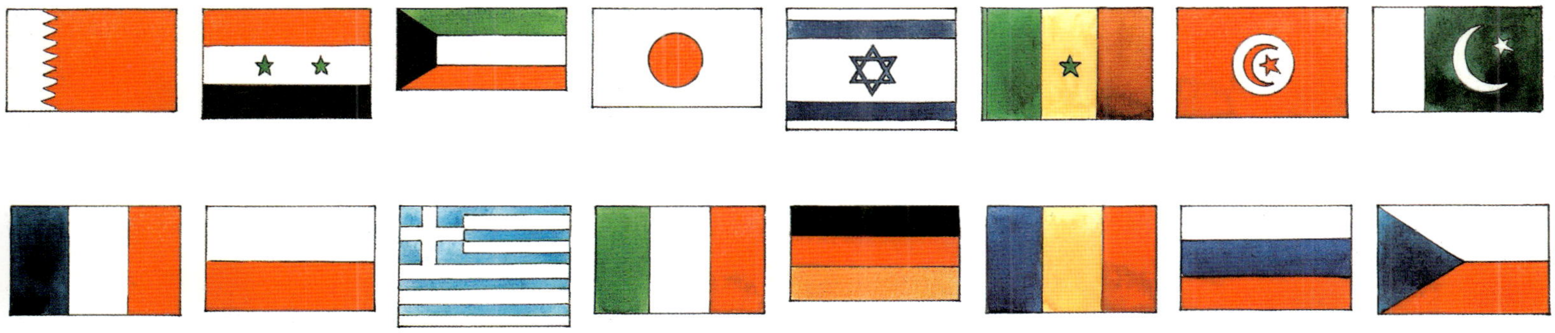

How Countries are Governed

As soon as people began to live in communities there was a need for a person or a group to organize things and to set out rules for the community. In small communities, the strongest or wisest man frequently became the chief or ruler and this position was often passed on in the same family. Wise rulers would seek the advice of ministers but sometimes these ministers would become as powerful as the ruler. Today every country has a head of state, some with greater power than others.

Nigerian king

Absolute Monarchs Have Power

A monarch is a ruler, such as a king or queen. Mostly, the title to the monarchy is hereditary — it is passed down through the family, usually to the eldest son. There are two forms of monarchy. In an absolute monarchy, all the power is in the hands of one person. In a constitutional monarchy, the monarch's powers are limited by law.

A Dictator Is Not Subject To Laws

A dictatorship is when a country is ruled by one person who is not subject to any laws. It is the opposite of democracy. In a democracy, ordinary people have a say in how the country is run.

The World's Oldest Parliament Is In Iceland

The oldest parliament in the world is the Althing of Iceland, which was formed in 930 AD. It was abolished in 1800 but re-established in 1843. The parliament with the longest unbroken history is the Tynwald on the Isle of Man, which was established over a thousand years ago.

Indians queueing to vote

Did You Know?

There are 191 independent countries in the world – but this figure tends to fluctuate!

In 1998, Amnesty International reported that 141 countries were not respecting human rights.

Democracy originated in the city-states of ancient Greece.

USSR was the first communist state, founded after the revolution of 1917.

Fidel Castro, who has ruled Cuba since 1959, has been in charge longer than any other leader.

In Denmark, any citizen can request a personal audience with the queen.

Democracy Was Devised By The Greeks

Democracy means government by the people. The country is run by a group that have been elected into power by the people. If the people dislike the group in power, they can vote against them in an election. Democracy is a system that was first devised by the ancient Greeks, in which all citizens had the right to vote. Not every inhabitant was classed as a citizen, however. Women, foreigners and slaves were not allowed to vote. In most modern democracies every sane, law-abiding adult can cast their vote for the government they want.

A Republic Has A President

Some democracies are republics, in which the head of state is an elected president. A few democracies have have a monarch instead of a president, but he or she has very little real power as the country is administered by a parliament.

Languages and Communications

Some people believe that most of the world's languages developed from one common language spoken in Asia in the distant past. As people spread out around the world, so different languages developed. It is estimated that there are some 3,000 different languages spoken around the world. Chinese, in its Mandarin, Cantonese and other forms, is spoken by the most number of people. The next most widely spoken language is English, followed by Spanish.

Mobile phone user

Technology Is Changing Language

Radio, television, satellites and mobile phones, as well as the increasing movement of people for business and pleasure, have brought the peoples of the world closer together through communication. Many words, especially technological ones, are the same in several languages. With the increasing use of the internet, on which the dominant language is American English, more and more people will use American English to communicate in the future.

Writing Started As Drawings On Walls

Writing probably started when primitive people began drawing pictures on the walls of caves. Later these pictures could have developed into warning signs or simple messages for others to read. The Egyptians used a form of picture writing and so did the Sumerians of Babylonia, who later simplified them into curved shapes. By around 1500 BC, the first alphabet was invented and 500 years later there were four well established alphabets — Hebrew, Cyrillic, Arabic and Greek.

Signpost showing different alphabets

Did You Know?

The most widely spoken language in the world is Chinese (Mandarin), which is used by over 1 billion people!

There are over 6,000 languages spoken in the world.

The sequoia tree in America is named after the Cherokee Indian Sequoyah, who invented the first Native American alphabet.

Clay tablets inscribed with writing have been found in the ancient Sumerian city of Uruk, dating from 3400 BC.

The discovery in 1799 of the Rosetta Stone, a tablet from 196 BC inscribed in three languages, enabled modern scholars to decipher the hieroglyphs of ancient Egypt.

In 1887, a Polish doctor invented a universal language called Esperanto in the hope that it would lead to world peace.

Native Americans Used Sign Language

Speech and writing are not the only forms of communication. The Native North Americans had a highly developed system of hand signals to communicate with tribes who spoke a different language. Shepherds in the mountains of the Canary Islands communicate with one another with a system of whistles. Many blind people learn to read Braille, a writing method composed of raised dots which was invented by Louis Braille in 1834.

Codes Send Messages Over Long Distances

Before the telegraph was invented semaphore, a code invented in 1822, was used to send messages over long distances. Semaphore stations, posts with moveable arms, proved very successful. Semaphore denotes the letters of the alphabet by the position of the two arms and it was later realised that this would work equally well with a person holding two flags. Morse code, a system of dots and dashes to represent letters was invented by Samuel Morse to transmit words by electric telegraph before the invention of radio. Morse Code was used by ships at sea until the end of the 20th century.

Home Sweet Home

Houses can take many forms and are traditionally built with materials that are readily available. The first homes were made in caves, but caves are not found everywhere so shelters had to be specially built using what material there was available. In forest areas wood and branches were used, in open areas mud huts were built. Buildings in wetlands are often made of reeds and the Inuit used the only material they had available — ice.

Mud homes in Mali, Africa

Igloos Are Built In A Spiral

The traditional Inuit igloo, which is only used as a temporary home, is made from large blocks cut from the ice. These are arranged in a circular form and shaped so that each layer moves up in a spiral. The blocks are also placed slightly overlapping so that they meet to form a domed roof. The blocks are cemented together with water which quickly freezes hard. Igloos provide excellent protection from the cold.

Some Houses Are Made Of Mud Bricks

Houses in many parts of Africa and the near East are often built with mud. The mud is usually formed into bricks and the roofs are thatched. This makes them cheap and easy to build and surprisingly cool to live in.

Bedouin tent

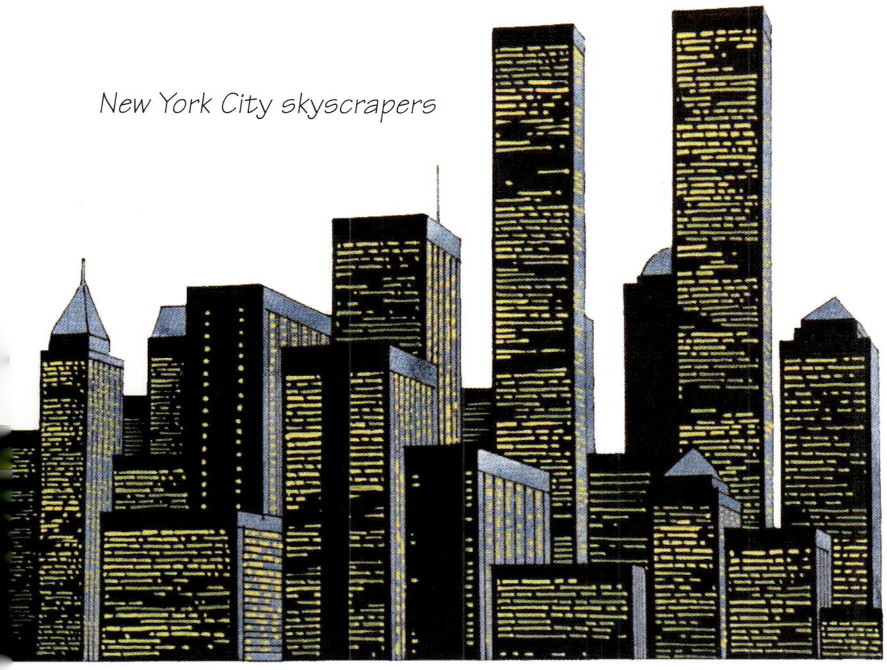

New York City skyscrapers

Many City Buildings Are Made Of Concrete

More and more people today live in cities where many of the buildings are built using reinforced concrete — concrete embedded with rods of steel to give it strength. Because land is expensive in city areas, many buildings are built tall, so that a lot of people can occupy a small area of ground. These buildings are called skyscrapers.

Bedouin Tents Are Made Of Camel Hair

Nomads — people who move from one place to another — carry their homes with them. The Bedouins who live in the arid areas of the Middle East live in tents woven from camel hair. These days, many Bedouins have given up the nomadic way of life to work in towns or on farms.

Did You Know?

In the Amazonian rainforest, the families of a Yanomami village all live under one enormous roof.

The Dogon people of Mali, Africa, construct their villages entirely out of mud.

An experienced Inuit can build a comfortable igloo out of a block of ice in one hour!

The nomadic Tuareg people of the Sahara live in tents made from goat skins or mats woven from palm leaves.

Tokyo contains the most people of any city, and 21 per cent of Japan's population lives there.

The ancient Romans invented many things we associate with modern cities, such as sewers and piped water.

Feeding the World

Food is something none of us can do without but the type of food we eat depends upon where we live, our beliefs and customs, our lifestyle and how rich or poor we are. Modern ways of growing food, new techniques to preserve it (such as canning and freezing), and faster means of transporting it (such as by aeroplane) have increased the variety of foods available to the richer countries.

Rice fields

Rice And Wheat Are Staple Foods

In many countries, for a lot of people, rice forms the staple diet — the basic food they eat each day. Rice is a form of grass. It is grown in flooded fields called paddies. In flat areas the fields are given walls of mud to keep the water in, but in hilly areas terraces are cut into the hillside and the water flows down through channels in the soil.

Another type of grass is wheat, which is used to make bread, something that has been a staple food for thousands of years. Huge areas of Canada, the USA, and southern Russia are used to grow vast quantities of wheat.

Did You Know?

Over 500 million tonnes of wheat are produced each year.

One in every 120 people is, or has been, a refugee, displaced by such things as famine and war.

In 1990, the USSR produced a record wheat crop – but stores in Moscow and Leningrad had no bread!

In 1982-4, 800,000 people died when war and drought caused famine in Ethiopia.

Band Aid, a world-wide concert held in July 1985, raised $70 million for famine relief.

The Huang He River is known as China's Sorrow because of the famines it causes when it floods.

People Starve Because Of Global Warming

In the world's poorer countries, many people are subsistence farmers. This means that they grow only enough for their families to eat. They do not grow surplus crops to sell. If their crops fail through drought or floods, or if they have to abandon their farms because of war, they have no money to buy food and will starve. There are ever more droughts and floods, due to global warming.

Large Fishing Fleets Damage Stocks Of Fish

The sea provides us with large amounts of food, but there is so much fishing that fish and other sea creatures are becoming scarce in some places. Traditional fishing methods do not take many fish from the sea. Even the large scooped nets used in China and India do not push the numbers down very much. It is the large fishing fleets that do much of the damage and in some places fishermen have been ordered to keep fishing down to a certain level, to allow stocks to replenish.

Combine harvester

Religions and Beliefs

Right from the earliest times, people have worshipped gods, and many different religions have come into being throughout the ages. The idea that there was just one supreme creator of the universe, who was greater than other spirits, was first taught by the Persian religious reformer Zoroaster in the 7th century BC.

Muslims Face Towards Mecca To Pray

Mohammed, the prophet of Islam was born in Mecca (in what is now Saudi Arabia) in AD 570. He died in 632. The holy book of Islam, the Koran, which sets out the revelations made by Allah (or God) to Mohammed when he went into the desert to meditate, was written in 650. All good Muslims must observe the five pillars of Islam. The five pillars are: confession of faith in one god and Mohammed, prayer five times daily, giving alms (money) to the poor, fasting, and pilgrimage to Mecca, where Mohammed was born. Muslims must face towards Mecca when they pray.

Muslims praying

Christians Believe That Jesus Was The Son Of God

The Bible is the most important book in Christian religion. It has two main parts. The Old Testament tells the history of the Jewish people, and the New Testament which describes the life and works of Jesus Christ and his disciples. Christians believe that Jesus was the son of God but the Romans who ruled Palestine, where Jesus lived, regarded him as a troublemaker and had him executed.

Jews Believe That The Messiah Has Yet To Come

Judaism, the religion of the Jews, is based on the teachings of the Old Testament of the Bible and the Talmud (the book of Jewish law and legend). Judaism teaches that there is one God (Jehovah) and that a Messiah (deliverer) will come but they do not believe, as Christians do, that Jesus Christ was the Messiah.

Stained glass window in a church

Did You Know?

Adam's Peak in Sri Lanka is visited by pilgrims from different religions who believe that a footprint there was made by Krishna (Hindus), Adam (Muslims), Buddha (Buddhists) or St Thomas (Christians).

94 per cent of Hindus live in Asia.

In 1992, after 359 years, the Roman Catholic Church accepted that Galileo had been right – the earth does travel around the sun!

Thousands of Buddhists gathered at Taiwan's main airport in 1998 to watch the arrival of Buddha's tooth.

The European Union decided in 1998 that Communion wafers must have a sell-by date.

The Holy Shroud of Turin, believed to be the burial shroud of Christ, has been carbon-dated to 1330.

Buddhism Is A Way Of Life

The founder of Buddhism was Gautama, the son of an Indian king. He gave away his riches and devoted his life to search for a solution to the world's unhappiness. While sitting beneath a bodi tree, he had a vision about the true purpose of life and began to teach the eight 'paths' to perfect peace. Buddhism is a way of life, not a religion. Its followers do not worship the Buddha.

Hindus Believe In Reincarnation

The basis of Hinduism is the belief in Brahma, the supreme spirit, who works through two gods, Vishnu the preserver, and Siva the destroyer. Hindus believe in reincarnation and that those who are bad will return in a lower state. The good return as higher beings, eventually to have their souls merged with the supreme spirit.

Money and Trading

When people first began trading with one another they simply exchanged goods. A farmer, for example, may have exchanged some meat for an axe. This system is known as barter, but as trading became more complicated it proved difficult to operate fairly. Token goods, such as shells, began to be used and these were gradually replaced by pieces of metal, often gold or silver. The first coins (actually stamped pieces of metal) were made as far back as the 7th century BC, in Asia Minor.

Each Country Has Its Own Currency

A currency is the money system used by a country. In Britain, the main unit of currency is the pound which is divided into 100 pence, the USA has the dollar made up of 100 cents, France has the franc, Germany the mark and Russia the rouble. Other currencies include the yen (Japan), peso (Spain), krone (Denmark), rupee (India) and the rand (South Africa). Because these currencies all have different values on the world market, an exchange rate is used. This is what it costs to buy or sell one currency for another.

Cattle Were Once Used As Currency

In times gone by many things have been used as money. Cattle was once regarded as the main form of currency and are still seen as a sign of wealth in parts of Africa and Asia. Cowrie shells were often used in the same way that we use coins, and on the island of Yap, in the Pacific Ocean, large stones, some too big to move, were used. Other items used as a means of exchange include tea, salt and soap. A few years ago in Italy, when small coins became scarce, people used stamps and sweets instead. These days trading can be done without coins or notes by using cheques, credit cards and direct bank payments.

Credit cards

Indian street market

Trade Involves Exchanging Money

Trading takes place at many levels. Buying something from a shop or market involves an exchange of money. So does the buying and selling of stocks and share on the world's stock markets, or the provision of services such as having your car washed or your garden dug. Millions of such transaction take place every day and all result in the movement of money.

Ancient World

Early Man

Modern humans originally came from a group of animals called primates. Over millions of years they developed into apes, then hominids (semi humans) and then into modern humans. In prehistoric times, the first humans lived by hunting animals and gathering fruit and plants to eat. They lived a nomadic life, moving from place to place in search of new food and land. They made their homes in caves or in basic shelters.

Ape (Australopithecus)

Hominid: Homo habilis

Human: Homo sapiens sapiens

Ice Age home

Birth Of Farming

As they developed, humans began giving up the nomadic life to settle in communities. Their lives changed and they became farmers rather than hunters. They cultivated the land and began keeping animals instead of relying upon hunting. They also began making things, such as weapons, for themselves instead of relying solely upon what they could find lying around. Groups of people started working together for the good of their community. As these communities developed, trade was built up between different areas. Such changes marked the first steps towards a civilized society.

First Civilizations

In the Ice Age, humans lived very basic lives, hunting and making fire for warmth and cooking food. When the Ice Age ended, 10,000 years ago, civilization (a way of life that includes art, science, learning and a sense of community), began to develop. One of the first civilizations grew up along the River Euphrates in what is now southern Iraq. The people who lived there, the Sumerians, invented writing and were renowned for their superb architecture.

Did You Know?

The oldest pottery ever was discovered in Japan, dating back to 10,000 BC.

Hand prints have been found from 10,000 years ago. People made these by holding their hands against cave walls and blowing pigment over them.

The oldest pieces of human art are 47,000-year-old engravings on rocks in Australia, believed to show kangaroo and bird tracks.

In about 2500 BC, prehistoric people at Stonehenge, England, somehow positioned 25-tonne blocks of stone in a perfect ring to line up with the sunrise on midsummer's day.

The oldest prehistoric human skeleton was named Lucy, because the Beatles' song 'Lucy in the Sky with Diamonds' was playing when it was found in 1974.

Invention Of Writing

An important invention that helped civilizations to further develop was that of writing. For the first time humans could keep a record of past events and pass on information other than by word of mouth. From this point, future generations could learn from the thoughts and discoveries of their ancestors.

The Discovery Of Fire

No-one knows how humans first discovered fire, but it is thought that it was between one and a half and two million years ago. It could have been the result of striking two stones together that caused a spark to ignite some dry grass. Whatever it was, it changed the way that humans lived because fire allowed them to keep warm, keep animals away from the settlements by scaring them off, and see in the dark. Later it was used for cooking, pottery-making and metal-working — a skill that gave humankind more sophisticated tools and weapons.

Life in Ancient Egypt

Egyptian civilization began to develop around 4000 BC along the banks of the River Nile and flourished for over three thousand years until Egypt was conquered by the Romans. At first there were two kingdoms, Upper Egypt and Lower Egypt, but these merged into one around 3500 BC.

Importance Of The Nile

The River Nile was vital to the people of Egypt. Each year the river would flood as a result of rains falling in the mountains to the south. When the water subsided the area would be coated with a thick layer of fertile soil in which crops would flourish. The farmers learnt to control the flood waters to irrigate (water) their crops. They used ditches and gates to adjust the amount of water going into the fields.

The Tomb Of Tutankhamun

The Egyptians believed that the human soul lived on after death. They preserved the bodies of the dead and buried them in coffins and then in tombs. Because of Egypt's dry climate, the contents of many tombs remained perfectly preserved through the centuries. Those that remain have given historians a unique picture of Egyptian life. Possibly the most famous tomb is that of the boy king (pharaoh) Tutankhamun who reigned from about 1360 to 1350 BC. It was discovered in the Valley of the Kings at Thebes, Egypt in 1922. It became famous for the treasures that were discovered in it.

An Egyptian scene

Tombs Of The Pharaohs

The pharaohs of Egypt were buried in tombs, often built in the form of pyramids.

Their bodies were mummified to preserve them for their journey in the next life. The body was then put into a mummy case and sealed up in a tomb. Many treasures and other objects were buried with the pharaoh too.

Mummy case

Writing With Pictures

The Egyptians developed a form of picture writing, known as hieroglyphics, and many of the tombs are decorated with this writing. Historians have learnt a great deal about life in ancient Egypt by studying these pictures.

The Biggest Pyramid

The largest Egyptian pyramid is that of King Cheops at Giza which was built around 2500 BC. It was originally 146 m (480 ft) high and 231 m (758 ft) long at the base. It contained 2,300,00 limestone blocks.

Did You Know?

The Great Pyramid at Giza contains over 2 million limestone blocks, each weighing between 2.5 and 15 tonnes!

The tallest lighthouse ever built, the 120-metre (393-foot) high Pharos of Alexandria, guided ancient Egyptian ships into Alexandria for over a thousand years!

The Egyptians believed the sun travelled across the sky each day in a beautiful barge.

Not just people, but crocodiles, dogs and thousands of cats were made into mummies.

The female pharaoh Hathshepsut wore a false beard to show she was king.

Egyptians wore cones of beautifully scented fat in their wigs, which gave off its aroma as it melted and slid down the hair!

Ancient Greece

Ancient Greek civilization was founded about 2000 BC. Because the area is so mountainous, communication between cities was difficult. So they developed city states which were ruled separately, but shared a common culture. The Greeks produced superb sculpture, great literature and monumental buildings. They also invented democracy (fair government).

Did You Know?

The ancient Greeks had criminal courts – with 200 people in the jury!

If enough people voted against unpopular politicians, the politician had to leave Athens for 10 years.

The Greeks believed that by going to shrines called oracles, they could ask the gods to tell them the future.

Some boys in ancient Greece were accompanied to school by a slave, whose job was to make sure they paid attention.

Wars in Ancient Greece were stopped every four years so that the Olympic Games could take place!

The Hippocratic Oath sworn by modern doctors takes its name from the doctor Hippocrates.

Athenian coins

Coins Of Gold And Silver

The first coins were minted in Lydia (part of present-day Turkey) around 650 BC. The Greeks copied the idea and made coins of their own from gold and silver. They bore images of the gods and heroes, or emblems of the cities where they were made. The coins for Athens, for example, showed the owl of Athene who was the patron goddess of the city.

Homes Of The Gods

The ancient Greeks worshipped many gods and goddesses. Among them were Zeus (god of the sky), Poseidon (god of the sea), Hebe (goddess of youth) and Aphrodite (goddess of love). Numerous temples were built in honour of these deities and sacrifices made to them. One of the finest temples was the Parthenon (built 447 — 438 BC) in Athens. It was dedicated to Athene, goddess of wisdom, arts and crafts.

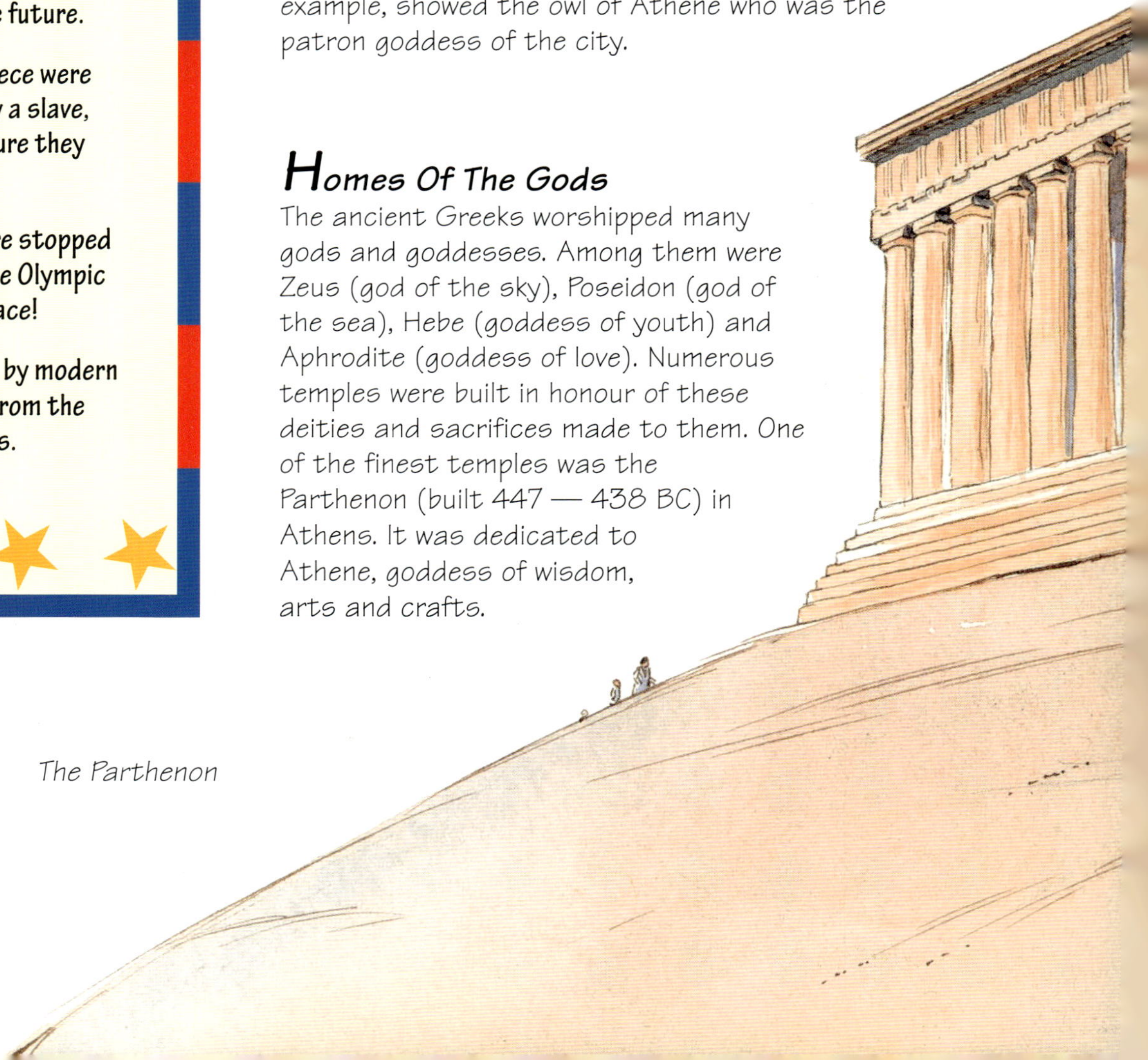

The Parthenon

Birth Of The Olympics

The Greeks were great athletes and there were over 200 different sports festivals in Greece and the lands around the Mediterranean Sea. Most famous of these was the Olympic Games, named after Mount Olympus, the home of the Greek gods. They first took place in 776 BC. At first, running was the only sport, but later other sports and even music, poetry and drama competitions were added. The games were held every four years until AD 393, when they were abolished by the emperor of Rome.

The Greeks At War

The ancient Greeks were often at war. In 490 and 479 BC they defeated Persian invaders. From 431 BC to 362 BC the Greek states were constantly at war with one another. These civil wars weakened the country and gave Philip II of Macedon (an area north of Greece) the chance to conquer it in 338 BC. Greece remained under Macedonian rule until it became part of the Roman Empire in the 2nd century BC.

The Roman Empire

The Roman Empire began when the Romans set out to conquer the rest of Italy, which they achieved by 272 BC. They then went on to conquer parts of north-west Africa and other lands around the Mediterranean Sea. Between 58 BC and 51 BC they invaded Gaul (the Roman name for the Celtic areas of northern Italy, France and Belgium) and Britain, but had to withdraw from Britain because of unrest in Gaul. Britain was not added to the Empire until AD 43. By AD 117 the mighty Romans ruled much of the ancient world.

Romans Spent A Lot Of Time at the Baths

Most big towns had public baths where the Romans could relax and meet friends. Before entering the actual baths, they had their slaves rub olive oil on their skin and scrape it and the dirt off with scrapers called strigils.

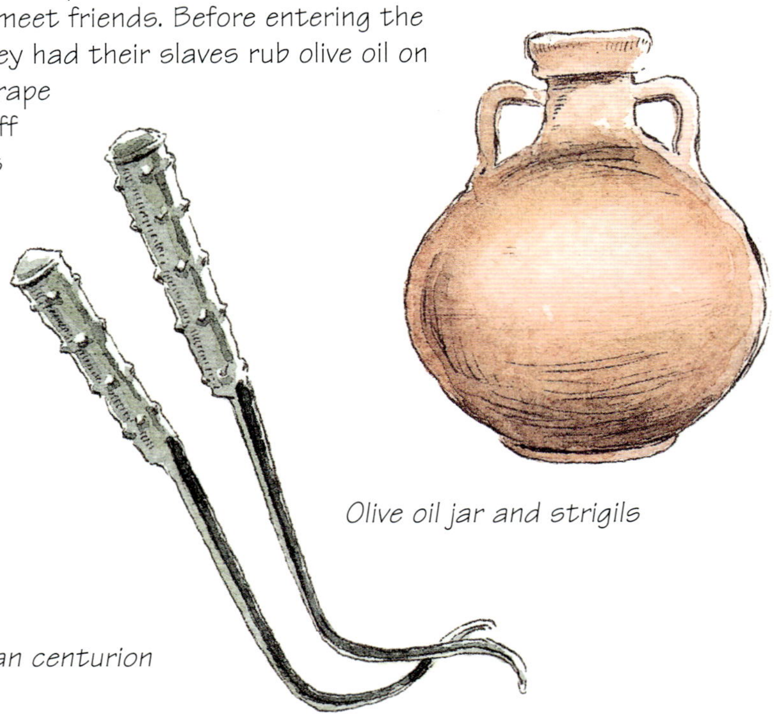

Olive oil jar and strigils

Roman centurion

They Were Great Builders And Engineers

The Romans built long straight roads, bridges and aqueducts, strong garrisons and beautiful villas. They also invented a system of central heating and public drainage.

A Mighty Army

The Romans established their empire thanks to their mighty army. This was made up of legions in each of which were 6,000 men. Each legion consisted of ten cohorts (military units) and in each cohort there were six centuries, each of one hundred men.

Did You Know?

★

The ancient Romans introduced public swimming baths, with hot and cold baths, steam rooms, manicure shops and gymnasiums.

Central heating was a Roman invention.

Roman householders kept weasels to catch rats!

The Romans built over 80,000 km (49,700 mi) of roads across their enormous empire.

The Acta Diurna, which was displayed in public places during Julius Caesar's days, was the world's first daily newspaper!

Hadrian's Wall, built around AD 120, was 6 m (3.5 ft) high and stretched across the entire width of northern Britain.

Founders Reared By A Wolf

According to legend, Rome was founded in 753 BC by two brothers, Romulus and Remus. They had been brought up by a she-wolf who found them unharmed after they had been thrown in the River Tiber by their uncle. The wolf fed them on her milk and a woodpecker brought them food. They were then brought up by a shepherd and later founded the city of Rome at the place where they had been taken from the river. The city was built on seven hills, the Capitoline, the Aventine, the Esquiline, the Caelian, the Palantine, the Viminal and the Quirinal.

Hadrian's Wall

Emperor Hadrian ordered the building of the wall in the north of Britain as a symbol of Roman authority. It was also an attempt to stop tribes from the north raiding Roman lands. Built by Roman soldiers, it probably took 16 years to complete. At every mile there was a fort staffed by at least eight soldiers. Between the forts were two turrets so the soldiers could keep a constant watch along the whole 120 km (75 mi) of the wall.

Hadrian's Wall

Raiders from the Sea

The Vikings were a group of people, the Norsemen, from the coastal areas of Norway, Denmark and Sweden. They were great seamen, explorers and traders. The first Viking raids on Britain took place in AD 789, but the main raids began four years later and continued right through to the 11th century. They also raided Ireland, Scotland, parts of France, Spain and what is now Russia. They also discovered islands to the west of Greenland and part of the North American continent.

Viking brooch

Skilled Shipbuilders And Sailors

The Vikings were skilled navigators and brilliant shipbuilders. Viking longships were up to 30 m (100 ft) long, built of oak and carried anything from 20 to 60 men. They could sail the oceans and were built to allow them to land on shelved beaches or sail up long stretches of river to get further inland. The front and back of the ship were carved to resemble the heads of strange and wild beasts and the ships were powered by oars.

Viking raiders

Talented craftspeople

Although the Vikings were warlike they were also beauty lovers. Their craftsmen produced superb pieces of jewellery and armour. Necklaces, cloak pins, finger rings and brooches of superb workmanship and beauty have been found by archaeologists. Even Viking swords were beautifully decorated and considered so valuable they were probably handed down from father to son.

Did You Know?

The Viking Leif Eriksson discovered America 500 years before Christopher Columbus!

The expression to 'go berserk' comes from the Vikings. They had special warriors called berserkers who would go into a frenzy when they went into battle.

Important Vikings were buried with an entire ship!

Iceland's parliament, the Althing, is named after Viking councils called 'things'.

The Vikings used an alphabet made up of characters called runes.

Viking sailors kept ravens on their ships, which they released and followed when they wanted to find land!

A Viking Heaven

According to Viking mythology, selected warrior heroes would go to Valhalla, the Hall of the Slain, when they died in battle. It was a glittering palace with walls covered in gold and silver shields. Each morning the warriors would go out and fight with one another before returning to the hall to enjoy a feast with Odin, chief of the gods.

The Valkyries, Odin's handmaidens, were the ones who decided which warriors were to die in battle. They would then take them to Valhalla.

Men who had been cowards in life were sent to the realm of Hel, goddess of death and queen of the underworld.

Trading Far And Wide

The Vikings were also great traders and travelled as far as the Mediterranean and the Black Sea to exchange their furs and honey for silver and spices. Their trade voyages also took them to the Middle East, where they traded with the Arabs in Baghdad.

Central American Civilization

The three great civilizations of South America were the Incas, the Aztecs and the Mayas. The Mayas were a major tribe of South Americans who established an amazing civilization in Central America from the 3rd to 9th centuries AD. The Aztecs settled in the central valley of Mexico from around 1200 where they built up a powerful empire. They were defeated by the Spanish in 1521. The Incas who had migrated from Peru in 1250 ruled a great empire in the Andes from 1438 up until the Spanish conquistador Pizarro arrived in 1532 and destroyed the Inca civilization.

The Aztecs Invented Chocolate

The Aztecs used to make a chocolate drink from ground cocoa beans and honey, flavoured with spices. Chocolate was taken back to Europe by the Spanish and our word 'chocolate' comes from the Aztec name for their drink — *chocolatl*.

The Inca Empire

The Inca Empire reached from the middle of present-day Chile right up to the north of Ecuador some 3,200 km (2,000 mi) away.

Mayan Astronomers

The Mayans are famous for their great knowledge of astronomy and mathematics. They built observatories on the top of buildings, like the royal palace at Palenque, so they could study the heavens.

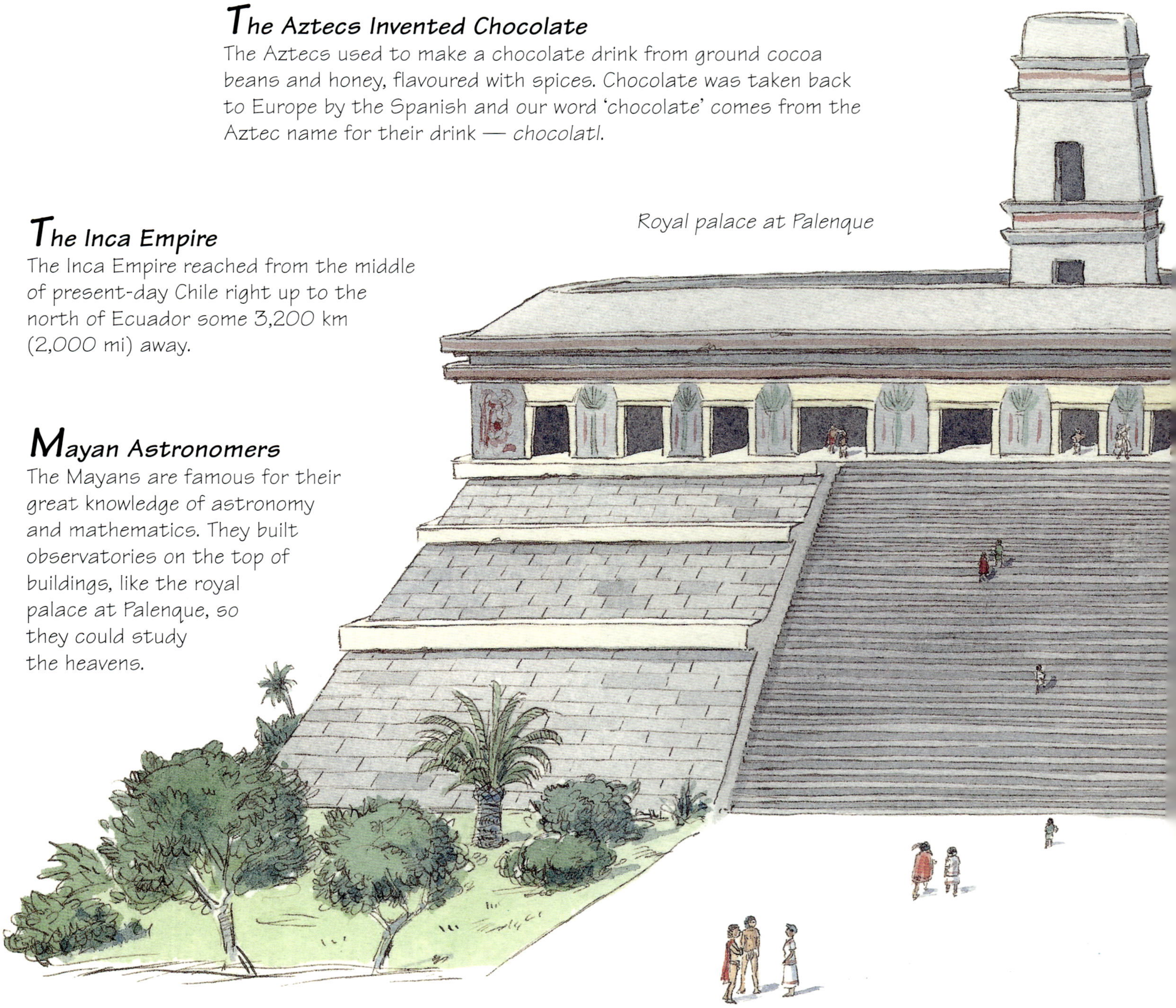

Royal palace at Palenque

Quetzalcoatl

How Mexico City Was Founded

In 1168 the Aztecs received a vision of Quetzalcoatl, the great feathered god, who commanded them to look for the permanent home he had selected for them. He said they would find an island on a lake where he would reappear as a golden eagle carrying a snake in its talons. The eagle would settle on a cactus and there they should build a capital city. Over 150 years later the prophecy came true and the Aztecs built the city of Tenochtitlán, which means 'cactus rock', on islands in Lake Texcoco. It had a population of about 300,000 people.

Tenochtitlán is known today as Mexico city and the Mexican flag shows the eagle perched on a cactus with a snake in its beak.

Did You Know?

The Pyramid of the Sun, built in the ancient American city of Teotihuacan, is almost as big as the Great Pyramid at Giza!

The Aztec city of Tenochtitlán was five times the size of London, and had canals, aqueducts and a zoo.

The Maya built enormous sports arenas and manufactured rubber balls to play games with.

To keep their gods happy, the Aztecs sacrificed thousands of people by cutting out their hearts.

The Inca had a social security system, where people paid taxes to help look after the poor!

The Inca built over 11,000 km (6,864 mi) of roads – as straight as those of the Romans – complete with magnificent suspension bridges!

The Lure Of Inca Gold

The Incas believed their king to be the son of the Sun god and they built great temples in which to worship the Sun. They had no system of writing but were very expert in architecture, pottery, weaving and similar crafts. But it was their gold that proved to be their downfall when the Spanish arrived. The Incas gave gold offerings, sometimes in the form of small animals, to the gods but the Spaniards wanted the gold for themselves.

The Centre of the World

Chinese civilization began around 1500 BC and flourishes to this day. The ancient Chinese believed that their country was the centre of the world. It was certainly a centre for excellence in many areas and was one of the largest, richest and most advanced civilizations in the world.

Wealth From The Silk Road

The Silk Road was the route Chinese traders used to take their products from China to Asia Minor and Europe to sell. Silk was just one of many products carried, but it was an important one because for centuries only the Chinese knew how to make it, which made it very valuable.

Ming vase

High Quality Chinese Pottery

Chinese pottery is to this day famous all over the world and many examples, such as Ming porcelain, are extremely valuable. In ancient times it was exported all over the world. One technique that made Chinese pottery so special was to allow the clay to 'weather' for up to 40 years. It was also baked at very high temperatures so it became incredibly smooth. Chinese potters also pioneered many new design techniques, including beautiful blue and white glazes that were much admired by people all over the world.

A Sign Of Good Luck

In China a five-clawed dragon is a sign of good luck, and lucky charms or clothing bearing pictures of them were believed to ward off evil spirits. In days gone by, the badge of the emperor was a dragon.

Ingenious Inventors

By about AD 150 the Chinese had discovered that some plants could be broken down into fibres and pressed into a sheet on which one could write — the first paper. They invented printing and gunpowder, knew how to make silk and were skilled mathematicians and astronomers. They also had kites, wheelbarrows, the decimal system, paper money and the seismograph. Agricultural inventions and techniques, such as the use of a foot-powered pump to lift water into the fields, made the land of China rich and productive.

Foot-powered water pump

History

Great Explorers

People have always wanted to explore new places, sometimes to achieve fame and fortune, sometimes to acquire new lands, and often just for the joy of discovering something new. The period from 1400 – 1800 is often known as the Age of Discovery. European explorers sailed to the Americas, around Africa and as far as Australia, and several European countries established colonies overseas.

Aboriginal hunters

Did You Know?

Early explorers navigated by looking at the sun and stars.

In the 1st century BC, the Ancient Chinese discovered that a substance called magnetite could be used to work out direction.

The first magnetic compasses were used by explorers in the 12th century.

Early sailors used an instrument called an astrolabe to measure the height of the sun or the Pole Star, and work out how far north or south they were.

In 1569, Gerardus Mercator was the first person to show the round globe on a flat map. His map is still used today!

When Mercator's maps were published, the cover showed the Greek god Atlas holding the world on his shoulders — that's how atlases got their name!

James Cook Made Three Expeditions To The Pacific

James Cook's abilities as a good scientific observer and excellent map-maker, charting the coasts of Newfoundland and Nova Scotia in Canada, earned him the leadership of an expedition to the Pacific in 1768. During that expedition he surveyed New Zealand and charted the coast of Australia. From 1772 to 1775 he discovered and charted new islands in the South Pacific. On his last voyage, which began in 1776, he discovered the Sandwich Islands (now Hawaii), where he was killed by local people in February 1779.

Burton Failed To Find The Source Of The Nile

From 1852 to 1856, Sir Richard Burton explored much of West Africa. He searched for the source of the River Nile, but this was eventually found by John Hanning Speke at Lake Victoria. Much of the centre of Africa, which up until then had been completely unknown to the outside world, was explored by David Livingstone, who discovered Victoria Falls. Other great explorers, such as Mungo Park, James Bruce and René Caille, did much to make the continent of Africa known to the rest of the world.

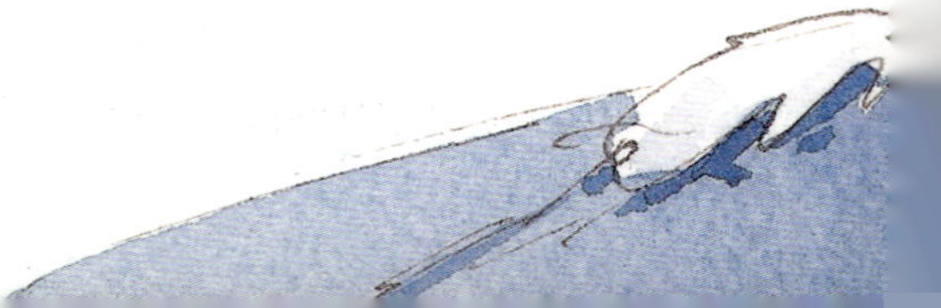

Columbus Was Looking For China When He Found The Americas

Christopher Columbus was an Italian explorer who set out to find a westward sea route to China. He persuaded the King of Spain to support him and sailed forth in 1492. When he reached the Caribbean Islands he thought he was near India, so he called them the 'Indies'. On later voyages, he explored other parts of the Americas but when he died in 1506 he still believed that he had found a route to the East.

Magellan's Crew Were First Round The World

Some of the crew led by the Portuguese navigator Ferdinand Magellan were the first to sail all around the world. Magellan sailed from Spain in 1519 with a fleet of five ships and then went round Cape Horn and across the Pacific to the Philippine Islands. There he was killed by local inhabitants, but some of the crew managed to return to Spain in The Vittoria, the one remaining ship of the expedition. The first captain to take a ship right round the world was Sir Francis Drake. He left Plymouth, England in 1577, sailed around Cape Horn, then across the Pacific and around the Cape of Good Hope into the Atlantic, arriving back in Plymouth in 1580.

Columbus's ship, the Santa Maria

The First Americans

The first people to inhabit the Americas travelled from Asia, crossing the Bering Straits, between Siberia and Alaska, some 12,000 years ago. They gradually populated the whole of the Americas right down to Tierra del Fuego on the southern tip of South America. Over 11,000 years later, when Christopher Columbus landed in America, he thought he had reached the coast of India, so he called the native Americans that he met 'Indians'.

Pilgrims Came From England

Europeans began settling in North America from around 1540. First came Spanish missionaries who settled in present-day Florida and California. French and English farmers settled in what is now Virginia from 1584. The most famous group of settlers were the Pilgrim Fathers who came from England in 1620. They sailed from Plymouth, England, to found a colony in New England to escape religious persecution.

Tea Was Thrown Overboard At The Boston Tea Party

In the 18th century, the British imposed taxes on tea imported into America. The people of Boston, Massachusetts, decided that none of this taxed tea should enter America. They tried to get the ships turned around but this proved impossible so, on December 16, 1773, a party of men disguised as Native Americans boarded the ships and threw the tea into the water. This action, known as the Boston Tea Party, helped unite all the American colonists and 18 months later, the anti-British movement had grown so strong it led to the American War of Independence.

Native American of the Plains tribe

Did You Know?

The native peoples of North America spoke at least 300 different languages, so they sometimes communicated with each other using sign language.

Over half the states in the USA have Native American names.

When Europeans arrived in America, they brought diseases against which the Native Americans had no natural resistance.

The words chocolate, moccasin, tobacco, squaw and papoose are all Native American words.

The first treaty between the United States and the Native Americans was signed with the Delaware tribe in 1778.

There are now over 2 million Native Americans in the USA, and fewer than half of them live on reservations.

Totem Poles Tell Stories

Native Americans of the Pacific Coast of the USA and Canada erected carved and painted poles, called totem poles, that depicted real and mythical animals, and people. These poles were used to record history and to retell ancient legends.

Totem pole

Slavery Caused A War

The American Civil War, from 1861 to 1865, was caused because of a dispute about the rights and wrongs of slavery. The Confederate forces of the southern states supported slavery and the Union of the northern states opposed it.

Confederate soldier

Union soldier

Meaning Of The American Flag

When the American colonies declared their independence in 1776, it was decided that the flag of 'the 13 United States be 13 stripes alternate red and white, that the Union be 13 stars, white in a blue field'. At first the stars were arranged in a circle, but as each new State entered the Union a new star and a new stripe were added to the flag. Before long the number of stripes was getting too many for the flag so, on 4 April, 1818, Congress ruled that the number of stripes should remain at the original 13 only. The stars increased to 50, the present number.

The Industrial Revolution

The Industrial Revolution, which began in Britain in the 18th century, marked a change from making goods on a small scale in people's homes to manufacturing goods in factories. It was helped by the invention of steam power and improvements in iron smelting. The digging of canals, the coming of the railways and improvements in road building all made it easier to transport goods.

The First Railway Carriages Were Drawn By Horses

The first iron railway in the world was built at Coalbrookdale, Shropshire in 1760. The carriages were horse drawn and used mainly for carrying coal from a mine. It was not until 1804 that a steam engine was first used on a railway. On September 27, 1825 the Stockton to Darlington Railway was opened for transporting freight, but people were so enthusiastic about this new mode of travel that the directors were forced to make it available to the public. In 1829, George Stephenson's *Rocket* steam locomotive reached 56 kph (35 mph)

Stephenson's Rocket

Did You Know?

★

Before the Industrial Revolution, 90 percent of people in Europe lived in the countryside.

When weaver James Hargreaves invented the Spinning Jenny in 1764, his fellow weavers broke into his house and destroyed the machine!

Sir Richard Arkwright, who invented the water frame for spinning in 1769, was a barber who also invented a new way to dye hair!

In 1769, Parliament made the crime of destroying machines punishable by death!

The output of James Watt's steam engine was measured in terms of the number of horses it could replace, or 'horse power'.

The Industrial Revolution Was A Time Of Invention

During the Industrial Revolution in Britain, many new inventions were developed. James Watt improved the steam engine in 1782, which meant it could be used to drive factory equipment. People such as Jethro Tull developed new machinery for agriculture. Great changes were made in the textile industry with the invention of the flying shuttle in 1733 and the power loom in 1785, which greatly increased the output of cotton. There were also significant changes in the home with improvements to lighting, and to sanitary systems, including the introduction of the flushing toilet.

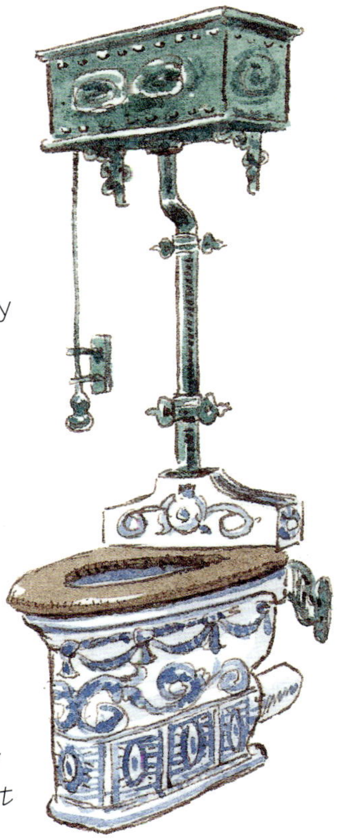

19th century flushing toilet

Children Worked In Factories And Mines

The growth of manufacturing industry brought with it an increasing demand for labour. Many of the jobs were dirty and dangerous and the wages were low, so children were often employed to do the work. Many young people worked 16 hours a day in mines, cotton mills and squalid factories. Women and children had been employed on the land before the coming of the factories, but the conditions in the factories and mines, and the frequent accidents, caused an outcry. The British government was forced to bring in parliamentary acts that restricted the hours of work, and prevented women and children from working underground. By 1900 most other countries had introduced similar rules.

Achievements of the 20th Century

The 20th century saw an amazing number of firsts in many areas of achievement. The first sustained aeroplane flight was made by the Wright brothers in North Carolina in 1903. After that, aviation expanded rapidly, especially when its military possibilities were realized in the First World War, and used to full advantage in the Second World War. The first scheduled passenger flights were as early as 1914 and now thousands of flights are made every day all over the globe. Communications have moved just as fast, with the first public telephone services opening at the end of the 19th century. With the coming of communications satellites in the 1960s, the invention of the mobile phone in 1979, and of the Internet, instant communication could be made to and from anywhere in the world — an incredible acievement indeed.

Astronaut on the Moon

The First Person In Space Was A Russian

The first artificial object to be placed in orbit around the Earth was the Russian satellite Sputnik 1 on October 4, 1957. Soon after that, in 1961, the Russians had a cosmonaut in orbit, named Yuri Gagarin. In 1962, the American astronaut John Glenn completed three orbits in Friendship 7. Progress continued to be made with longer flights and unmanned probes to the Moon, and in 1969 the Americans Neil Armstrong and Buzz Aldrin became the first people to walk on the Moon.

The Atomic Bomb Ended The Second World War

The first atomic bombs were dropped by the US Air Force on the Japanese cities of Hiroshima and Nagasaki in August 1945. The atomic bomb succeeded in bringing the Second World War to an end, with the Japanese surrendering unconditionally, but at a terrible loss of human life. Unfortunately, this first use of atomic weapons in war did not lead to the end of conflicts, because people have never been able to live in peace with one another. Disputes have continued to arise over land and trade, and over different beliefs and forms of government. In the past 50 years or so there have been both minor and major wars in many parts of the world.

Atomic bomb exploding

Did You Know?

The first Internet arrest took place in 1996, when a convicted bankrobber's photo was posted on the FBI's web-site.

The first widely known computer virus flashed the word 'cookie' constantly on computer screens at Stamford University, California.

A famous red telephone has provided a direct link between Moscow and Washngton DC, since 1963. To be sure the lines are working, the Americans and Russians send tests to each other every hour.

On a space shuttle mission in February 1984, American Bruce McCandless was seen riding a 'scooter' in space.

During the First World War, British scientists tried to keep their new invention a secret by calling it a 'water carrier', and then a 'tank'!

Knights and Armour

Knights were the fighting warriors of the Middle Ages. They had to conform to a code of conduct and often became the champions of noble ladies for whom they fought in battle and took on challenges. Knights usually received gifts of land in return for their military service.

How Armour Developed

Armour in the Middle Ages covered the whole of a knight's body and also much of his horse. The knight would wear a personalised emblem or device on his helmet and shield so that other knights would know who he was.

Over a period of time the armour became heavier and more cumbersome and if a knight was dismounted he was at a disadvantage when fighting with someone who was not wearing armour. With the increasing use of firearms in battle, against which armour was of little protection, its use declined.

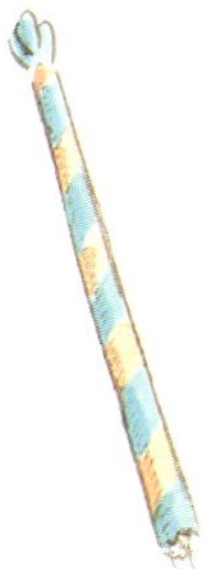

How To Become A Knight

To become a knight a young man had to be of noble birth and undergo a period of long and rigorous training. This usually started with work as a page from about the age of seven. The boy would act as the servant of a noble lady and she in turn would teach him good manners and see to his education. After about seven years he would become squire to a knight. He would then be responsible for looking after the knight's armour and his horse as well as serving at the tables and assisting the knight at tournaments. During this time he would be learning how to fight with lance, sword, mace, battleaxe and dagger both on horseback and on foot.

By the age of 21 he was eligible to become a knight. This was conferred upon him by being tapped with a ceremonial sword on each shoulder, exactly as the British monarch dubs knights to this day. These days, however, knights are not bound to do military service and may be awarded for political, social or artistic services to the community.

Knights jousting

Science

Matter

Matter is everything that takes up space in the universe, from the tiniest speck of dust to the biggest star or planet. Matter exists in three states: solid, liquid and gas. When substances are heated or cooled, they can change from one state to another. Hard rock can melt into lava; runny water freeze into solid ice. Scientists call this change between states of matter 'physical change.'

Buildings Can Expand In Hot Weather

Most solids expand when they are heated. This is why bridges and skyscrapers built with steel have to be designed so they can expand in hot weather and contract in cold weather. Ice is an exception. As solid ice, water takes up more space than when it is liquid. This is why water pipes can burst in freezing weather. The water has expanded by turning into ice, then splits open the pipes as it melts.

The Celsius Scale Has Been Reversed Since It Was First Invented

The Celsius or centigrade scale for measuring temperature was invented by the Swedish astronomer Anders Celsius in 1742. He called the temperature at which water boils into vapour 0 °C, and the point at which it freezes 100° C. In the modern Celsius scale, this has been reversed, so water freezes at 0° C and boils at 100 °C.

Glaciers contain ice – water that has frozen to become solid

Did You Know?

The freezing point of a substance is identical to its melting point. So, water freezes and ice melts at 0 °C (32 °F).

Gold turns into a liquid at 1064.43 °C (1,950 °F), and boils at 2,807 °C (5,084 °F)!

Helium is so light that it floats out of the Earth's atmosphere.

Hydrogen is the lightest element, and weighs 1/15 as much as air.

Hydrogen used to be used to fill air balloons, but has been replaced by helium which has the advantage of not being explosive!

Scientists can make it rain by adding substances such as dry ice to clouds!

All Matter Has A Melting Point And A Boiling Point

All substances are made of tiny particles called atoms or molecules. When a substance is solid, these particles fit together tightly so the solid keeps its shape. If the substance is heated, the bonds between the particles begin to break up, so the solid melts into a liquid. Every solid melts at a certain temperature, called its melting point. Liquids in turn can be heated until they reach their boiling point. This is the point at which they cannot get any hotter without changing state. Water reaches its boiling point at 100°C. When it has reached this temperature, it begins to evaporate and turn into a gas — steam.

Clouds form when rising air cools down and the water vapour it contains condenses into water

Water in seas and river evaporates to become water vapour, which forms clouds

Atoms

Everything in the universe, from a football to a distant planet, is made up of atoms. Atoms are tiny particles from which all matter is made. They are so tiny, it is impossible to see them even with the most powerful optical microscopes. Each atom is a million times smaller than the thickness of a hair. There are just over 100 different kinds of atom. Some materials, such as iron, contain just one kind of atom. Most are made up from different kinds of atom that have joined together to form molecules.

Scientists Can Scan Atoms Using Powerful Microscopes

Atoms are too tiny to see even with the most powerful optical microscopes. But in 1981, the scanning tunnelling microscope was invented. This magnifies objects 10 million times, and allows scientists to scan the atoms contained in molecules. A probe scans the surface of the molecule, and its tip follows the contours of the atom, tracing its shape.

Did You Know?

A nanometre is a billionth of a metre, and an atom measures between 0.1 and 0.5 nanometres!

Atoms are made up of subatomic particles called protons, neutrons and electrons.

The protons and neutrons at the centre of an atom are 100,000 times smaller than the atom!

Protons and neutrons are made up of three even smaller particles, which are called quarks!

Electrons are over 1,800 times smaller than the protons and neutrons!

An electron weighs 0.0000000000000000000000000009 g (0.000000000000000000000000000003 oz)!

Atoms Contain Huge Amounts Of Energy

At the centre of every atom is its nucleus. The nucleus contains subatomic particles called protons and neutrons. A third kind of subatomic particles, called electrons, spin around the nucleus. Electrons are bundles of energy which move as fast as the speed of light. They spin round in different shells, or layers, usually in pairs, with one travelling clockwise and the other anticlockwise. Electrons have a negative electrical charge and protons have a positive electrical charge. The attraction between them holds the atom together. Scientists now believe protons and neutrons are made of smaller particles called quarks, and electrons are made of leptons. A third kind of particle holds them all together. Atoms contain a huge amount of energy because of the strong force between the particles inside the nucleus.

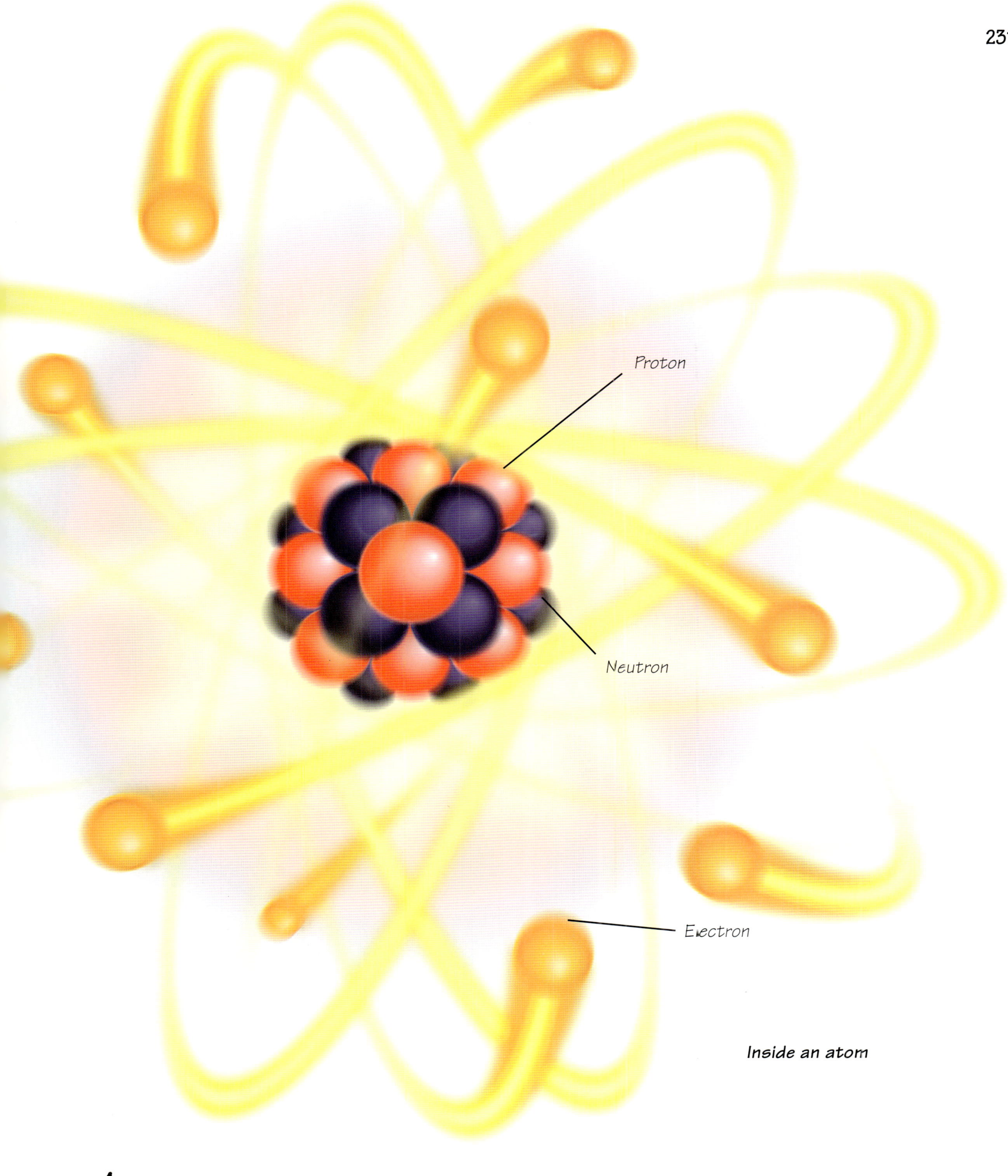

Inside an atom

Atoms Are Made Up Of Even Tinier Particles

Scientists once believed that atoms were the smallest possible particle of matter. In 1919, Ernest Rutherford split the atom, using a radium gun. Scientists now use powerful machines called particle accelerators to smash atoms. These have shown that there are at least 200 subatomic particles, and scientists are discovering more all the time.

Elements

There are thousands of different substances on the Earth, but everything is made from just over 100 different elements. An element contains only one kind of atom. All the atoms it contains have the same number of protons and electrons, which give the element its character and make it unique. An element can't be broken down, but it can combine with other elements.

Most Elements Are Metals

About three quarters of all elements are metals. The most common metals include iron, copper, zinc, aluminium and lead. Most metals are hard and shiny. They are made of tiny crystals that are held together by tight bonds that make them very strong. Metals can carry heat and electricity and can be bent or moulded into shape, so they can be made into everything from cutlery to spacecraft.

Scientists Group Elements Into Families

Scientists divide elements into metals and non-metals and arrange them in a chart called the Periodic Table. The chart puts elements in order, according to the number of protons in their nucleus.

				H hydrogen 1					
Li lithium 3	Be beryllium 4								
Na sodium 11	Mg magnesium 12								
K potassium 19	Ca calcium 20	Sc scandium 21	Ti titanium 22	V vanadium 23	Cr chromium 24	Mn manganese 25	Fe iron 26	Co cobalt 27	Ni nickel 28
Rb rubidium 37	Sr strontium 38	Y yttrium 39	Zr zirconium 40	Nb niobium 41	Mo molybdenum 42	Tc technetium 43	Ru ruthenium 44	Rh rhodium 45	Pd palladium 46
Cs caesium 55	Ba barium 56	La lanthanum 57	Hf hafnium 72	Ta tantalum 73	W tungsten 74	Re rhenium 75	Os osmium 76	Ir iridium 77	Pt platinum 78
Fr francium 87	Ra radium 88	Ac actinium 89							
				Ce cerium 58	Pr praseodymium 59	Nd neodymium 60	Pm promethium 61	Sm samarium 62	Eu europium 63
				Th thorium 90	Pa protactinium 91	U uranium 92	Np neptunium 93	Pu plutonium 94	Am americium 95

The Periodic Table

Copper ore

Elements Can Be Mixed To Make Stronger Materials

Some substances, such as gold, contain just one element. Most substances, such as salt, are mixtures of two or more elements. Salt is a mixture of sodium and chlorine. Elements can also be mixed together to make stronger or better materials. Copper can become dull and tarnished, but when it is mixed with zinc it makes brass, which is stronger and keeps its shine longer.

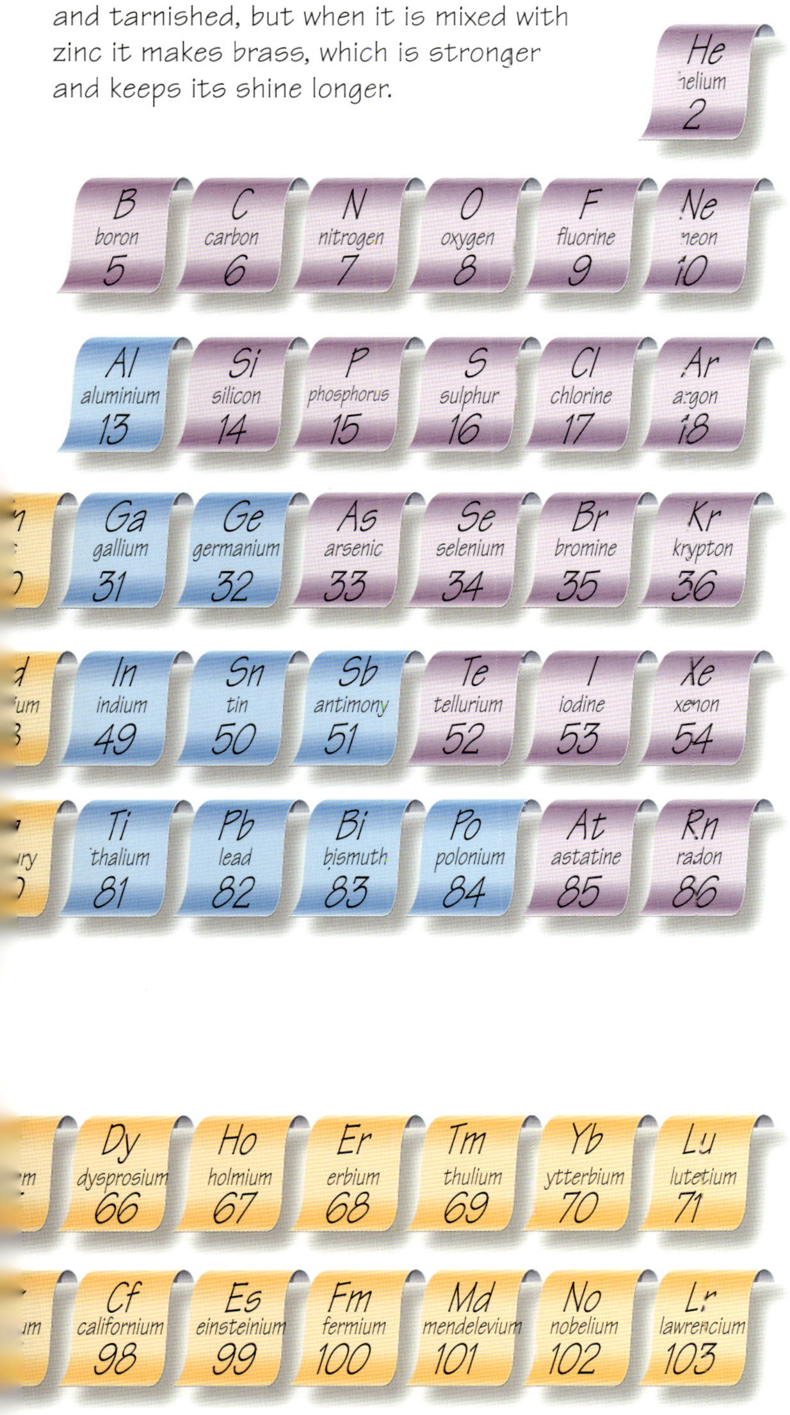

Did You Know?

Hydrogen is the most common element in the universe, but it has no smell, no taste, and it is invisible!

The element calcium is the most abundant metal in our bodies, but is also found in marble!

Mercury is the only metal that is liquid at room temperature, so it is used in thermometers and barometers.

Arsenic is an element that can be used both for medicines and deadly poisons!

Chlorine is a poisonous, foul-smelling gas – but it can be safely used to purify the water we drink and swim in!

Krypton is not just the planet where Superman comes from, it is the name of an element used in fluorescent lamps.

Hydrogen Was The First Element To Form After The Big Bang

Hydrogen is the first element in the Periodic Table because it has just one proton in its nucleus. After Big Bang, hydrogen was the first element to form, followed by helium. These gases make up to 98 percent of the stars in the universe. All the elements that make up Earth were created from exploding stars in space. The Earth's crust is made mainly from oxygen and silicon. In the human body, carbon, oxygen and hydrogen are the most common elements.

Radioactivity

In some types of atom, the nucleus is unstable. In time, tiny particles or waves of energy start to shoot out, and the nucleus begins to break up. This is called radioactive decay. The gamma rays and alpha and beta particles that escape are forms of nuclear radiation. Radiation is dangerous for living things but it can be used for medicine, and to make nuclear energy for electricity or defence weapons.

Radioactivity Was Discovered In 1896

Radioactivity was first discovered in uranium by the French scientist Antoine Becquerel. Marie and Pierre Curie then studied uranium ore and found that it contained the powerful radioactive elements radium and polonium. Becquerel and the Curies shared the 1903 Nobel Prize for Physics for their discovery of radium.

Did You Know?

After the discovery of X-rays in 1895, a London firm began selling X-ray proof underwear!

Marie Curie became the first woman to win a Nobel prize, and the first person to win two.

For thirty years after its discovery, people experimented with radioactivity and X-rays without realizing that it was dangerous.

Lethal radioactive substances such as radium were sold as miracle cures!

The Geiger counter, which measures radiation, was invented in 1912 by the German physicist Hans Geiger.

Marie Curie died from leukaemia, probably caused by her experiments.

Radioactivity Helps Scientists Date Things From The Past

In some materials, the break up of unstable nuclei happens faster than in others. Scientists measure radioactive decay in 'half lives'. Carbon 14 has a half life of 5,700 years, because it takes that length of time for half the atoms in a sample to decay. Animals and plants all contain a certain amount of carbon 14 when they are alive. When they die, they stop taking in carbon 14 and it begins to decay. By measuring the amount of carbon 14 left in remains, scientists can find out how old they are.

Inside a nuclear power station

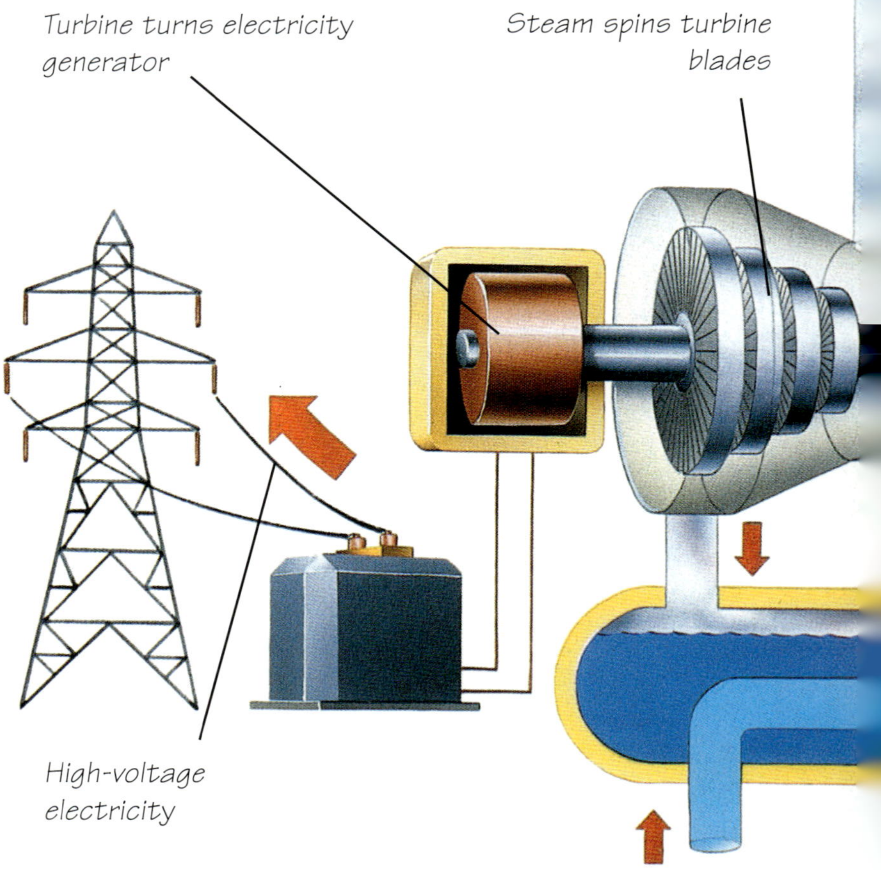

The Energy Released By Nuclear Reactions Is Used To Make Weapons

In nuclear power stations, radioactive substances, such as uranium, are bombarded with neutrons. Their nuclei split, releasing radiation and more neutrons, which set off a chain reaction. This is called nuclear fission. It can also be used to create powerful atomic weapons. In World War II (1939 – 45) the USA dropped atomic bombs on the cities of Hiroshima and Nagasaki in Japan, killing hundreds of thousands of people.

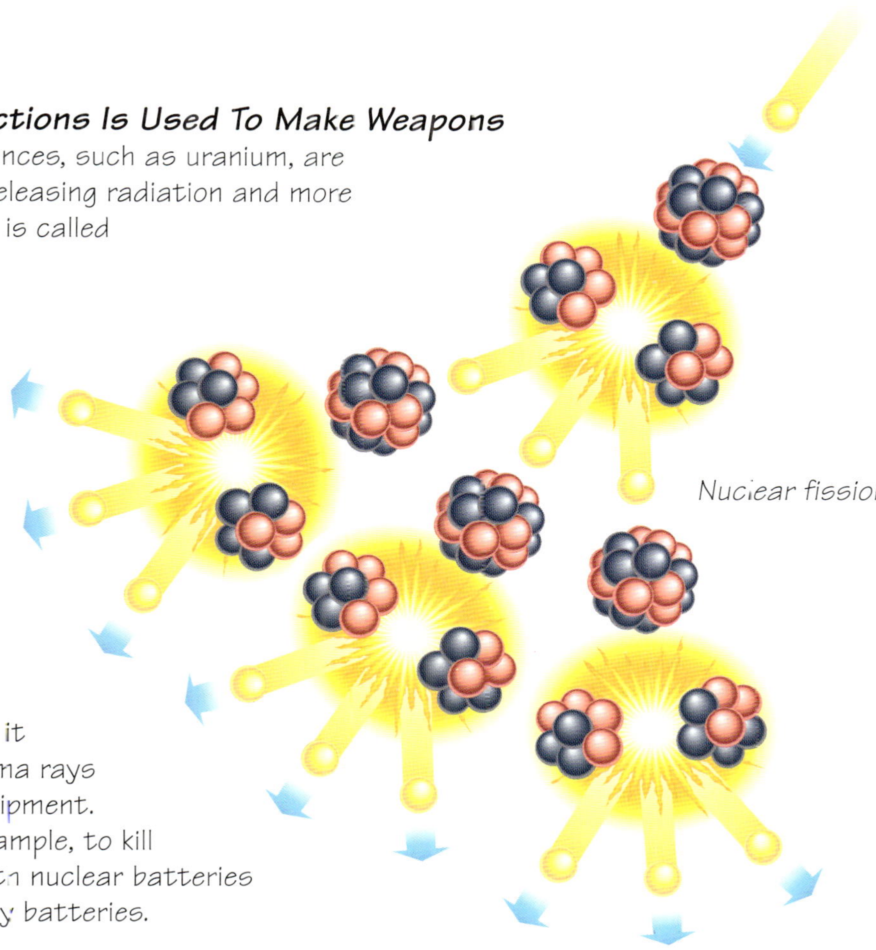

Radiotherapy Is Used In Medicine

Radiation is deadly because it can pass into living tissue and damage it. Exposure to radiation can cause sickness and death, but it can also be used for medical purposes. Gamma rays are used in hospitals to sterilize medical equipment. They can also be used in radiotherapy, for example, to kill cancer cells. Heart pacemakers are fitted with nuclear batteries because these last much longer than ordinary batteries.

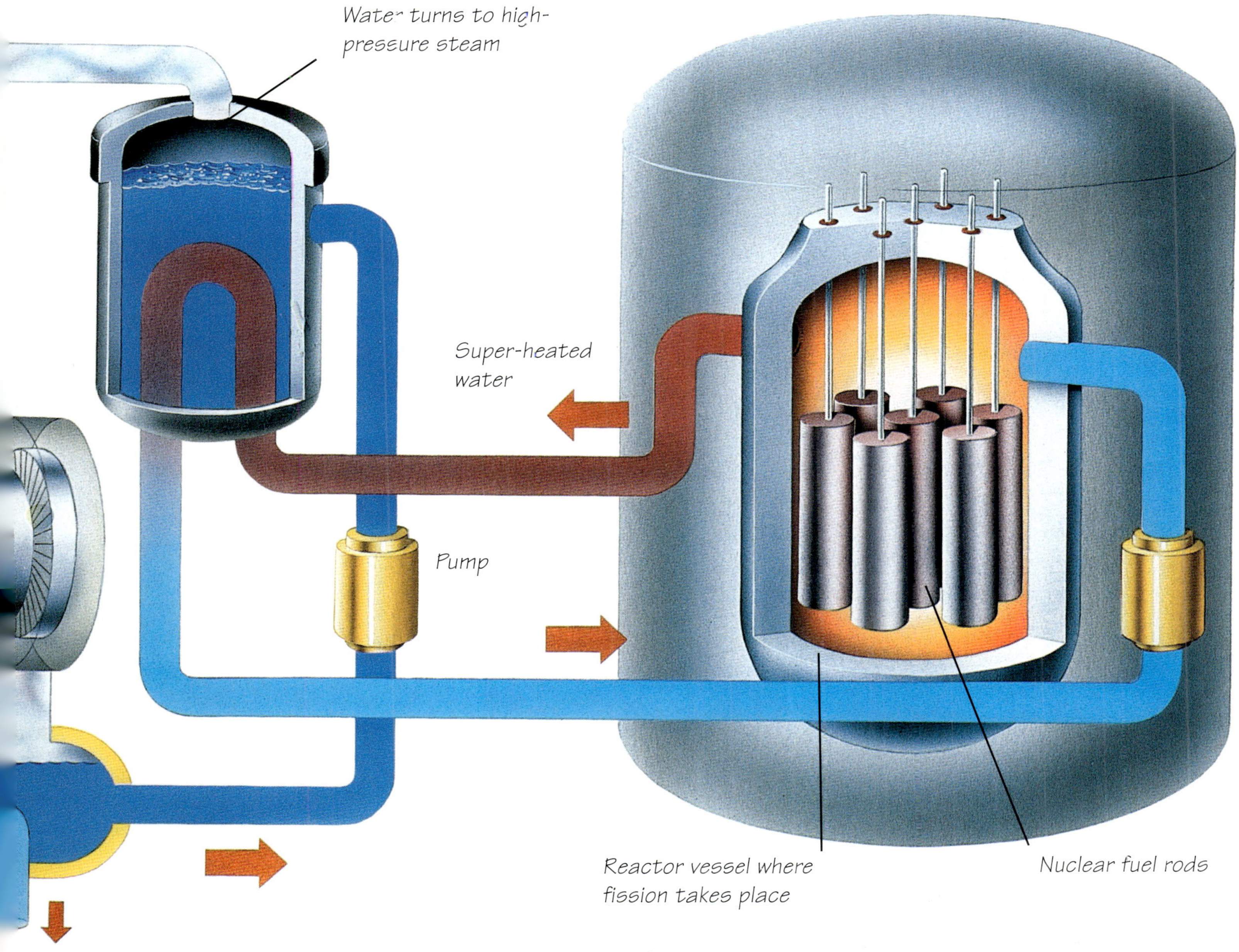

Gravity

Gravity is a force of attraction between two objects. An object that falls to the ground is being pulled downwards by the Earths' gravity. Gravity is the force that keeps the planets orbiting round the Sun, and the Moon orbiting round the Earth in our Solar System.

A Falling Apple Led To The Discovery Of Gravity

The scientist Sir Isaac Newton (1642 – 1727) is said to have discovered gravity when he was a student on holiday on his mother's farm. When he saw an apple fall from a tree, he guessed that the force that pulled it down was the same as that which pulled the Moon into the Earth's orbit. The Moon doesn't fall to Earth, and Newton was able to work out that the strength of gravity depends on the mass of the objects being pulled together, and how far apart they are. Mass is the amount of matter an object contains, measured in kilograms (pounds). The nearer objects are to each other, the stronger the force of attraction. The strength of attraction between two objects is their weight, which we measure in Newtons, named after the great scientist.

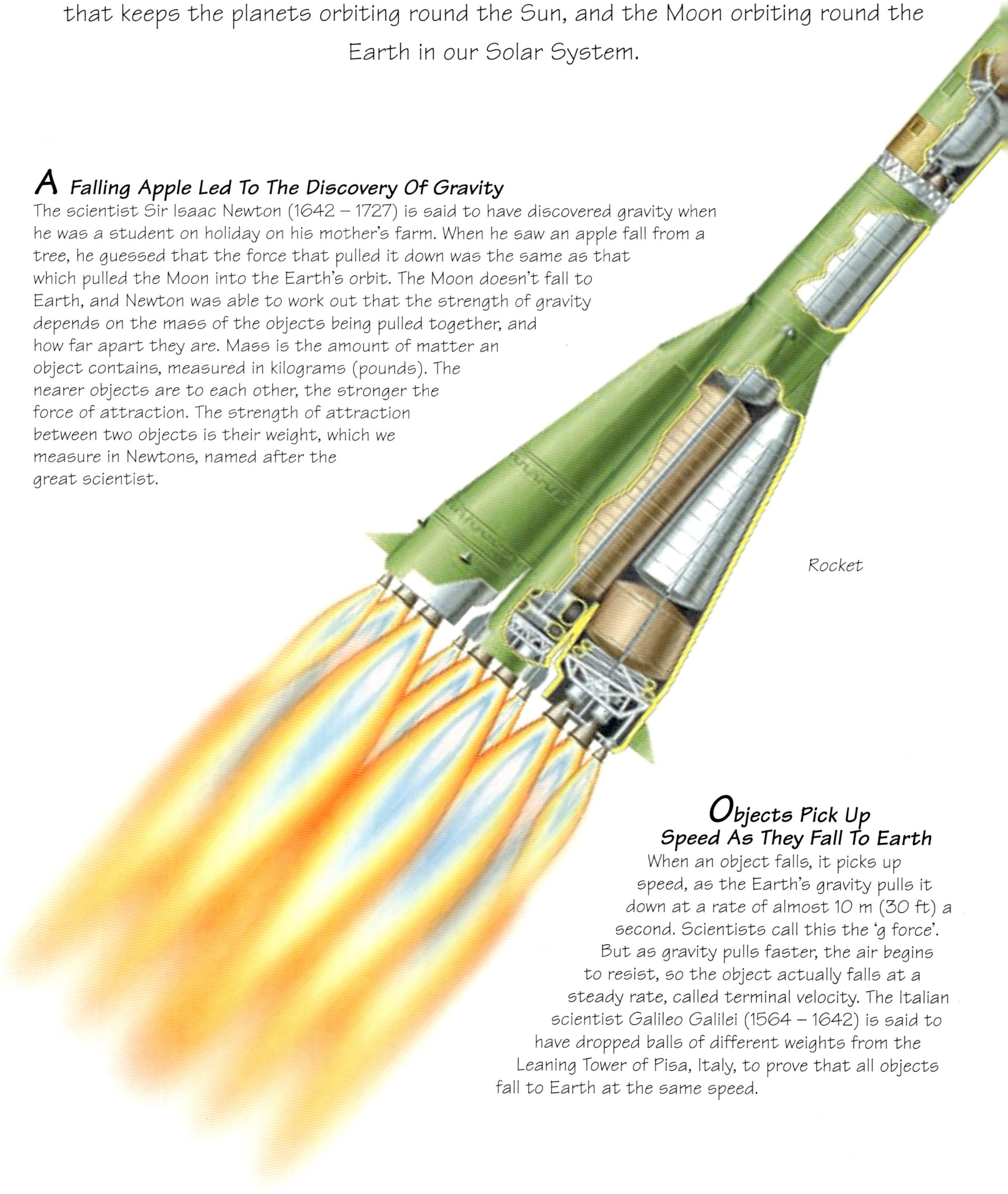

Rocket

Objects Pick Up Speed As They Fall To Earth

When an object falls, it picks up speed, as the Earth's gravity pulls it down at a rate of almost 10 m (30 ft) a second. Scientists call this the 'g force'. But as gravity pulls faster, the air begins to resist, so the object actually falls at a steady rate, called terminal velocity. The Italian scientist Galileo Galilei (1564 – 1642) is said to have dropped balls of different weights from the Leaning Tower of Pisa, Italy, to prove that all objects fall to Earth at the same speed.

Rockets Use Speed To Overcome Earth's Gravity

A rocket cannot leave the Earth's atmosphere to fly in space unless it moves with a force greater than the force of gravity that pulls it back to Earth. To do this, a rocket must reach a speed of 40,000 kph (25,000 mph) or more. Rockets are used to send astronauts and satellites into space. The rocket engines burn fuel to give them the force needed to push upwards and away from Earth. So much fuel is needed that it is carried in separate containers, called stages. As each stage is burned up, it drops off to reduce the weight of the rocket, and the rocket uses its next stage of fuel.

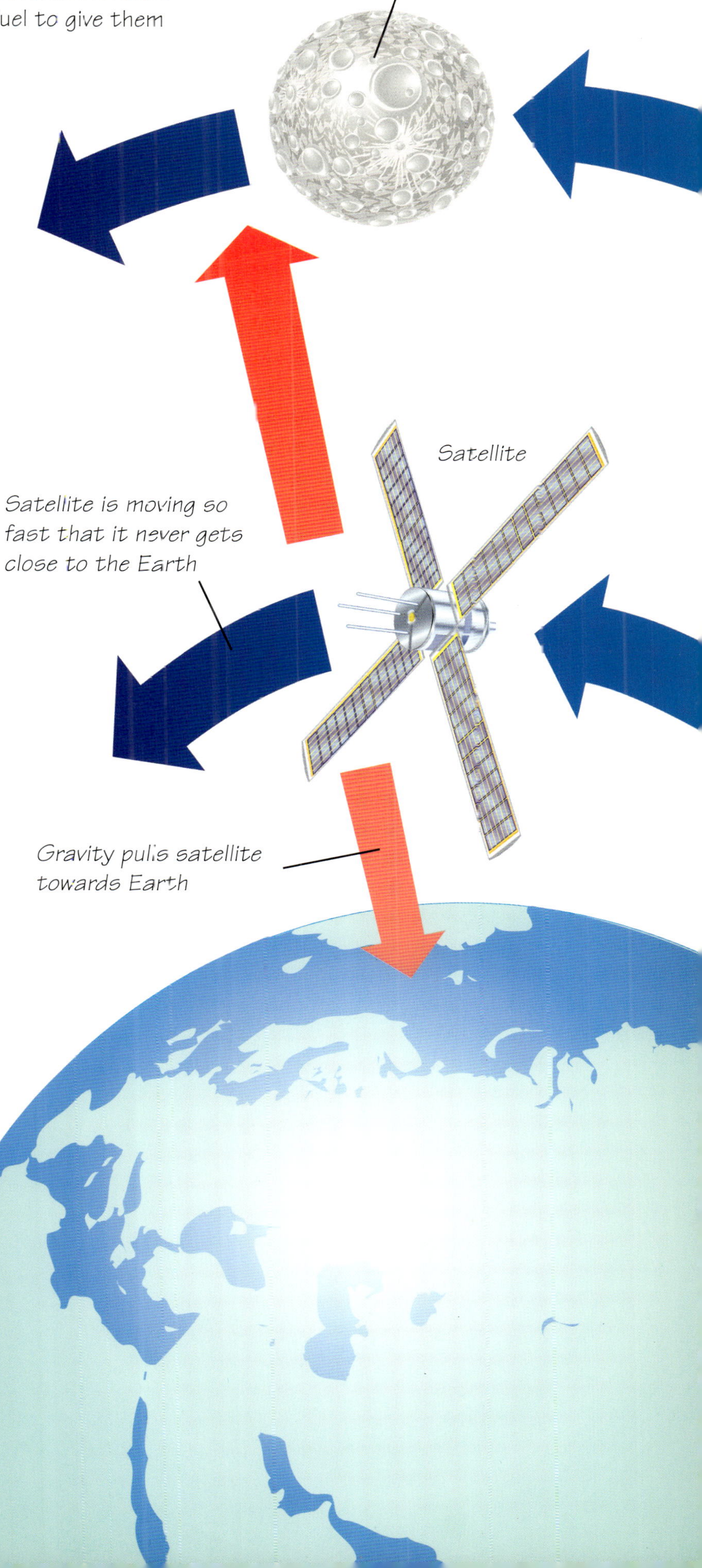

Did You Know?

Galileo discovered the principles of the pendulum by using his pulse to time the swings of the great lamps of Pisa Cathedral during an earthquake!

Sir Isaac Newton was born in the same year that Galileo died.

Newton was only under his famous apple tree because plague in the city had forced him to flee to the countryside.

Some of Newton's important books were published by Sir Edmund Halley, who discovered the famous comet.

Neptune and Pluto were calculated to exist using Newton's theory of gravity before they were discovered!

At the earth's surface, gravity causes a falling object to accelerate by 9.8 m (32 ft) every second.

Light

Light travels in waves. Some waves are short, some are long. When we see colours, we are actually looking at light of different wavelengths. Sunlight appears to be colourless, or white, light. It is really a mixture of light of different wavelengths, making up all the colours of the spectrum. We can see these colours when a rainbow forms.

Refraction

Blue Skies And Red Sunsets Are Caused By Particles In The Air

As sunlight passes through the Earth's atmosphere, a mixture of gases, dust, ice crystals and water droplets absorb some of its colours, and reflect others. Clear skies look blue because gases in the air reflect mainly blue light from the sun. Sunsets look red when the air is full of dust and water droplets. The dusty, moist air reflects all but the longest red or yellow light waves, so it is these that we see glowing in the sky.

Light Is The Fastest Thing In The Universe

Light travels at nearly 300,000 km (186,000 mi) per second. It travels fastest through air, slowing down slightly when it passes through transparent materials, such as glass or water. When a ray of light passes from one material to another, the change in speed forces it to change direction. This is why objects in water, such as a straw in a glass of water, appear to bend.

Sunlight Is Made Of Many Colours

We can see the different colours that make up sunlight when a rainbow forms in the sky. Sunlight passes through the raindrops at different angles, changing speed as it does so. Different colours have different wavelengths and colours with long wavelengths, such as red, bend more than colours with short wavelengths, such as violet. This makes the colours separate and fan out in the sky as a rainbow. Sir Isaac Newton proved that sunlight is made up of many colours. When he shone a ray of light through a glass prism, the light split into different colours.

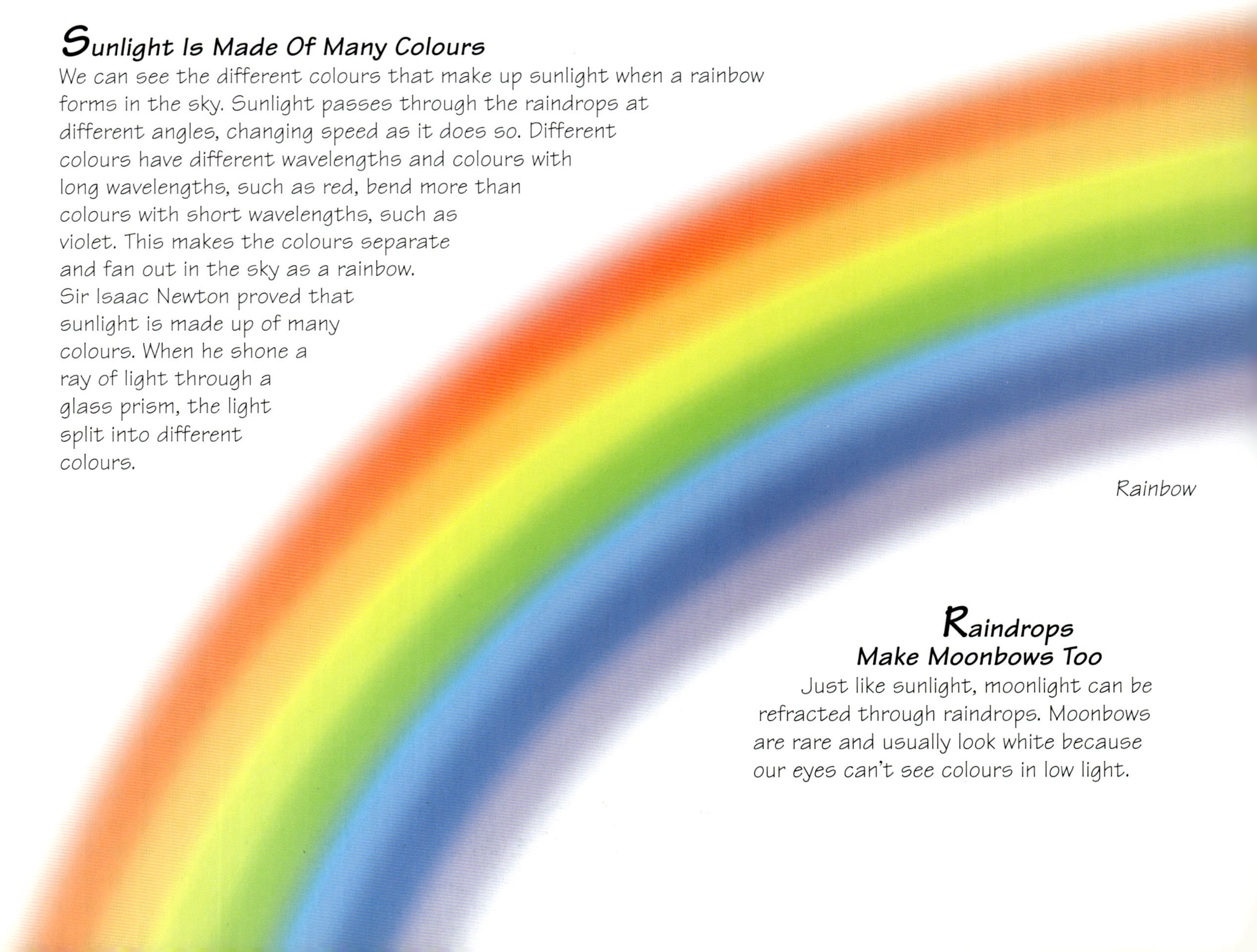

Rainbow

Raindrops Make Moonbows Too

Just like sunlight, moonlight can be refracted through raindrops. Moonbows are rare and usually look white because our eyes can't see colours in low light.

Machines

Sea and Air Transport

In the last 200 years, the world has become a smaller place with the development of air transport. Aircraft have developed from slow balloons carried by the wind, to jets that can travel at two or three times the speed of sound. Ships and boats, meanwhile, have developed for war, trade, travel and sport.

Jet aircraft

The First Powered Flight Lasted 13 Seconds

The first powered flights were made by the American brothers Wilbur and Orville Wright in 1903. The brothers were running a cycle business in Ohio, USA, when they designed their first powered plane, *Flyer 1*. The first flight, made by Orville Wright, lasted for just 13 seconds.

The First Boats Were Probably Hollowed Out Logs

The earliest boats were probably simple rafts, floats and hollowed-out logs. They were powered by poles, paddles or oars. Sailing ships, such as the Chinese junk, were developed for trade. Others were developed for war. By the 19th century, the fast trading ships called clippers were being replaced by steam ships. The SS *Great Britain*, designed by Isambard Kingdom Brunel in 1845 was the first steam ship with an iron hull, driven by propellers, to cross the Atlantic Ocean. Propeller power was soon being used for cargo ships, war ships and passenger liners. Passenger liners grew bigger and more luxurious, but it was not until after the *Titanic* sank on her maiden voyage in 1912 that there were safety regulations for the number of lifeboats.

Chinese junk

Hovercraft

A Hovercraft Floats On A Cushion Of Air

Many people have tried to develop craft that can travel on both sea and land. The British inventor Christopher Cockerell had the idea of making boats go faster by raising them above the waves, which would reduce the drag of the water. He experimented by using an air blower to blow air through the gap between two tin cans which were placed one inside the other, on a pair of scales. This showed that a vessel could be lifted on a cushion of air pumped from jets round the edge. In 1954, these experiments led to the first designs for the hovercraft, which travels over sand or water by floating on a rubber cushion of air. Gas turbine engines power the air cushion fans and propellers. Hovercraft are now used for sea crossings all over the world.

Jet Travel Began In The 1950s

In 1952, the world's first jet airliner began a regular passenger service. Jet engines work by sucking air in one end and blowing it out the other at a much faster speed. This pushes the aircraft in the opposite direction. Only the rich were able to afford air travel, until jet airliners such as the Boeing 707 began to be used in the 1950s. The first Jumbo Jet was the Boeing 747 which was introduced in 1970. Jumbos are over 70 m (210 ft) long and can carry up to 500 passengers.

Did You Know?

The first-ever air passengers were a sheep, a rooster and a duck! They took off in the hot-air balloon pioneered by the Montgolfier Brothers in France, in 1783.

The time taken to travel round the world is now 390 times faster than 500 years ago.

Because of the time difference, passengers on Concorde can board their plane in London, have lunch, and arrive in New York City – in time for lunch!

In 1785, an American and a Frenchman were the first to cross the English Channel by balloon. As the balloon lost height, they had to lose weight, so they threw everything overboard – including their clothes!

If Titanic had hit the iceberg head on (instead of side on) she would most likely have stayed afloat.

Land Transport

In just over 100 years, cars and trains have developed from the first 'horseless carriages' driven by steam power to sleek modern machines that can travel at hundreds of kilometres an hour.

The First Cars Had Steam Engines

The first cars were made in the 1880s. They had steam or electric engines, but steam made them slow and heavy, and electric motors needed huge batteries to recharge them. The first internal combustion engines, which could run on petrol, were introduced in 1889. In Britain, a law was passed to stop motor vehicles from travelling faster than a walking pace, and all cars had to have a man walking in front with a red flag to warn pedestrians and horse-drawn transport. In 1896, the British speed limit was increased to 20 kph (12 mph).

Modern family car

The Model T Ford Was The First Popular Car

The American engineer Henry Ford introduced the Model T Ford in 1908. The car went on sale for $850 but by 1925, faster assembly -line production meant the price had come down to $250. Model Ts became the first popular family cars. Eighteen million Model Ts were made between 1908 and 1927. They were known as 'Tin Lizzies' and could reach 72 kph (45 mph). Modern family cars can reach about 200 kph (120 mph).

In Future, Cars Will Drive Themselves And Trains Will Fly

Technology has made it possible for onboard computers to drive cars automatically. Ultrasound sensors keep the cars a few metres (feet) apart on motorways, while computerized route maps direct the driver. Some cars already use sensors to measure parking spaces, and park automatically. In Europe and Japan, trains are being developed which fly a few centimetres (inches) above the tracks on a cushion of magnetism. 'Maglev' trains can reach speeds of around 500 kph (300mph).

Did You Know?

★

Leonardo da Vinci drew a perfect picture of a modern bicycle – 400 years before it was invented!

A policeman was killed in 1868 when the first traffic signal, installed outside the Houses of Parliament, blew up.

Frenchman Jacques Garnerin tested the first ever parachute in 1797 – by jumping out of a balloon at over 900 m (2,700 ft). Fortunately, it worked!

The first ever bicycle could not be pedalled or steered!

The first pneumatic tyres, invented in Scotland by John Dunlop, were called 'mummy' tyres, because they were wrapped around the wheel!

One of the least popular inventions was made by a Mr Magee in Oklahoma City, USA, 1932 – the parking meter!

The First Railway Locomotives Were Horse Drawn

When steam engines replaced horse-drawn locomotives in the 1820s and 30s, many people thought that their speeds of 32 kph (20 mph) would kill animals, and that passengers would not be able to breathe properly. The first public railway opened in 1825 and ran between Stockton and Darlington, England. The railway craze swept Britain and the USA and by the 1850s, trains were part of everyday life. It was nearly a century before steam locomotives began to be replaced by electric trains. The last steam trains in Britain ran in 1969.

The Longest Rail Journey Is In Russia

The longest rail journey that can be made without changing trains is 9,297 km (5,777 mi) on the Trans-Siberian line from Moscow to Vladivostok in Russia. The journey takes 6 1/2 days.

Trans-Siberian Railway

Telecommunications

In just over a century, the telecommunications industry has changed the way we live and work. Telecommunications means sending words and pictures by radio waves or along wires or optic fibres. Telephones, fax machines, computers and televisions are all part of the telecommunications network. Satellites enable us to view events as they happen, anywhere in the world. Mobile phones and the Internet mean we can communicate instantly with others anywhere in the world.

The Telephone Was Invented In 1876

Alexander Graham Bell invented a way of converting the human voice into electrical signals that could be sent along copper wires. When the first telephone exchange opened in Connecticut, USA, in 1878, just 21 people were connected. Telephone calls can now be sent as pulses of light along fibre optic cables that are made from strands of glass. A few fibres can carry 100,000 calls at once. They can also be sent as radio waves, relayed by satellites in space. Mobile phones send radio waves to radio aerials on their cellular networks. In remote areas, mobile phones use communications satellites to send and receive signals.

Mobile phone

The Internet Started As A Computer Link Between Four Universities

The first computers using electronic signals were built in the United States in 1946. Early computers were giants, often taking up entire offices. Modern computers contain microchips that store and process information.

Microchip

In the 1960s, the U.S. government began developing the first network of computers, or Internet. They wanted to find ways of linking computers without a control centre, in case of war or nuclear attack. The first network was built in 1969, linking four universities. By the 1970s, the network had become global. The Internet uses modems to connect computers by converting electronic signals into audio signals that can be sent along telephone lines. Telephone lines are gradually being replaced by high-speed cable links which send data as pulses of light along fibre optic cables. Computer data can also be sent by satellite links.

Did You Know?

Alexander Graham Bell was fascinated by sound, and spent his early years teaching deaf children.

The first words transmitted by telephone were Alexander Graham Bell's: 'Mr Watson, come here — I want you.'

Less than 25 years after the invention of the telephone, one in every 50 homes in the USA had one.

ENIAC, the world's first electronic digital computer generated enormous heat from the 18,000 vacuum tubes it used!

The Internet was developed from the network of computers used by the US Department of Defence.

In 2000, Bill Gates was ordered to divide the computer software monopoly held by his Microsoft organization.

Satellites Work Like Giant Magnifying Mirrors

Satellites circle the Earth, sending us photographs of the weather, and relaying telephone calls and television programmes around the world. Communications satellites orbit at heights of around 36,000 km (22,500 mi). Radio signals are beamed up to them from huge dish-shaped aerials on Earth. The satellite uses solar-powered cells to make these signals stronger, then beams them back around the world. Satellites can send pictures of live events as they happen. They can also carry tens of thousands of telephone calls at once. In future, they may have even more uses, such as reading energy meters in remote areas.

Communications satellite

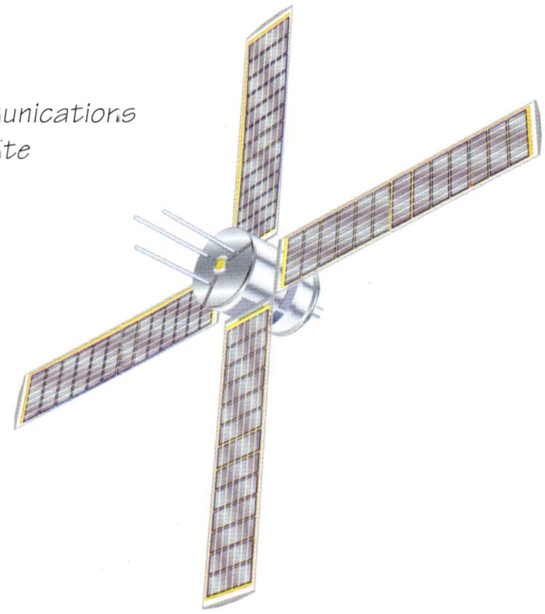

Domestic Machines

We use machines in our homes every day. Machines, such as dishwashers, vacuum cleaners, washing machines and microwave ovens have made domestic chores like cleaning, washing and cooking faster and easier. Television has brought home entertainment to everyone. In future, one slim computer panel may operate every machine in our homes, linking the television, computer, fridge, dishwasher and cooker.

TV Pictures Used To Be Black And White

The first television sets had bulky cases with small screens. In some countries, they were sold as kits which the buyer had to put together. Television is a way of sending moving pictures from one place to another. A television camera converts pictures into electrical signals which can be sent along cables or via radio waves to a television receiver, which converts them back into pictures on a screen. John Logie Baird was the first person to demonstrate television, using a mechanical camera, in 1926. In the 1930s, the first television sets were sold to families who could afford them. Each country had one channel, and programmes were only on for part of the day. All the programmes were shown in black and white and were live because there was no way of recording television pictures. Today, programmes can be sent via satellite or along cable links, making it possible for every home to have access to hundreds of different channels.

Mini portable TV

Popcorn Was The First Microwaved Food

Microwaves use powerful radiowaves with very short wavelengths to cook food quickly. The microwaves bombard water molecules in food making them vibrate so fast that the food heats up. Microwaves were invented by an American named Percy Le Baron Spencer, who experimented by cooking maize in a bag with the energy from a radar tube. The maize cooked into popcorn. The first microwave ovens were made in 1945 for hospital and military canteens, but by the 1960s they were becoming popular for the home.

Microwave oven

Did You Know?

★

Beautiful bronze safety pins have been found dating back to the 8th century BC!

The first successful vacuum cleaner, invented by Hubert Booth, had a 250-m (750-ft) hose and was so loud it scared horses in the street!

Microwaves were first developed for use in Britain's radar defences in the Second World War, not for cooking!

The invention of the microwave oven was the first completely new way of cooking since prehistoric people discovered fire!

John Logie Baird built his first television almost entirely out of scrap!

98 percent of homes in the USA have a television set!

Vacuum cleaner

The First Vacuum Cleaners Were So Big They Needed Two People To Work Them

Herbert Cecil Booth invented the first vacuum cleaner in London, England, in 1901. His firm provided a cleaning service for people's homes. All his employees wore uniforms. The first machines were so big that they had to be carried to people's houses on horse-drawn carts, and it took two people to operate them. In 1907, an American inventor named Murray Splangler developed designs for lighter machines powered by electricity. He sold his invention to William B Hoover, and the Hoover vacuum cleaner was launched. Some modern vacuum cleaners have a cylinder instead of a replaceable bag, in which the dust is collected.

Machines for Mining and Building

Mining and building work which once needed huge teams of workers, can now be done by machines guided by computers. Vast drills and tunnel-boring machines cut through hundreds of metres of rock in a day. Cranes are powerful enough to lift loads weighing a thousand tonnes.

Mining Trucks Can Work By Remote Control

The earliest miners used simple picks to mine metal ores. Today, huge drilling rigs bore holes into the mountain side, then dynamite is used to blast away the rock. Giant 980 tonne electric shovels can move up to 40 cubic metres (1,412 cubic feet) of rock at a time, loading it onto 240 tonne dump trucks. Many mining trucks are operated by remote control. In future, it may be possible for all the trucks in a mine to be controlled by one operator working on a computer screen.

Giant Drills Cut Through Mountain Sides

Drill and blast tunnelling is used to cut through hard rock, such as under mountains. Giant drills working together as a drilling jumbo bore holes into the rock face, guided by a computer. The holes are then filled with dynamite to blast away the rock. French engineers pioneered drill and blast tunnelling when they built the Mont Cenis rail tunnel under the Alps in 1871. They used pneumatic drills which had been invented just ten years earlier.

Mining truck

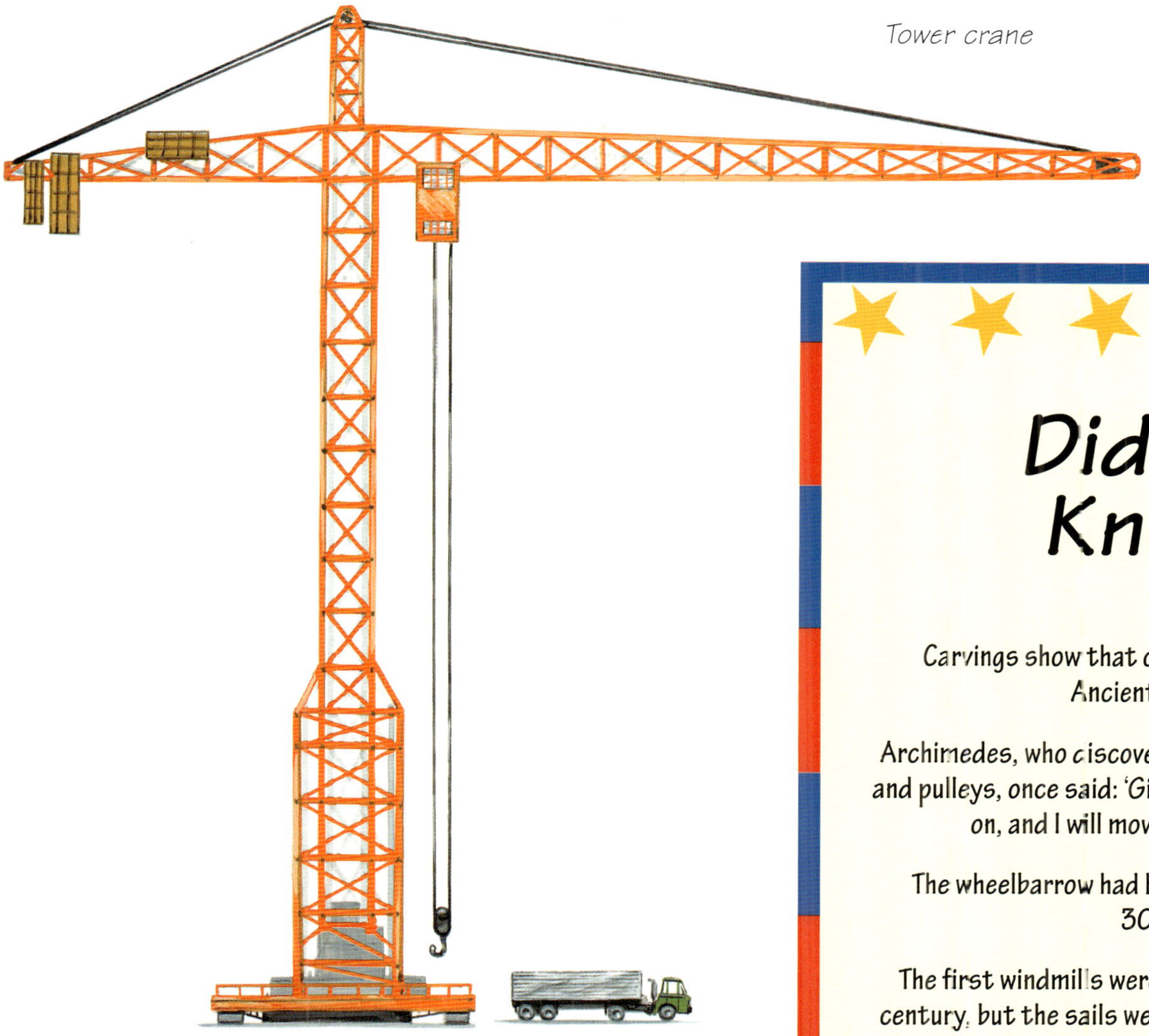

Tower crane

Did You Know?

Carvings show that cranes were used by the Ancient Romans.

Archimedes, who discovered the principles of levers and pulleys, once said: 'Give me a fixed place to stand on, and I will move the entire earth.'

The wheelbarrow had been invented in China by 300 BC.

The first windmills were used in Persia in the 7th century, but the sails were fixed horizontally rather than vertically.

The success of the Ancient Romans was partly due to their discovery of a way to mix concrete.

The invention of a safety lift by Elisha Otis in 1857 paved the way for builders to develop skyscrapers!

Cranes Were Invented 3,500 Years Ago

No-one knows when cranes were first invented, but the Assyrians were using simple rope and pulley systems to move building materials by about 1500 BC. In Roman times, cranes were often powered by human treadmills. The great Italian artist and inventor Leonardo da Vinci designed the first pivoting crane in about 1480. Today, cranes are used to load ships and move heavy machinery or materials around factories and building sites. The tallest cranes, called tower cranes, are used to construct skyscrapers.

The Channel Tunnel Was Cut By Huge Machines

In 1988, work began on the Channel Tunnel, a 50 km (30 mi) tunnel linking the UK to France. The "Chunnel" was dug out 100 m (300 ft) beneath the sea by huge tunnel boring machines (TBMs). Each TBM is as long as two football pitches and can cut through up to 100 m (300 ft) of rock a day. TBMs have rams that drive the cutting head round, and waste rock is fed onto a conveyor belt. In making the tunnel, 7.5 million cubic metres (265 million cubic feet) of rock had to be removed.

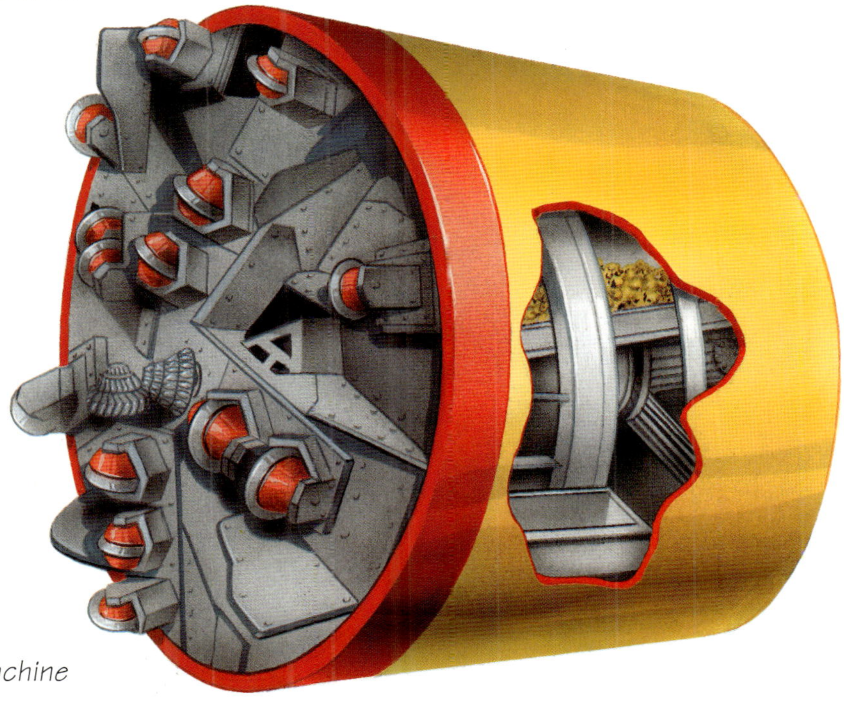

Tunnel boring machine

Medical Machines

Machines play an important part in modern medicine. X-ray machines and ultrasound scanners can be used to investigate inside patients' bodies, diagnosing the cause of their illness. Lasers can be used to fight cancer cells and perform precise surgery on eyes and other parts of the body.

The First X-Ray Image Was Of A Hand

X-rays were discovered by accident during experiments by the scientist Wilhelm Konrad Roentgen in 1895. He called them X-rays because at first he did not know what they were. X-rays are a form of radiation that can pass through human tissue and leave an image on a photographic plate or a screen. The first image that Roentgen produced was of his wife's hand wearing a ring.

Laser Beams Are Used In Surgery

Laser beams are used by surgeons to burn away cancer cells or to make precise cuts in surgery, such as in eye operations. Ordinary light is a mixture of wavelengths but in laser light, the waves are all the same length and travel in the same direction. This makes laser beams very powerful and precise. In a laser tube, electricity is passed through laser material, such as helium or neon, to release pulses of laser light.

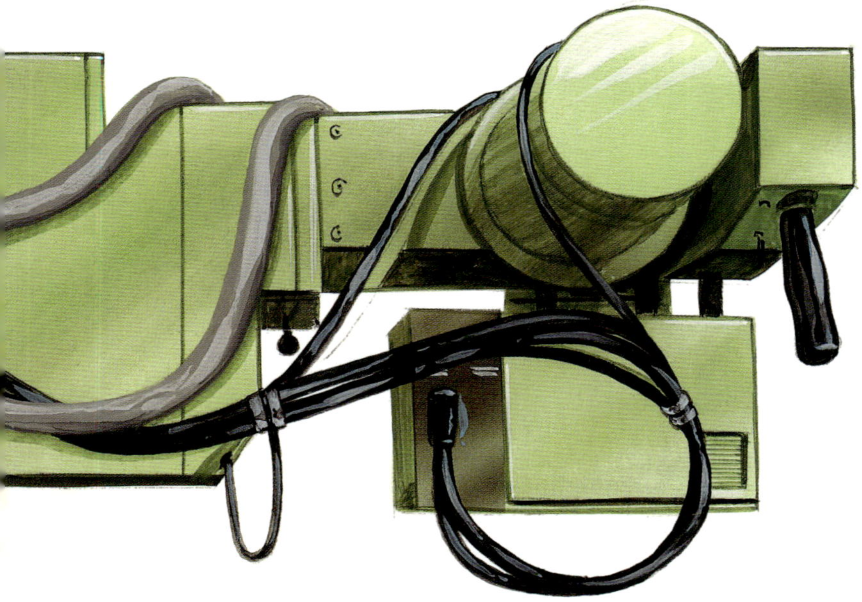

Ultrasound Can See Inside Your Body

Ultrasounds are sound waves which are beyond the range of human hearing. Ultrasound can be used to look inside the human body. Scanners use ultrasound probes to send out ultrasonic vibrations, which bounce back when they are reflected by tissue or organs inside the body. Ultrasound can be used to show how an unborn baby is developing in the womb, or to scan the brain or body for cancer cells. Scanners use high-speed computers to project detailed images on a screen. Ultrasound is widely used in modern medicine because it does not damage human tissue, as over exposure to X-rays can.

X-ray machine

Index